EXPLODING THE COMPUTER MYTH

EXPLODING THE COMPUTER MYTH

Discovering the 13 Realities
of High Performing Business Systems

GLENN E. WEADOCK

omneo

AN IMPRINT OF OLIVER WIGHT PUBLICATIONS, INC.
85 Allen Martin Drive
Essex Junction, VT 05452

Oliver Wight Publications books may be purchased for educational,
business, or sales promotional use.
For information, please call or write: Special Sales Department,
Oliver Wight Publications, Inc.,
85 Allen Martin Drive, Essex Junction, VT 05452.
Telephone: (800) 343-0625 or (802) 878-8161; FAX: (802) 878-3384.

Library of Congress Catalog Card Number: 94-61549

ISBN 0-939246-82-1

Printed on acid-free paper

Manufactured in the United States of America
1   2   3   4   5   6   7   8   9   10

Many of the product names mentioned herein are registered trademarks
of their respective companies.

ACKNOWLEDGMENTS

Lines from "'Choruses' from The Rock" by T.S. Eliot is from *Collected Poems
1909–1962*, by T.S. Eliot. Reprinted by permission of Faber and Faber Limited,
Publishers, London. Copyright 1936 by Harcourt Brace & Company.
Copyright 1964, 1963 by T.S. Eliot, reprinted by permission of the publisher.

Lines from "Look What You Did, Christopher!" by Ogden Nash is from *Verses
from 1929 On* © 1933 by Ogden Nash. Reprinted by permission of Little,
Brown and Company, Boston.

Lines from "The Wood Pile" by Robert Frost is from *The Poetry of Robert Frost*,
edited by Edward Connery Lathem. Reprinted by permission of Henry Holt
& Company, New York.

To Emily,
with love and appreciation

Acknowledgments

None of the research in this book was supported by grants from public or private institutions. (It probably had to be that way because at some point just about everyone connected with business computing takes their lumps in these pages.) The book was, however, supported by a number of terrific individuals.

My thanks to Al Heuer for early encouragement and advice, and to Lucille Enix for editorial direction and consultation. Special thanks to Mike Snell for believing in the message, invaluable help refining it, and an indefatigable effort finding the right publisher in an industry that publishes computer books and business books but only rarely business books about computers. Special thanks also to Jim Childs for excellent editorial direction and a much-appreciated participatory style. It's a pleasure to work with such professionals.

To all my friends who encouraged me to write this book and who were gracious enough to read parts of it and contribute their comments, including Ted Wilson, Marti Baker, Dan Baker, and Ed Weadock, sincere thanks as well.

My wife, Emily, ultimately made the effort possible by helping with writing, editing, proofing, illustrating, and by doing the hundreds of things authors' spouses do to make the creative process run smooth rather than rough. She's graciously endured the deranged and obsessive behavior that accompanies any book project.

If there are errors of fact, which I've made every reasonable effort to eliminate, I'm responsible for them. If there are errors in reasoning, it would not be the first time, and I welcome discussion about them. If there are errors in spelling, I blame my computers. The belief that they can catch every mistake is a—well, *you* know.

Glenn E. Weadock

Contents

List of Illustrations

Introduction

When a river floods, as the Mississippi did so dramatically during the summer of 1993, vast quantities of water rush over hydroelectric plant spillways, leaving as little as 10 percent flowing through the turbines and generating useful electricity. In the same way, most of the benefits of automation are bypassing U.S. companies, which are harnessing only a small fraction of the torrent of computer power flooding their organizations.

The Computer Myth states that automation's benefits are *automatic*, that computers are *inherently* a smart business investment that is likely to improve operations, reduce costs, or both. If this were true, organizations would be enjoying performance gains—revenues, earnings, cost savings, faster time-to-market, new products—proportional to their massively increased expenditures on Information Technology (IT).

But they aren't. The Computer Myth *isn't* true, not by a long shot. It's a dangerous misconception that leads businesses to waste billions of dollars each year. *Automation only benefits companies with a deep understanding of its true costs, limitations, capabilities, pitfalls, and requirements.* Most organizations have not yet developed such an understanding, and it is costing them dearly.

This book is for any business person who has to deal with computer systems. Some readers will be planning how technology fits into their organization's future; others will be authorizing new systems. Some have inherited systems that they must somehow make more useful and workable; others face an up-coming conversion or migration from one system to another. Many have little or no background in computers but must wrestle with the issues they create.

Whether decision makers or implementers, strategic planners or project leaders, *all* business managers can help make their organizations more successful once they understand, and reject, computer mythology. The truths that emerge in this book are all the more powerful and practical because they transcend business functions and apply to *every* computer application, from manufacturing to marketing, from e-mail to spreadsheet, from PC to mainframe.

ORGANIZATION: MYTHS AND SUBMYTHS

Part I begins with a detailed look at the Computer Myth and how it relates to modern business trends. Part I also explores why the myth persists, and why examining it is a worthwhile and profitable endeavor.

Part II familiarizes the reader with the basic knowledge needed to read the main part of the book without confusion or frustration. Like most disciplines, high tech is not as complicated as its practitioners make it seem. Obviously, however, every industry has its own set of terms and ideas that the informed customer must understand to use that industry's products intelligently. Part II is based on a technology briefing document I've used for years in my consulting practice. If some of the stubbornly old-guard, antitechnology executives I've had to deal with can understand this presentation, so can most intelligent business readers.

This second part (or the entire book, for that matter) will not make you a computer expert. It is very important that you *not* become a computer expert; we have enough of those already, and, besides, you don't have the time! Rather, you, the business person, should become computer-*aware*. You can benefit by understanding the myths and the truths that they obscure. The details—admittedly daunting and complex—are almost entirely irrelevant for our purposes.

The primary Computer Myth rests upon many subsidiary myths, which fall into two sets. The first has to do with "the big picture," and part III (see Plan) addresses these long-range issues:

Plan of Part III
"Myth and Truths: The Big Picture"

Myth 1: Computer Productivity Is Unmeasurable	Myth 2: Leave Technology to the "Experts"	Myth 3: Computers Belong in the Back Office	Myth 4: Fit People Around Technology Myth 5: The More Information, The Better
SKEPTICISM	INVOLVEMENT	CREATIVITY	HUMAN ORIENTATION

- ❑ How does an organization begin measuring computer impact if automation does not ensure productivity gains?

- ❑ Who should participate in computer decisions, to what extent, and how can business people discuss technology productively with the "experts"?

- ❑ If computers are good for tasks other than traditional "back-office" chores, what should companies be using computers *for?*

- ❑ If the human factor is too important to ignore, how can organizations plan systems to take into account the way people interact with them?

❏ Finally, if more data is not necessarily a good thing, how can computer users filter information to avoid the paralysis that follows information overload?

Although these are all strategic issues, they should concern any business computer user with a PC on the desk.

The second set of myths, investigated in part IV, (see Plan) has to do with *tactics and implementation.*

Plan of Part IV
"Myth and Truths: Applying Automation Now"

PLANNING	PURCHASING	MANAGING	IMPROVING
		Myth 10: Computers Are User-Friendly, So We Don't Need Training	Myth 12: If It's *Not* Working, Throw Money at It
Myth 6: We Don't Have Time for a Plan	Myth 7: Get the Most Powerful Computers We Can		
	Myth 8: Computers Are Becoming Standardized		
		Myth 11: Computers Are Reliable, So We Don't Need Support	Myth 13: If It *Is* Working, Leave It Alone
	Myth 9: Custom Software Gives Us an Edge		

❏ If planning is important, how do we do it?

❏ If we don't need the fastest computers for every job, how can we decide how much technology is appropriate for a task?

❏ Computers aren't user-friendly yet; we will still need proper training for our users, but how much and of what type?

❑ Computer reliability is another myth; what are the options for providing support when things go wrong, how can those support costs be contained, and what are the key elements of a disaster plan?

❑ Industry standards alone will not ensure that our computers can connect and communicate; how can an organization develop corporate standards to minimize obsolescence and product incompatibility?

❑ Custom software has an undeniable appeal, but it also carries serious hidden costs—should we avoid it in favor of commercial software?

❑ If more money doesn't always fix computer problems, how can we avoid throwing good dollars after bad, and when should we abandon old systems for new ones?

❑ And, if the systems that we *think* are working well can work even better, how should we evaluate them, and how often?

Readers can apply the truths behind these myths on whatever scale they need: individual, project team, department, division, or organization-wide.

Finally, the book presents a new paradigm for making computers work in business. Part V will help companies apply the computer power they have (or will have) to enhance competitiveness by cutting costs, improving speed, making better decisions, boosting quality, and unlocking creativity. It summarizes the critical success factors that appear as each myth is systematically destroyed; these are the secrets to capturing more of the power rushing unused over the spillway. There are thirteen such factors:

1. Measure and monitor computer systems' impact on productivity.

2. Get involved in information systems; don't leave key decisions to "experts."

3. Apply technology in new ways instead of simply automating the past.

4. Fit technology around people, not the other way around; think *systems*.

5. Use computers to convert raw data into meaningful information.

6. Plan information systems rather than let them evolve haphazardly.

7. Invest in appropriate technology, not overkill, to avoid wasting capital.

8. Emphasize usability over "features," and battle computer illiteracy.

9. Support information system users intelligently and listen to their ideas.

10. Break down communications barriers by rooting out incompatible systems.

11. Manage software projects to reduce cost and improve reliability.

12. Recognize that money is the least important computer system success factor.

13. Overcome organizational inertia to introduce beneficial technology.

The book explores each of these key issues in detail, using illustrations and examples from companies that have faced the challenges,* and drawing sometimes surprising conclusions

---

* Companies and individuals are named wherever confidentiality agreements or "off-the-record" interviews do not prevent doing so. All examples are real and factually correct even if, in some cases, names are not named.

about how to reduce the "productivity gap." Companies can often improve dramatically with relatively little additional investment: after all, the computer, like the power plant, does not cost much more to run at 30 percent capacity than it does at 10 percent. Surprisingly often, the solutions to these thirteen challenges involve *organizational* or *procedural* changes and have nothing to do with bits and bytes.

In every case, the solutions can be implemented immediately. They apply to all sizes and types of businesses. They apply to all types of computer applications, whether a company is automating its accounting, budgeting, document processing, manufacturing, or market research functions.

Part V also describes a philosophy businesses can adopt to make sense of high-tech and use it in the best way possible. This final section can serve as a blueprint for success in dealing with automation, whether in the form of a small microcomputer network or a global mainframe operation.

This is a practical book for practical people. Seven years in the making, its foundation is the accumulated observations of years of consulting for and teaching hundreds of business clients in the United States, Canada, and the United Kingdom. As you read this book, you will learn how to use technology more profitably. You also will learn facts about the computer industry that have nothing to do with chips and circuits but everything to do with successful information systems. There are many suggestions for change; some will inspire action, some will provoke argument and even controversy. The goal is to leave behind conventional wisdom in search of actual wisdom; to destroy myths and reveal realities, even if that means sacrificing a few sacred cows along the way.

So much for preliminaries; let's get started.

Part I

The Computer Myth

"It's not the things we don't know that get us into trouble; it's the things we do know that ain't so."

—WILL ROGERS, AMERICAN
HUMORIST (1879–1935)

When touring the central computer facility of the Superconducting Supercollider Laboratory, the massive atom-smashing project in Waxahachie, Texas, I saw rack upon rack of small computers linked in a sophisticated and complex network that must have taken considerable effort to program and configure. This network was the computing "engine" scientists used for designing the giant magnets that would accelerate subatomic particles around a huge ring. Finally, those particles would collide at close to the speed of light, providing physicists clues to the very origin of the universe and the nature of matter.

Staring at the impressive array of workstations, I asked if it would not have been easier, cheaper, and faster to have purchased a single, powerful supercomputer to do the magnet design work. Probably, came the reply; but it was much easier to get budget authorization from the federal government for hundreds of the smaller machines than for a single supercomputer.

The Supercollider eventually was killed by Congress, ostensibly for being behind schedule and over budget. It turned out that building a sophisticated and complex computing facility by itself wasn't enough; the computer system wasn't really right for the job, and the reasons had their roots in bureaucratic red tape. It seems plausible that if the project managers had been able to get the machine they needed at the outset, the project would have tracked closer to both schedule and budget. It might even still be proceeding toward its goal of redefining our concept of who we are and where we came from, instead of culminating in a dead-end fiasco that wasted billions of taxpayer dollars.

For me, the Supercollider incident reinforced a conviction that years of consulting have confirmed: *how* an organization automates is more important than *whether* it automates, and computerization per se is no guarantee of anything. That's a major change from the way businesses traditionally have looked at computers.

Turning points in business civilization occur when innovators shatter widely held myths and rebuild something nearer the truth from the pieces. During the Industrial Revolution, managers believed that people should adapt to the machines they operated, instead of the other way around. Later, managers thought that "quality control" was a separate activity that they could tack on at the end of a process, rather than a philosophy to be applied at every stage. More recently, businesses have assumed that productive work teams must function in a single geographic location. In each case, exploding the myth has opened opportunities for dramatic productivity improvement.

Today, one of the most pervasive business myths is that *computer systems automatically improve bottom-line productivity,* where productivity is the amount of whatever the organization generates (typically profits, but possibly other measures—for a university, the number of students properly educated, for example) per unit of cost or input (personnel, capital equipment, overhead).

Many reasonable and intelligent people believe this Computer Myth. When I started my computer consulting practice in 1982, I certainly did, with enthusiasm. You probably did, too, until one day you had an experience with computers that made you wonder.

The doubts may have begun forming when an IS guru tried to explain to you how to use a management information system; when you tried to get some technical help with a computer problem; or when your printed document looked disconcertingly different from its screen image. Perhaps you were struggling through a setup manual for a home PC, listening to an administrator advise that it would take a month to get the report you'd requested, or watching your department scramble to recover important data lost during a power outage.

You may have begun to harbor a suspicion that the computers in your business might not be working to maximum advantage, or even that they might not be worth what they cost. But you dismissed those suspicions by reminding yourself that *everyone* is buying and using computers; that they are a necessary component of an efficient, modern operation; and that the people making the computer decisions are far better versed in the technology than you could ever be. You decided your suspicions were incorrect. After all, as one of my consultant friends has said, you don't try to cost-justify your phone system. (Or *do* you?)

Your suspicions were not only valid, but *they also did not go far enough*. After a career spent astride the two mutually alien worlds of computer technology and business management, it's clear to me that business computers do not always, or even most of the time, improve bottom-line productivity. In many cases, they hinder more than they help, or perform woefully below their capabilities. Most of the time, no one really knows what their net effect is; businesses push forward with some vague notion that they are doing the right thing by using these computers, awkward and expensive and difficult though they may seem.

CYBERWASTE

In a Florida State University survey of thirty Information Systems executives, *not one* could demonstrate that computerization had improved their organization's overall productivity! One reason for this is the tremendous waste of computer resources in typical organizations. Consider the following cases, which unfortunately are not at all isolated:

- A major insurance firm bought hundreds of large mainframe computers they aren't using, and probably won't ever use, because they don't connect well with the firm's other systems.

- Auto-parts giant Federal-Mogul ripped out millions of dollars of plant computer equipment that created more problems than it solved—it prevented technicians, for example, from quickly retooling the plant for different parts.

- A top U.S. civil engineering firm has so many incompatible computer networks (nearly a dozen) that it can't manage them.

- At the offices of a large telephone company in Irving, Texas, hundreds of employees have expensive PCs at their desks, which they use solely for word processing: $3,000 typewriters that should also be scheduling meetings, handling faxes, booking flights, and keeping Rolodex lists, but aren't.

- At one of the U.S. National Laboratories, scientists and engineers used hundreds of top-line Macintoshes mainly to send and receive electronic mail: $4,000 computers doing the work of $400 terminals.

- At a huge cosmetics manufacturer, a large mainframe prepares just annual budgets: a $700,000 calculator.

- At a leading engineering consulting firm, each department has its own computer network—and none of them can communicate with another, a fact that stifles interdepartmental project teams and drives support and maintenance costs skyward.

The waste of computer resources becomes more significant and more disturbing as businesses employ computer systems ever more widely. Nearly every modern business has some form of computing equipment on the balance sheet. About 150 *million* microcomputers (PCs) are at work in the United States at this writing, and dealers sell thousands more every day. Hundreds of thousands of larger minicomputers and mainframes hum and whir at this moment in offices and computer rooms nationwide. These machines rank among the most sophisticated devices man has ever made. The computer resource *could* be as liberating as oil reserves, farmland, or fresh water. It *could* mean the competitive edge that helps us compete in the new global marketplace.

GROWING IMPORTANCE OF THE MYTH

Some would say that because computer systems have been dropping in price and growing in power so quickly, the productivity question becomes less and less important; we can *afford* more waste. This position certainly sounds reasonable and is therefore dangerous as well as wrong and naïve. Consider a few modern business trends and their implications for the relevance of managing information technology effectively.

TRENDWATCH *Team Computing.* Geographically dispersed teams are doing more and more of the U.S.A.'s work. Such teams typically rely heavily upon information technology for communications, from simple e-mail and data file transfers to remote access to corporate networks and mainframes, and even video conferencing. The efficiency, reliability, and usability of information technology—all of which businesses unwittingly sabotage by adhering to the Computer Myth—are critical success factors for many teams.

Teams need to be able to share their work, but unless the company's computers facilitate such sharing, it can become a stumbling block. A new class of software pioneered by Lotus

Development Corporation, *groupware*, incorporates data sharing into its design, recognizing, for example, that a typical document is not written and edited by a single person. Implementing groupware requires careful planning, corporate standards for computer components, and a high degree of hardware and software compatibility across systems. These are not typical attributes of today's business systems, and they are most certainly not automatic. Groupware itself is fairly new technology; only in the early nineties have software companies begun providing viable, if imperfect, tools for viewing documents created on different systems.

Extend the team concept for a moment to consider computer systems as *members* of a team, rather than as mere tools; as entities that, like employees, must be hired (bought), paid (maintained), and which must provide valuable service (perform). Most team leaders would "fire" their computers instantly if they thought of computers in this way:

- They are overpaid and underworked, sitting idle much of the time.

- They are costly when one considers life cycle costs such as user training, documentation, maintenance, troubleshooting, repair, and technical support instead of just purchase prices.

- Understanding and communicating with them is difficult: They know several highly limited languages, very bad English (if any), and cannot communicate by hearing or speaking.

- They have no initiative or creative ability, and they never come up with new ideas themselves.

- They are unable to modify their behavior to fit changed circumstances.

- They can only perform the most minutely detailed instructions and will carry them out to the letter, heedless of the user's original intention. If a potentially disastrous mistake lurks unnoticed in their instructions, computers proceed anyway; they have no judgment.

☐ They require many highly trained support people to keep them fit, frequently need some kind of medical attention, sometimes demand their own (expensive) special rooms to function properly, and yet they live only a few years.

As computer systems become more and more an essential component of business teams, their performance determines to a greater degree whether the technology functions as an enabling, or disabling, factor.

Reengineering. As organizations examine their work flows and information flows, information systems can either enable change or thwart it. The flexibility of an organization's computer systems is a critical success factor for many reengineering efforts. Organizations that believe the Computer Myths tend to institute customized, nonstandard, incompatible, and inflexible information systems that reinforce old ways of doing things.

Networks, Networks Everywhere. More and more, organizations are interconnecting their vast populations of personal computers, workstations, minicomputers, and large "legacy" mainframes. Some 35 percent of corporate PCs belonged to networks as of 1993, and the number is increasing rapidly. As any network administrator or PC coordinator will attest, linking systems adds a thick layer of technological complexity that renders the computing environment more challenging to manage and troubleshoot effectively. The more complex the system becomes, the more important it is to dispel the conventional "wisdom" that planning computer systems is a waste of time in a fast-changing marketplace. Unplanned systems guarantee in advance the expensive failure of computer networks.

Digital Paper. The "paperless office" has been TRENDWATCH an unrealized fantasy since the term was coined many years ago by technology enthusiasts with a misguided view of appropriate automation goals. I would not like to work in an entirely paperless office until computer systems advance considerably beyond their present state. However, as the cost of computer scanning, storage, and graphics systems has plummeted, the feasibility of managing masses of documents electronically has increased. Larger banks are replacing microfiche systems with digital document management systems—for example, to store images of customer checks and charge slips. Electronic Data Interchange (EDI), which replaces paper documents with electronic ones, is changing the way companies such as GM's Saturn division buy and pay for component parts.

While organizations could protect against, or at least work around, computer unproductivity with a paper backup system, this option vanishes when an organization throws that backup system away. The performance, reliability, and expandability of document imaging computer systems take on new urgency. Would you be confident enough in your IS department to do away with all of the paper in your business?

Sayonara to Support. The year 1993 saw most TRENDWATCH software companies retreat from the practice of supporting their products at low or zero cost to the customer. Even companies that built their popularity on the back of free customer support—like WordPerfect and Microsoft—abandoned the expensive policy. There is every reason to expect the trend to continue, meaning that the responsibility for supporting end-users will shift from the vendor to the customer. Companies that believe in the myth of computer reliability, and have not provided adequate technical support in the past, will find it much more expensive to rely upon software vendors for those services in the future.

All the above trends underscore the growing importance of automating effectively. Why have most businesses left such an important task to the technocrats? Let's explore some reasons.

CONVENTIONAL MYOPIA

"Nobody was permitted to see the Emperor of China, and the question was, What is the length of the Emperor of China's nose? To find out, you go all over the country asking people what they think the length of the Emperor of China's nose is, and you average it. And that would be very 'accurate' because you averaged so many people. But it's no way to find anything out."

—RICHARD P. FEYNMAN,
NOBEL LAUREATE IN PHYSICS, IN
Surely You're Joking, Mr. Feynman!

Ask a few dozen IS executives if they feel that computerization has contributed to organizational productivity, and they're likely to say yes (in part, perhaps, because their jobs depend on it); but they usually can't prove it, so this feeling is about as useful as the Chinese villagers' speculations about the Emperor's nose.

Failing to address the Computer Myth is costing businesses billions of dollars annually. Computer systems now comprise 30 percent of American businesses' capital budgets and typically account for about 5 percent of annual revenues; yet study after study reports a negligible productivity gain from automation. Why does the myth persist? How is it possible that the extraordinary achievements of high technology have not done more to improve business productivity? Why do intelligent business managers continue to spend massively on computer systems if they don't really improve productivity? Can so many intelligent people be so wrong?

Sure they can. In the computer field alone, many used to believe that mainframes were the only serious business computers; that developing new computers required huge capital resources; that customers would never buy computers by mail. Then along came DEC and Apple and Dell to wake everybody up. In the world of business, many used to believe that Americans would never buy small cars; that the United States would always dominate consumer electronics; that the Chinese market was impenetrable. Honda and Sony and Coca-Cola changed everyone's minds. "Conventional wisdom" is wrong all the time. A better name for it is "conventional myopia."

The U.S.'s competitiveness problems in global markets despite its extraordinarily high IT expenditures in recent decades should at least *suggest* that business might be automating ineffectually. But there *are* reasons that help explain why the Computer Myth persists, reasons that businesses must consider to advance their understanding and stop making the same mistakes over and over.

WHY THE MYTH FLOURISHES

Blind Faith in Progress

One reason is the belief that technological progress is necessarily *forward* progress. Few organizations try to measure the impact of computers in the work environment, admittedly an extremely challenging task, and find it easier to take as an article of faith that the net effect is positive. This belief does not hold up to scrutiny: technology can take us in a variety of directions, some positive, some negative, depending on how businesses *implement* it (see figure 1 on p. 14).

A small California software company automated its customer service center to track problems and complaints more efficiently. However, the system required ten pieces of information (name, company, serial number, version number, and so on) for every call, even for inquiries that the support representatives used to answer in a few seconds (for example, "When's the new version due out?"). Customers grew irritated at having to supply the extra information, the support representatives became frustrated at having to demand it, and before long the system fell into disuse. Its data and reports are now incomplete and essentially useless.

The scientific and engineering successes fueling the breakneck pace of digital computer hardware and software advancement do not alone guarantee business productivity. During the computer recession of the mid-1980s, corporate America expressed its collective frustration by slashing computer spending during some of the most dramatic technological advancements in computing's history. Consider also that in the country's service sector, where 85 percent of information technology spending occurs, productivity increased less than 2 percent during the entire decade of the eighties.

In fact, the rapid pace of technological change may be working *against* us in the sense that technology is outpacing our ability to assimilate and integrate it with business operations. Due to business's relative inexperience with high technology, most managers know only what the industry tells them about computers; and it is an imperfect, immature industry. Not only is the technology new, the industry is new as well, and both are changing so fast that it's difficult to understand either. Yet, understanding both is essential. Managing the technology productively is

Figure 1   Computer Myth and Computer Reality

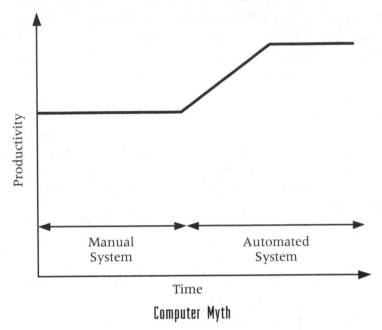

Computer Myth

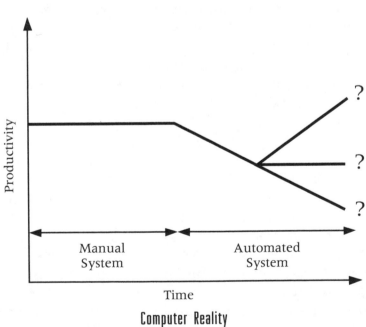

Computer Reality

important, but dealing effectively with hardware and software suppliers, technicians, and consultants is no less so. Astute planning, purchasing, installation, and management of computer systems require an awareness of the computer industry's problems and traditions, strengths and weaknesses.

Trusting the computer industry to move in directions that will safeguard its customers is a very risky proposition. Trusting the computer industry to design products appropriate for human beings, and asking our employees to adapt to the technology's characteristics instead of looking for technology that works with people, is another common but disastrous error (Myth 4, "Fit People Around Technology"). Most of the thousands of books, seminars, and classes on maximizing employee productivity ignore how people and computers work (or don't work) together. Unfortunately, so do most computer companies.

The dazzling pace of change, then, blurs the critical vision we apply to most other aspects of business management. Companies *assume* computerization is a positive thing while knowing precious little about how to use computers productively in the human environment. Computer customers do not expect enough from their systems, or use them as creatively as they should.

Belief That More Is Better

Another reason the Computer Myth persists is that computer systems have been dropping dramatically in price as they have been increasing in power. It is difficult for us to imagine that a software program that does ten times as much as it did five years ago, and costs only a quarter as much, isn't providing us with a giant boost in productivity. To equate more features and lower costs with higher productivity, however, is a good example of computer mythology. Let's think about it more carefully.

Our new program has ten times more "features" than our older one; but one can't assume that all of those new features are really useful. Many are not. A new version of a spreadsheet, for example, might be able to create five new types of 3-D stacked bar graphs; that *seems* useful until one tries to read such a graph and compare a bar on one end with a bar on the other end! Even the users who do need some of the new features will only use them a small percentage of the time. (How many of the features on your VCR remote control do you actually use regularly?)

The benefit, then, is not nearly tenfold, but perhaps twofold if we're generous. A product with more features will take longer to learn, meaning higher training costs that negate most if not all of the cost savings from the new lower product price. Support technicians must learn to support the more complex product, and troubleshooting will probably take longer, meaning more downtime when things go haywire. Modifying system documentation, fixing new compatibility problems, and converting old data files to work with the new product add further to the cost.

The new product, then, might end up with a life cycle cost much higher than its precursor and deliver a net productivity decrease in real life. The purchase price of a computer product turns out to be the smallest component of its true life cycle cost, and "rampant feature-itis" often adds little real-world value.

Turning our focus to hardware for a moment, the dramatically faster, cheaper machines of today often seduce business customers into buying more power than they need for the job at hand. Buying twice the power needed for only 30 percent more might seem like a good deal, until you discover three years later that you're retiring hundreds or thousands of devices with capabilities you never began to tap.

Technophobia

A third important reason the Computer Myth persists is that most managers are confused and intimidated by computer systems. One of my first consulting jobs was to set up a simple program on an Apple II computer that would track declining oil well production and predict when it would no longer be adequate to cover well maintenance costs. This was long before the days of sophisticated spreadsheets that could handle such a chore with ease. The owner of the company told me at the outset: "I've never understood a word computer programmers said; I've never seen a computer program I could use; I don't want to know anything about what you're doing; I don't want to talk with you until you're done; and frankly I don't think this project is going to work. I'm only hiring you because my vice president wants me to." It took a month to set up the system and about four months to convince the owner to sit down at the machine and run the program himself. Once he did, he loved it, but he was the first to admit that his technophobia almost killed the project before it was started.

While such vigorous resistance to automation is becoming less common, managers still tend to defer critical decisions to the high priests of technology rather than venture into the mysterious and forbidding world of high tech and try to make sense of it all. IS departments and computer companies have helped perpetuate that confusion because it often accrues to their benefit, creating a crisis of confidence.

The free-market model assumes educated buyers, but many companies (and managers) remain remarkably ill informed about the life cycle costs and benefits of the systems they buy. Companies *are* buying technology that's not nearly as cost-effective as they think it is; and once they do buy it, they don't know how to implement and manage it to their best advantage— all because they simply don't understand computers. Which leads to the following question:

CAN A NONTECHNICAL PERSON UNDERSTAND COMPUTER SYSTEMS?

Emphatically YES. It's time for nontechnical managers to understand information technology and take responsibility for applying it. It really *is* feasible to raise your business-computing

consciousness without an engineering degree from MIT, or without devoting hour upon hour to painful details about bits and
bytes.

> *"We are lost in the mazes of our ingenuities because,*
> *being trained to look at details rather than at wholes, we*
> *are confused by the complexity we have created."*
>
> —ARNOLD PACEY, PROFESSOR AT
> THE UNIVERSITY OF MANCHESTER
> INSTITUTE OF SCIENCE AND
> TECHNOLOGY, *The Maze of*
> *Ingenuity* (1974)

Anyone with reasonable intelligence can understand the potential benefits and pitfalls of automation without knowing all the
jargon or how transistors work. (Conversely, knowing how transistors work is no guarantee at all that one really understands the
dynamics of information systems, and, in fact, may get in the
way of such an understanding.) The details presented in this
book are the minimum necessary to get across the essential
points.

Given that business professionals can understand computers,
at least to the extent necessary to overcome computer myths and
dramatically boost productivity, the next question becomes:

WHY IS UNDERSTANDING THE COMPUTER
MYTH WORTH MY TIME?

Having found gadgets and gizmos fascinating from a young age, I
admit enjoying working with computer systems (and, occasionally, against them). However, my work has shown me that
high tech isn't something most business people enjoy thinking

about, talking about, or reading about. Small wonder; the industry is awash in "acronymania" and off-putting technospeak. Those on the management side who do make the valiant effort to acquaint themselves with the technology typically get little support from their own IS organizations; still less from system vendors; and practically none from the books and magazines, which all seem written exclusively for those already belonging to the technological cognoscenti.

Computers are about as interesting for most business managers as quantum physics. Why put out the effort to understand them? Why invest your valuable time to read this book? Unlike quantum physics, understanding the realities of computers could help you accomplish your business goals, whether as part of a global business rethinking process or as part of an evolutionary growth plan. Continuing to believe all, or even a few, of the computer myths is likely to keep those goals farther from your reach than you would like. Here are four simple examples; the rest of the book provides many more.

❏ *Clarify business directions.* Thinking about information systems leads companies to *define* their business goals and directions more clearly. The IS managers at a hardware chain who are debating whether to install more powerful computers in retail stores versus enlarging the mainframe at corporate headquarters are also forcing management to think about its business model: whether to decentralize and give store managers more responsibility and control. *Planning information systems is a good way to spark thinking about business growth.*

❏ *Speed information flows.* Sometimes the greatest benefit of a computer system feasibility study is not the new computer system that results, but the analysis of an organization's information flows. A multi-million-dollar hotel chain wanted a feasibility study for a new computer system to get financial data to managers faster. To start the study, the firm's top accountant and I started drawing information flow diagrams. It soon became clear that the company's consolidated month-end financials could be ready about four days earlier if the hotels sent sales data to corporate headquarters by modem instead of by mail, where it could be fed directly into the headquarters' central computer. This simple change avoided a mail delay and saved the time of the bookkeepers at headquarters who were receiving the paper reports and re-keying data from them into their computer. The change also removed one extra transcription step, reducing the chance of data entry errors. The firm didn't buy the new computer system, but they didn't really need it because they improved the speed of information flow using the system they already had. Whether you call this *process re-engineering* or just thinking about automation, the results were positive.

❏ *Avoid expensive mistakes.* A California pharmaceutical company that implemented a computer network relied on custom software to manage its financials. It turned out later that the software couldn't grow with the network unless it was substantially rewritten, at great expense. That company believed the myth that custom software is always better than off-the-shelf software. They don't believe it any more, but it was a costly misconception.

❏ *Use human resources more intelligently.* Business managers who believe the myth that computers and programs are becoming easier to use and more reliable—a myth promulgated at tremendous expense by the computer industry—fail to allocate enough technical personnel for supporting users with questions or problems. These same managers, believing another myth that so-called standard products from different vendors work together seamlessly, mix and match hardware and software components that ultimately don't work well together. As a result, computer professionals who should be designing new networks and systems spend their entire working days putting out fires and fixing problems in the field. System users can't do their jobs because they're waiting for the technical experts to fix their computer problems. Companies like Aetna Insurance, which institute their *own* corporate standards for computer software, enjoy much lower support costs and can free up technical experts to do the jobs they were hired to do.

You might be surprised to find, as you read these pages, that business computing issues are as often organizational in nature as they are technological, and that making computers work for your business is as much a challenge to your imagination and creativity as to your rational intellect.

Once you get past the myths and begin dealing with computer realities, making these systems work for you may turn out to be not only profitable but also gratifying—in the way that one who understands any tool takes pleasure in wielding it to a productive purpose. The power of information technology *is* impressive once we begin using it intelligently. It may offer the greatest prospects for productivity improvement of *all* modern technologies.

While one respects the intellect of the scientists and engineers who have designed today's computer systems, technological virtue lies ultimately in utility. The intellect and creativity businesses demonstrate in putting that technology to good use are equally important. Applying technology is more challenging because it involves the enormous variable that human beings introduce to any equation. And that's one area where business expertise is desperately needed.

Like many popular myths, the Computer Myth contains a kernel of truth. Computers *can* certainly improve business productivity, and do in many organizations. It's been my business, and perhaps yours, to see to it that that happens. But business people have to understand these machines a bit better if that is to happen with regularity. If they can stop:

◻ Disdaining the technology that makes them uncomfortable;

◻ Abdicating their responsibility for automation decisions to the technology specialists;

◻ Accepting the promise of productivity as an article of faith not to be questioned; and

◻ Believing everything the computer industry (and the IS department) tells them, then (and only then) business managers can move to a more profitable and honest dialogue with their technical elite.

The Computer Myth is real, and today's business trends are increasing the importance of its consequences. Fortunately, it *can* be overcome, and businesses stand to benefit in many ways by doing so. The next step is to lay the foundation for coping with each of the submyths by coming to grips with the basics of modern computing technology. That's the subject of the following part.

Part II

Computer Essentials for Business Readers

"Wagner's music isn't as bad as it sounds."

—Mark Twain

Computer jargon isn't as bad as it sounds, either.

As in all specialized fields, the computer industry has its own set of terms and concepts, efficient in communications between experts but obscure and formidable to lay persons. There is just no way a completely computer-illiterate person can expect to use or manage automated systems effectively, any more than one can expect to manage money well without knowing something about compound interest.

The computer industry hasn't made it easy for outsiders trying to learn the lingo. IBM has always given its computers and peripherals interesting, easy-to-remember names such as *9370* and *AS/400*. Technicians use terms such as *VDT* (Video Display Terminal) instead of just *terminal, primary storage* instead of *memory, IPL* (Initial Program Load) or *boot* instead of *restart*. One might assume that most computer professionals flunked English. There are more acronyms in the computer industry than in the U.S. military.

Fortunately, a broad knowledge of computer fundamentals is all that's needed to understand and overcome business computer myths. Even better, those fundamentals don't take too long to present, and they can be described without too many acronyms or tedious technical minutiae. Read through this chapter once, then return to it if necessary when reading later chapters.

DEFINING *COMPUTER*

Computer is an unfortunate misnomer that I wish could somehow be changed, overnight, in all books and magazines and minds. The computer's ability to perform arithmetic is *not* its most important ability in business applications. It just happens to be chronologically first in the history of the computer's development. People in business use computers to do many jobs that have little to do with computation:

- Create, edit, and produce textual and graphical documents;

- Electronically file everything from sales forecasts to employee photographs;

- Rapidly communicate with other individuals, teams, organizations, and countries;

- Design products more quickly and with fewer errors;

- Quickly access reference services, from zip code directories to jet airplane assembly instructions;

- Educate employees and customers with "multimedia" presentations;

- Screen applicants for bank loans using preprogrammed advice;

- Improve marketing by targeting prospects and tracking sales;

- Monitor the safe operation of industrial facilities; and so forth.

A computer, then, is a device that can accept, store, move, and produce just about any kind of data, and modify or manipulate that data in just about any kind of way. Whenever you see *computer*, think *datatool*. It's provocative to the imagination. If a computer is a datatool rather than a calculator, what could it do for your organization? What data do you deal with every day? How could you track it, reorganize it, transport it, analyze it, present it, in a useful way?

NO MACHINE IS AN ISLAND

Whereas a computer is a machine, an *information system* may consist of one or one thousand individual computers with their associated input and output devices, programs, support staff and users, plus the power and communications grids to which the machines connect. One of the biggest problems in automating today's business activities is the tendency to focus on computers instead of on information systems.

COMPUTER TAXONOMY

The eighteenth-century Swedish botanist Carolus Linnaeus successfully created a classification structure for all living things: the neat structure of kingdom, phylum, class, order, family, genus, species that biologists still use. If Linnaeus were alive today and charged with developing a similarly elegant classification scheme for computers, he would go rapidly insane.

Though no single, simple, clear scheme for classifying the various kinds of computers exists, it is possible to look at a few of the more common schemes and gain some idea of how a "workstation" differs from a "personal computer." The broad spectrum of datatools is divided by boundaries that blur further each year; but it's important to know about the whole range because the versatile "personal computer" does not provide the best answer for every business need, any more than the traditional mainframe does. The smartest companies take advantage of more than one type of datatool, exploiting the advantages of each type.

Generalists and Specialists

General-purpose computers may be instructed, or programmed, to handle a wide variety of problems. Most business computers are general-purpose machines. They're like people, capable of doing almost anything if properly programmed (educated).

Special-purpose computers are highly customized to meet a specific need and are not easily modified to perform other tasks. Examples are the on-board "black box" that controls a car engine's fuel intake system, the timer in a microwave oven, and the automatic pilot in a commercial airplane.

The gray area between these two categories includes specialized general-purpose computers. Examples are database machines specially designed for rapid data storage, manipulation, and retrieval; artificial intelligence computers that run programs approximating human intelligence functions, such as deductive reasoning; and gateways that connect different kinds of computers that need to exchange data.

Generation Gaps

A historical classification considers *generations*. First-generation computers were built from vacuum tubes, such as one might find in old radios or TVs, and had very limited memory capacity. These were large and slow, generated a great deal of heat, and consumed mass quantities of electricity. While some hi-fi enthusiasts still prefer vacuum-tube stereo amplifiers, no one still makes vacuum-tube computers, and no one misses them.

Second-generation machines used transistor technology, which reduced size and power requirements while improving reliability and reducing heat output. Printed circuit boards connecting the transistors eliminated much of the tangle of wires associated with first-generation machines.

Integrated circuits, or "IC" chips, characterized the third generation and combined many transistors on one small rectangular silicon chip. It still took hundreds of integrated circuit chips to comprise a computer "brain." Large-scale integration (LSI) enabled the production of special chips, called *microprocessors*, which contain practically all the logic functions of the computer's brain on a *single* silicon wafer. One chip could do the work of thousands of vacuum tubes.

LSI, microprocessors, and large quantities of inexpensive memory distinguish the fourth-generation computer in common use today. Fifth-generation computers do not exist yet, and their characteristics are a matter of speculation; probably, they will embody faster processors, greater memory, more "intelligent" functions, such as voice and handwriting recognition, and perhaps neural-network designs that work more nearly like the human brain.

Operating Mode

Another means of distinguishing computers is by mode of operation: batch, interactive, or real-time.

◻ *Batch* computers work job by job, and process large quantities of accumulated data at one time; the batch computer always controls its next step—disciplined, deterministic, and inflexible. Supercomputers and some mainframes work in batch mode; because they don't need to worry about managing a large number of interactive users, designers can optimize these machines for speed.

◻ *Interactive* computers allow random entry, modification, and reporting of data at any time. I can sit down at an interactive computer and request sales figures for the southwestern region at any time; whether I'll get the figures quickly or not is another question. Multiuser interactive computers use some form of time-sharing technique to divide the computer's attention equitably between users; users and programs may have different priorities to resolve conflicting demands. Interactive machines work better for most office automation tasks than pure batch-mode machines.

◻ *Real-time* systems must respond quickly to user requests or changing physical situations. (*Time-critical* would be a more accurate term for these machines.) Real-time (and interactive) computers do not know in advance what their next activity will be because they respond to unpredictable inputs, or *interrupts*, just as humans do when the phone rings. Computers that control robots, manage nuclear power plants, or perform simulations are real-time computers. Unlike the simple interactive computer, the real-time computer is designed to get me my answers *fast*.

Many computers combine aspects of all modes: Business systems may have real-time operating systems that respond quickly in interactive mode, as well as special batch capabilities to perform recurring tasks such as deleting old data or downloading information from disk to tape. Heavily interactive, real-time computers such as airline reservations systems are called *On-Line Transaction Processing* machines.

Word Size

Engineers often classify computers technically, by word size. The *word* is the smallest meaningful data unit used in the machine's internal language, just as in English the word is the smallest meaningful element of a sentence. Word size is measured in *bits*, or *b*inary dig*its*, each bit having two possible values (1 and 0). Think of a bit as a miniature switch that will always be set to one of two positions, either *on* or *off* (1 or 0). An 8-bit word might be represented as "01001100." Part of the word can hold an *instruction*, and the other part can hold a data location, or *address*, within the computer's memory.

An esoteric discussion of word length isn't necessary here. It's enough to say that as word size increases, a trade-off emerges between the simplicity of the data pathways and the power of the instruction set. A 32-bit machine can have a larger instruction vocabulary and can address a larger amount of memory; however, the logical structure of the machine is more complex and the data paths more convoluted.

Word size need not remain constant throughout the computer. The processor may work with a different-size word for internal computations than it uses to communicate with other devices. A 32-bit processor may have a 22-bit data path; a 16-bit processor, a 20-bit data path. This can affect the efficiency of the machine. The speed advantage of a large processor word size may diminish if data moves in and out of the processor using small words. As with other computer specifications, word size can mislead the nonexpert customer. It's probably the least important classification scheme from the business user's standpoint.

From Super to Micro

Another functional categorization consists of four broad tiers. In order of decreasing power, these are: supercomputers, mainframes, minicomputers, and microcomputers.

❑ *Supercomputers* are very high-speed devices used for jobs requiring intensive computation with many variables, such as weather forecasting or airplane stress simulations. They may cost millions of dollars apiece and require special facilities, such as their own liquid cooling system. Major vendors are Cray, Hitachi, and Fujitsu.

❑ *Mainframes* are large, high-speed, multiuser machines capable of supporting two hundred to six hundred users. They typically operate in large, air-conditioned computer rooms, and are attended by full-time system managers and computer support staff. The mainframe environment is one of centralized control and management, with typically wide availability throughout the organization. Most of the computing "action" takes place in the centralized machine; mainframe terminals act as simple windows into the central system. Global or nationwide electronic mail systems, airline reservations systems, and car manufacturers' inventories are sample mainframe applications. IBM has dominated mainframes throughout computer history.

❏ *Minicomputers* are also multiuser machines supporting from two to two hundred users. Many can operate in normal office or factory environments, and smaller minicomputers may not require full-time staff support. Small to medium businesses may employ minicomputers rather than mainframes for their data processing needs. Minicomputers use central processors to serve smaller groups in individual departments or work groups, but the user sees the minicomputer (as the mainframe) through so-called "dumb" terminals that just send information back and forth to the central machine. Although mainframes are usually large machines, "mini" computers may be quite large themselves, and large minicomputers are often referred to as mainframes. Digital Equipment Corporation single-handedly created the minicomputer, but its famous VAX line of machines is now in decline. IBM markets a successful minicomputer line called AS/400.

❏ *Microcomputers* are small, individual-sized computers primarily designed for one user at a time and with a full complement of local processing hardware and software. They can operate independently and are characterized by low cost (though not necessarily on a per-person basis!), high flexibility, and great variety. Often referred to as personal computers or "PCs," micros cost between $1,000 and $10,000. Small enough to fit on a desktop, their low initial cost relative to larger machines has made them popular choices for businesses just beginning to automate.

In fact, the advent of the microcomputer has transformed the computer industry. These machines were designed originally for use in an environment in which one person (single user) is doing one job at a time (single tasking) on one machine (stand-alone). Now, however, microcomputers linked in networks form a viable modern alternative to the mainframe and minicomputer, though whether PC networks are as cost-effective as minicomputers or mainframes is not always clear, as they can be more complex to manage. The microcomputer offers a degree of independence and freedom unprecedented with minicomputers or time-sharing systems.

Recent years have radically distorted this traditional model and it can't adequately describe most modern organizations' information systems. The distortions arise from two main trends: the filling in of gaps between the traditional computer types with hybrids that blur the traditional boundaries, and the connecting of all these various systems in different ways.

Some high-end microcomputers can support more than one operator; many now offer provisions for multiple CPUs or co-processors, blurring the distinction between microcomputers and minicomputers. Similarly, the dividing line between high-end minicomputers and traditional mainframes is dissolving as minicomputers become more powerful. Subclasses within each broad tier include the following:

☐ *Minisupercomputers* are smaller supercomputers built for highly technical jobs such as fluid dynamics research, computational chemistry, and three-dimensional machine design. These are usually 64-bit machines costing between $150,000 and $4 million.

☐ *Superminicomputers* (different from minisupercomputers!) form the elite corps of the traditional commercial minicomputers. Used for commercial applications, superminicomputers are typically interactive real-time machines costing from $100,000 to $1 million but approximating supercomputer performance.

Superminicomputers, pioneered in the eighties by Convex Computer, have their roots in office systems and networks.

◻ A subclass of microcomputers, *engineering (or scientific) workstations* offer extra computational power and high-quality screen displays for use in product design, computer drafting, and scientific analysis. Workstations (typically 64- or 32-bit computers) are the smaller siblings of minisupercomputers, and emerged in the early eighties. Though single-user machines, workstations offer higher-speed mathematics and more sophisticated graphics than PCs. Sun Microsystems and Hewlett-Packard are leading workstation makers.

◻ *Supermicrocomputers* are extremely fast micros with capabilities approaching those of the engineering workstations. Some companies use this term to describe their smaller minicomputer offerings.

Fortunately, classifying a particular computer precisely using one of the above terms is never critically important. Digital Equipment Corporation's Alpha AXP machine, introduced in 1993, costs under $10,000 but offers power equivalent to the mainframes of five years ago; is it micro, supermicro, or workstation? Who knows? At least one *can* say that it functions as a workstation, has the power of a mainframe and the cost of a microcomputer; that has meaning to those who understand the traditional definitions.

As should be (perhaps painfully) clear by now, the range of computers available to today's businesses is both broad and deep. Most computer companies specialize in certain sectors of the computer spectrum; there are no one-stop shopping centers for computer systems, and the prospective customer must expend considerable energy to canvass the entire market. Usually, the customer can narrow the field considerably at the outset; the small retail clothing store won't need a Cray X/MP supercomputer. However, customers who mistakenly assume that they need a certain class of machine (64-bit word size, for example) without first considering the many reasonable alternatives may spend too much money and may end up with inappropriate products.

ELEMENTS OF A TYPICAL COMPUTER

Hardware, I: The System Unit

First, let's look at the physical, tangible computer *hardware*. A typical computer room has a drab, off-white, faceless box in its center, from which a variety of cables twists like giant spaghetti, connecting the box to screens and printers and other devices. The faceless box contains the core of the machine, or *system unit*; the other connected devices clearly facilitate communication between the large box and the outside world. As those devices exist along the periphery of the system unit, they're called *peripherals*.

If we remove the cover of the faceless box to expose its innards, we'd discover a number of thin, flat plastic boards (*circuit boards*) having conductive copper traces: narrow pathways like flattened wires to carry electrical impulses.

The boards line up neatly in a row, plugged into slots that connect the circuit boards to what appears to be a common communications channel (the *bus*, or *backplane*). This channel allows the individual circuit boards to exchange information with each other as needed: the computer equivalent of a telephone party line. The circuit boards indicate a sensible, modular design: to add capabilities to the computer, one merely adds an appropriate board.

The largest circuit board seems to be designed around a large black plastic *chip*, an inch or so square, which encases layers of silicon etched in intricate and tiny patterns. The patterns are hundreds of thousands of on-off switches; this chip is a *microprocessor*, a rudimentary "brain" that can perform arithmetic, receive data, modify it, and send it out again. The *central processing unit*, or CPU, directs most of the data traffic throughout the computer.

A number of the other circuit boards also have microprocessors, which perform specialized functions to assist the primary CPU. One such board connects to a flat, wide cable leading to a sealed metal box. Disassembly of the enclosure reveals several disk-shaped platters stacked one above the other on a common spindle and connected to a motor; and a movable arm assembly with electromagnetic heads that can move in toward the center of the platters or out to their edge.

The platters are magnetized, and this *hard disk drive* uses magnetized surfaces to store data. This makes sense for information one might want to keep: Magnetic fields persist even when no power is applied to the device, just as audio tapes retain recorded music. And the stored magnetic fields can be changed at will, by magnetizing the *read/write head* on the movable arm as it passes over the platters—meaning that the drive can be reused over and over to store different information as desired. The disk drive is housed in that sealed box to prevent dust from contaminating the platter surfaces.

The circuit board to which the drive connects via cable controls the reading and writing of information to and from this storage device; it's a drive *controller*, and data moves between the drive, the controller, and the "brain," or CPU. Further examination reveals several more disk drives and controller boards within the system unit, providing more storage capacity.

One cable leads to a similar, smaller drive that is *not* enclosed, but has an open slot on the front of the box, apparently for a removable magnetic storage device. Casting a glance around the room, we discover a stack of such small disks, or *diskettes*, useful for sending information between two unconnected computers. Taking apart a diskette, we'd see a single platter similar to the ones in the hard drive, but smaller; it would be easy to find information quickly on such a platter, but surely the limited storage capacity would be a problem? It would take hundreds of these little diskettes to contain all the information on a single hard drive. And what if a hard drive broke? Surely the information on it must be stored in another place. . . .

Such as the *tape drive* nestled just beneath the diskette drive, clearly designed to accept the small tape cartridges lined up on a shelf on one wall. Disks are much faster than tapes in locating specific data elements, because the read/write head can move across the disk in a few thousandths of a second, while a tape drive may have to search through several hundred feet of tape. (A stereo owner can select a song much more rapidly with a phonograph than with a cassette deck.) Tapes work better for reading or writing large quantities of data in one continuous stream; they're therefore good for making duplicate copies of hard disk data and archiving data to be removed from the hard disk. Hard disks store data that the computer must read and write quickly during the normal course of business.

All this is well and good, but even the relatively quick hard disk drives, being mechanical devices, after all, would not really be fast enough to do the computer's daily work. Pull another circuit board out of the bus, and we find it harbors row upon row of identical chips: smaller than the microprocessors, and infinitely simpler in design. These *memory chips* (or RAM chips, short for Random Access Memory) provide high-speed data storage, twenty or thirty times faster than the hard disk drives; they have no moving parts and so must be very reliable. This is where the actual work occurs, where data is entered, retrieved, modified, and massaged.

Why isn't the entire computer made up of such high-speed storage devices? Memory chips are much more expensive than the magnetic disks, so there can only be enough of them to store the information that the human operators are currently working on.

There are no magnetic or electrical signals from the memory chips on the removed circuit board; without power, their contents disappear. When a user has entered or modified information in this high-speed memory chip area, that person must copy or *save* the information to the magnetic drive so it will be available for *loading* back from the magnetic drive the next time the system unit restarts.

The last type of circuit board in the box has a cable that runs outside the system unit. This seems to be a link between this computer and other computers, outside terminals, printers, and so on; in fact, it's a *network interface card* that does just that, providing a channel for input and output (*I/O*) to and from the main box.

It is now clear that the bus constitutes a common communication channel for the Central Processing Unit, device controllers such as the hard drive controller, the high-speed chip memory, and the network board. Some computers use several different buses for different functions: there may be a special high-speed bus connecting just the CPU and memory, for example, or a special bus to which only storage devices connect. Some system units (such as those in PCs) use a *motherboard*, a large printed circuit board housing the main processor and some memory as well as the bus slots into which other optional boards connect.

The CPU receives instructions from humans over the network cable to read stored data and programs from the inexpensive hard drives into the expensive, high-speed memory for manipulation, and then to copy the manipulated data back to the hard drives or send it out to printers or other computers, also over the network cable.

There are a few remaining components of the system unit— a silver metal *power supply* box that provides electricity to the bus, disk and tape drives, and several cooling fans that dissipate the heat energy all those components generate. Now let's examine the other pieces of hardware in the room, the peripherals.

Hardware, II: Peripherals

So-called peripheral devices include:

- *Terminals*, which consist of keyboards for data entry and screens or monitors for communication from computer to user;

- *Printers*, for recording the results of computer operations on paper;

- *Modems*, for telecommunication of data across telephone lines; and

- Additional *storage* in the form of disk drives, tape drives, or optical drives, especially if they reside outside the system unit.

An optical drive sits on a shelf above the system unit; this is a read-only "CD/ROM," which uses the same type of compact disk technology made popular in the audio industry. A low-power laser beam reads surface irregularities stamped into the disk during manufacture, interpreting them as ones and zeros. More and more software vendors are shipping programs, data files, and even documentation on CD/ROM because of its durability, convenience, high capacity, and low cost.

The network console near the system unit is a special terminal or PC used to manage the computer network. Its display is one-color (monochrome), but all the PCs on the network have color displays. The detail displayable on a screen, or *resolution*, is a function of the number of dots, or *pixels* (picture elements), that the screen may draw horizontally and vertically. All PCs have *graphics* displays that can show images or pictures along with text; mainframe terminals may have graphics capabilities but are usually text-only, or *alphanumeric*.

One peripheral that has become popular in the PC and work-station environments is the *mouse*, a pointing device with a roller on the bottom and one to three buttons on top, which the user rolls around on a desktop or special pad to move an arrow or other indicator on the computer screen. *Trackball*s are, in effect, stationary mice that are built in or hang off the side of portable computers for use in tight spaces (on an airplane, for instance).

For hard copy output, *printers* come in all shapes, sizes, and speeds:

- ❏ *Dot-matrix* printers use tiny pins in a rectangular array striking an inked ribbon to place dots on the paper to create letters and numbers.

- ❏ *Laser* printers use xerography to generate black-and-white images.

- ❏ *Ink-jet, thermal wax transfer,* and *dye sublimation* printers provide different-quality levels of color output.

- ❏ *Pen plotters* move ink pens across a moving page to create color diagrams on a wide variety of paper sizes.

All these devices can connect to their host computers in a variety of ways: Their communication "ports" may link directly to a network cable, or they may connect to a *serial* or *parallel* cable running to the system unit. In a serial connection, devices send data one pulse at a time over a single pair of wires, while in a parallel connection, devices send data in groups of pulses simultaneously over several sets of wires, a technique that's usually faster.

A large networked laser printer squats in one corner of the room; it's really a sophisticated computer in its own right, with its own CPU, memory, and programming language. This particular machine uses a popular language called PostScript; any PC on the network that has PostScript-capable software can send output to this printer and create correct pages.

Modems are classified by speed and rated in "baud" units; 9,600-baud modems can transmit or receive about 1,200 characters per second. Error-correcting modems use special circuitry to handle line noise, which can be problematical over long-distance connections. Leased phone lines are dedicated to one customer and can provide faster and cleaner data transmission. A single leased line may connect several mini or mainframe terminals to a remote computer by using *multiplexers,* which divide the communication channel among users so that each appears to have a direct, dedicated link. PC modems nowadays typically include fax send-and-receive capability. Network modems allow any user on the net to dial out.

The world of peripherals doesn't stop with terminals, printers, and modems:

- ❏ *Scanners* read paper-based text and pictures into the computer. Image scanners read documents as a pattern of tiny dots on a page, whereas text scanners with Optical Character Recognition (OCR) can distinguish and recognize letters and numbers.

- ❏ *Film recorders* perform the reverse function of printing digitally stored images on film.

- ❏ *Graphics tablets* are used by artists and draftspeople for more precise illustration and design.

- ❏ *Touch screens* are specialized monitors that can sense a user's finger on the screen surface using a grid of light beams.

- ❏ *Speech synthesizers* and *voice-recognition devices* allow computers to speak and "hear" speech.

- ❏ *Scan converters* allow computers to create video tapes, etc.

There are even specialized peripherals to scan and organize business cards! Chances are good that just about any device one can think of has been connected to a computer at one time or another.

At this point, we perch in front of the main console, tap a few keys, and restart the computer to see what happens. We're about to come face to face with the computer's most important component: *software*.

Software

Software is nothing more than the sets of instructions that tell the computer to do something. If hardware makes up the brains and body of the computer animal, software defines its intelligence and instinct—its "mind." Software is by nature more abstract and generally less understood than hardware; yet, its importance exceeds hardware's in ultimately defining the productivity and value of a computer system.

All software comes on disks or tapes and becomes useful or active when the computer *loads*, or reads, it into main memory. Loading software into memory is analogous to a chronic amnesiac waking up in the morning and reading a "to-do" list of instructions (get dressed, brush teeth, and so forth). The list is on paper and never changes, but this individual forgets it each night after falling asleep and must reread the list each morning.

SYSTEM SOFTWARE

The basic software that allows the computer to move information from one place to another and communicate with peripheral devices in an orderly way is the *operating system*. All computers have operating systems; a given computer may be able to use several different operating systems, though usually only one at a time. For example, an IBM-compatible PC may run either MS/DOS, OS/2, or UNIX (among others), each of which manage computer housekeeping operations in very different ways.

Operating systems create organized data structures on disks for storing information such as names, dates, and dollar amounts; such structures are called *data files*. The programs themselves, whether part of the operating system or applications programs, are called *code files* or, more concisely, *code*. Some computers use a hierarchical, branched file structure that allows data and code files to be grouped into *directories*; for example, October transactions might reside in a different directory than November transactions. Directories organize disks much as manila folders organize file drawers.

Operating system software, networking and communication software (which handles data movement between connected computers), and system utility programs (which help the operator manage the computer's resources) collectively comprise *system software*. In the heyday of mainframes, the same company that built the computer (usually IBM) would write and sell system software for it. Although many companies (for example, Apple) still work that way, it's no longer generally true with small computers; one may buy a PC from Compaq but the operating system from Microsoft. The process that the computer goes through at power-up, when the system software loads into RAM, is called *bootstrapping*, or *booting* for short; the machine figuratively pulls itself up by its bootstraps.

APPLICATION SOFTWARE

In contrast to system software, programs that enable users to do specific and useful tasks with the computer, such as word processing and inventory management, are *application software*. They use the facilities provided by the operating system behind the scenes, but the user may not even know the operating system is there. Activating application programs is also done by reading the program from disk or tape into primary memory; this is *running* or *executing* the program.

Many kinds of application programs exist. *Horizontal market* programs, which may apply to a wide variety of industries, cover such areas as:

- Bookkeeping and accounting;

- Inventory;

- Word processing;

- Desktop publishing;

- Spreadsheets;

- Communications;

- Databases;

- Desktop utilities, such as calendars and phone lists;

- Business graphics;

- Computer-aided design (CAD);

- Illustration and paint;

- Project management;

- Investment management;

- Decision support systems (DSS);

- Educational software, and many other types.

Vertical market programs address specific industries, such as real estate or manufacturing. These programs may combine elements of horizontal market software with special features for a particular industry's needs. For example, a property management program is a specialized database system that tracks tenants, leases, contract services, payments, and so forth.

Much of the general-purpose computer's flexibility derives from the fact that the operating system and applications programs are not "cast in stone": the machine reads them into memory from disk each time it is turned on, and they may be modified to suit different needs and markets. This flexibility can create problems: It's easy to modify the way the machine behaves but difficult to predict all the possible results of a seemingly simple, single change. The quality and reliability of the computer's work are directly proportional to the quality and reliability of the software instructions that guide it—*Garbage in, garbage out.*

PROGRAMMING LANGUAGES

Technical experts (and, all too frequently, nonexperts) write their own applications programs using *programming languages*. A language is itself a program; it allows the programmer to compose English-like instructions that tell the computer what to do in a very flexible and customizable way, without the programmer having to worry about all the underlying details. Sometimes, programmers *want* to manipulate those details for the fastest speed possible or to keep their programs smaller; they will then write in a less abstract and more detailed language called *machine language* or *assembly language*.

High-level languages (such as BASIC, COBOL, Pascal, or "C") enable programmers to use single, concise instructions for common operations that might correspond to several machine-language instructions, thereby saving time and money. Still higher-level languages are the *program generators* or *fourth-generation languages* (4GLs); these enable programmers to perform more powerful tasks with even fewer commands at a higher level of abstraction from the machine language.

The first programming language most people learn is BASIC, which does *not* mean "a basic language" but rather (believe it or not) "*B*eginner's *A*ll-purpose *S*ymbolic *I*nstruction *C*ode." My personal favorite language name is APL, used in mathematical and statistical work. Its acronym stands for "*A Programming Language.*"

Programs called *compilers* translate the work of the programmer, called *source code*, into instructions that the machine can understand directly (*object code*). Companies that buy applications that they'd like to modify extensively can often pay significantly more money and buy not just object code but source code as well, without which modification becomes much more difficult and expensive if it's even possible at all.

Networks

When computers connect in networks, users can share files as well as expensive resources such as high-quality printers; they can also send messages to each other. Networks are aggregations of CPUs and other devices, connected by cabling systems, which may communicate and share resources using specialized software.

Local-Area Networks (*LANs*) connect computers within a single geographical location; *Wide-Area Networks* (*WANs*) span different cities or countries by way of dedicated phone lines, satellite links, or public data networks. Networks have both hardware components (network circuit boards, cables) and software components (file-sharing facilities, security features to control network access). PCs, minicomputers, workstations, and mainframes may all participate on the same network, though this is not always as easy as it sounds.

Networks have *distributed* or *decentralized* processing abilities because the intelligence (processing power) divides out among the various CPUs on the network rather than concentrating in a single centralized, high-speed CPU. Client/server networks, the preferred type in most organizations, use dedicated machines called *servers* to share files, printers, and applications. Peer-to-peer networks allow any user to share his or her files with any other user and may make sense for small businesses or project teams, but these lack security and are more difficult to administer.

Bridges and *gateways* link different networks, and networks to mainframes. A bridge, or *internet*, connects two or more identical networks to each other, allowing the two to continue operating independently while also providing a path for transferring data between them as necessary. One kind of gateway connects two or more different networks to each other; another kind links a network to communication services, such as a public data net.

Businesses will have an easier time dealing with the computer industry if they have some inkling of its short history, which concludes this chapter.

A QUICK HISTORY OF COMPUTING

Beginnings

The history of computers teems with dramatic stories about inventors, scientists, businessmen, generals, and lawyers. It's an extraordinarily compressed saga in which thousands of remarkable events and developments occur in the short span of a very few decades; in which small companies became huge and individuals made incredible fortunes in the span of months; in which industry giants have endured a painful comeuppance for resting on their laurels. Here, however, there is only time to summarize the highlights in order to place modern machines into perspective and suggest the origin of some of the problems afflicting the industry today.

Though in one sense computers have been around for about five thousand years, since the invention of the abacus, electronic computers are relatively new to the business scene. The Census Bureau dedicated the first business computer, Remington Rand's UNIVAC, for use in March 1951.

The decade from 1951 to 1961 saw amazing leaps forward in computer technology. The late Dr. An Wang introduced core memory in 1953 at MIT, allowing computers to become smaller, more reliable, and less power-hungry. Programming languages began to develop in 1951, and the first commercial language compiler was IBM's FORTRAN (*FOR*mula *TRAN*slator) in 1957.

Nineteen-fifty-seven was also the year that the transistor, introduced in 1948 by Bell Labs, began to find its way into computers; it would replace the expensive and unwieldy vacuum tube in computers just as it would do in radios and televisions. In 1961, the integrated circuit was in commercial development, leading to dramatic improvements in the miniaturization and power consumption of computer circuits. These developments fueled the rapid acceptance of computers as viable tools.

Government agencies, primarily the military, funded computers of the early fifties. They calculated weapons trajectories, planned aircraft interception courses, and assisted in the design of atomic weapons. Many people are unaware that IBM actually got off to a slow start in business computing; during this period, Remington Rand was the market leader and IBM was playing catchup, not forging into the lead until around 1956. From 1958 to 1963, twenty-six of the largest computers ever made were installed nationwide as part of a defense network to monitor aircraft. The Social Security Administration was another early computer purchaser (though many retirees will attest that despite its long experience, the SSA still hasn't really figured out computers).

Business and the Mainframe

Slowly, as the commercial applications of computer technology became apparent, business got interested. Nineteen-sixty-four saw the introduction of IBM's SABRE, a reservations computer built for American Airlines. That year also marked the debut of IBM's System/360, the first major computer product family, which cost the company over $5 billion to develop. System/360 was truly a "bet the company" project and ultimately an extremely important machine; its influence remains visible today in many IBM mainframes and operating systems. The System/370, which followed in the seventies, used the new integrated circuits.

The late fifties and early sixties were the days of big mainframe computers, a market dominated by IBM and the so-called "plug-compatible" manufacturers such as Burroughs, Control Data, and NCR, which built IBM workalikes. Mainframe makers typically leased rather than sold their computers, and installed full-time, on-site technical staffs for their care and feeding. Because the machines were so expensive, and because IBM's training and support (typically and cannily included in the lease agreements) kept the relationship between vendor and customer a close one, IBM customers tended to remain IBM customers; it would have been too expensive and risky to switch. In the mid-sixties, IBM owned over 60 percent of the computer market.

A secondary industry of service bureaus sold time on their mainframes ("time-sharing") to companies that couldn't afford or justify having one of their own and developed specialized services for those companies. From the mid-fifties to the early sixties, most machines operated in batch mode: jobs ran through the machine all at once and processed in sequential order. Any given job might take hours to finish. Candidates for batch processing are payroll, billing, financial reporting, and other monthly activities. Even today, most service bureaus perform jobs such as payroll processing in batch mode. For many firms, outsourcing computer services entirely with firms such as ADP was much less expensive and painful than leasing their own machines and trying to do things themselves.

A Change in Scale

As the need for access to up-to-date information increased, commercial business computers emerged that could function in *interactive* mode, where users update or enter information on the computer randomly and frequently over the course of a week or day or hour. In this way, data is always current. Minicomputers helped make interactive computing possible.

The minicomputer arrived on the scene in the 1960s, courtesy of Digital Equipment Corporation (DEC). The "mini" was originally developed for specialized applications in which small size was essential, such as on-board airplane navigation systems. It soon metamorphosed into a vehicle to bring commercial computing power to small and medium-size businesses or departments that could not afford a mainframe but which could benefit from in-house automation.

Many business computing needs were small enough to be met by a minicomputer like DEC's PDP-8, which cost $20,000 at its introduction in 1963. (PDP stood for *Programmable Data Processor*.) Because they were less expensive than mainframes, companies could buy minicomputers outright instead of leasing them and devote them to single jobs instead of dividing computer time among many jobs. These were fundamental changes. The minicomputer companies—DEC, HP, Data General—enjoyed rapidly expanding growth throughout the seventies. As customers migrated some of their computer applications off mainframes and onto the more economical minicomputers, a twenty-year trend, now called "downsizing," began. That trend will probably continue for another twenty years as advances in small systems continue outpacing advances in large ones.

Minicomputers have come a long way since their introduction. Early minis required specialized personnel to set them up, service and operate them. Many smaller minis may be set up and run by non-computer experts, and all can operate interactively. Networks of minicomputers proved so successful during the eighties that DEC was the darling of Wall Street when most other computer firms were suffocating from weak demand. Another reason DEC was so successful was their policy of listening to customers who didn't want to rewrite all their software when they moved to a larger computer. Within the DEC VAX product line, the same software could run on the largest or the smallest model—a growth path that IBM had never offered. My own consulting clients valued that philosophy so much that they bought DEC minis over IBM machines many times during that period, despite IBM's still-strong image as the safe choice.

One of the important side effects of the mini was a change in customer attitude. Technical people within organizations started to feel more comfortable buying systems from companies other than IBM. DEC's popularity in the eighties was the beginning of serious competition for IBM, competition from companies designing new *kinds* of computers rather than plug-compatible mainframes, companies with ears a little closer to the customers. (Regis McKenna chronicles this attitude shift in his entertaining book, *Who's Afraid of Big Blue?*)

Largely as a result of this attitude shift, the seventies engendered a new kind of computer company: the *systems integrator*, who assembled bits and pieces from several computer companies and put together systems that more closely met a given customer's needs. In today's multivendor market, systems integrators continue to play a strong role.

Times change, and the minicomputer market is now showing signs of decline. DEC, for example, is seeing sales shift from its proprietary, high-profit VAX minicomputer line to smaller and less profitable microcomputer networks. This shift is a primary reason for DEC's financial woes and heavy layoffs of the early nineties, and for the bankruptcy of firms such as Wang, which underestimated the importance of the now-ubiquitous PC, or microcomputer.

The Microcomputer Revolution

Intel introduced the microprocessor chip in 1971 with its model 4004, paving the way for the next revolution in computer technology. Recall that a microprocessor is a single silicon chip with a complete general-purpose computer brain inside, consisting of thousands of transistors and logic circuits. The micro*computer* (which is based on the micro*processor*) traces its origins back to the Mark-8 hobbyist kit of 1974 and the $600 Altair 8800 of 1975. The colorful duo of Steve Jobs and Steve Wozniak introduced the Apple II somewhat later (1977), and it became a great commercial success—Apple manufactured it in one form or another until 1993! Apple went from zero to over $100 million in revenues in less than two years.

How does the micro differ from the mini? Minis are multiuser systems with more than one terminal, while the micro functions most often as a single-user device. Minis also are characterized by larger physical size, greater centralization of data, higher levels of security, more sophisticated "diagnostics" (self-testing software), and a higher price tag.

Although many industrial and technological developments laid the groundwork for the microcomputer, such as improved integrated circuit production methods, in the final analysis *software* makes or breaks a computer in the marketplace. The history of computing is full of examples of perfectly good and interesting machines that never caught on because, for one reason or another, no one ever wrote any compelling software for them.

VisiCalc, the first electronic spreadsheet and the spiritual ancestor of programs like Lotus 1-2-3 and Microsoft Excel, really launched the microcomputer and was responsible for the remarkable success of the Apple II. The program enabled users to perform mathematical modeling, financial ledgers, projections, and tabular reports with one programming tool. A very simple program technically, VisiCalc's genius was that it made the power of the microcomputer available in an understandable and broadly usable way.

IBM introduced its personal computer into the marketplace, in typically conservative fashion, in 1981—after Apple had demonstrated the market's viability. IBM manufactured almost nothing for the new PC itself; its role was much more like a systems integrator, choosing commercially available pieces and gluing them together. IBM's open architecture, in contrast to Apple's secretive and proprietary designs, ensured both the success and failure of the IBM PC: manufacturers created more software and peripherals for the PC but soon began "cloning" its design and competing with IBM in the marketplace. IBM's predictable slowness in improving the original PC left the door wide open for companies such as Compaq to take market share away by building a better product. Today, IBM-compatible and Apple microcomputers dominate the marketplace.

The Recent Past

The story of computing since 1977 has been one of dramatic but evolutionary improvements in speed, reliability, and affordability. Laptops and notebooks have made microcomputer power practical for the road. Graphical displays, pioneered by the 1984 Apple Macintosh, provide a new and richer way for people to interact with computers, compared with older text-only displays. Microprocessor architecture is moving from CISC (Complex Instruction Set Computer) to RISC (Reduced Instruction Set Computer) for better speed and less costly design. Networks, pioneered by DEC and others in the seventies to connect all those minicomputers, have grown up into mature, mostly reliable, and nearly manageable systems. Today's faster machines are making digital sound and video possible at reasonable costs, spawning a new software category called *multimedia*. Minisupercomputers, introduced in the early eighties, offer nearly the speed of multi-million-dollar supercomputers but at a fraction of the cost.

Much of this rapid change is the result of companies using computers to build better computers; the technology is self-accelerating.

Despite all the new wrinkles, important though they are, no fundamentally new *kind* of general-purpose computer has appeared as a commercially viable category, despite the attempts of Apple's Newton and the like to create a new genre of "Personal Digital Assistants." Computers all still work much the same as they did twenty years ago. When people mention the fast pace of change in this industry, it's true that the pace is incredibly fast in an evolutionary sense, but it's not fast at all in terms of revolutions. The last real revolution was the microcomputer, in 1977.

Rather, miniaturization, improved manufacturing processes, better materials, and economies of scale have combined to provide far more computing power per dollar today than ever before. The hard disk drive that cost $1,000 per "megabyte" (a unit of storage) in 1983 costs $1 per megabyte in 1993, and lasts forty times longer. A computer with 100 kilobytes of main memory would have cost about $1 million in the late sixties; in the early nineties, machines with eighty times as much memory cost $2,000 (five hundred times less). The laser printer that cost $400,000 in 1974 costs $900 in 1994. And the list goes on. To a large extent, the popularity of microcomputers has driven rapid increases in performance per dollar because those machines were inexpensive enough to attract a large customer base quickly, fueling sales and accelerating advancement.

It's therefore no wonder that computers have become so prevalent. There were perhaps twenty thousand computers in the United States in the mid-sixties. That number had doubled by 1970. By 1987, it had grown to 12 million; by 1994, there were over 50 million.

Strangely, almost unbelievably, this population of computers is simultaneously a powerful ally of modern business and an enormous millstone around its neck. Now that the basic types of computers are understood, their fundamental component parts explained, and their history laid out (if only briefly), it's time to explore vigorously why this remarkable army of computer systems is so ineffectually deployed in today's workplace—and what businesses can do about it. It's time, in short, for some myth busting.

Part III

Myths
and Truths:
The Big Picture

MYTH 1

Computer Productivity Is Unmeasurable

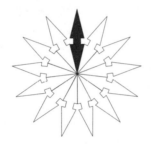

"What is essential is invisible to the eye."

—Antoine de Saint-Exupéry,
French author and aviator,
The Little Prince (1943)

THE MYTH

A popular business computer text from the late 1960s suggested that although it's impossible to evaluate a computer's efficiency by looking at it, the curious manager can learn a great deal from the orderliness of the computer room and the work habits of the system managers. If tape reels and reports are haphazardly strewn about and data processing staff are putting in long hours, computer operations are inefficient. If everything is tidy,

59

and the staff rarely works overtime, operations are efficient and the computer system is contributing to the organization's effectiveness.

Simpleminded suggestions like this one have led many a manager to give up entirely on the prospect of measuring automation's productivity impact. If an organization never measures that impact, thinking the task to be impossible, then that organization will never discover how small the impact really is. Its managers will continue to believe the primary Computer Myth—that computer systems automatically improve bottom-line productivity, that automation and efficiency are cause and effect. The first step in challenging the primary myth is to demonstrate that there *are* steps businesses can take to begin evaluating automation's productivity impact. This, then, is the first myth to explore: *computer productivity impact is unmeasurable*.

These mysterious, high-tech products and the strange industry that creates them seemingly conspire to obscure the answer to the simple question: What *do* computers really contribute to the organization? Yet, what more relevant and important question can businesses ask about the technology that increasingly dominates the landscape?

This chapter first explores *why* organizations know so little about computer productivity that they believe this first and most pervasive myth. Second, we examine the consequences of this ignorance. Finally, based on the reality that automation's benefits are never automatic but can only be verified by careful observation and measurement, this chapter suggests solutions to this first and, perhaps, most challenging problem.

ROOTS OF MYTH #1

Technotrust

The first reason many organizations don't work at measuring computer impact is that they believe the impact is inherently positive. One doesn't test what one takes for granted, especially when there are so many more obviously pressing tasks at hand.

Of course, many business computers *do* improve productivity. Companies that switch from manual to automated systems often have a sense that things are being done more rapidly and accurately. But because this sometimes holds true, and because the actual improvement is so difficult to measure experimentally, as we'll see, it's tempting to assume that automation *always* improves productivity. Part I of this book suggested that this is a very dangerous leap of faith. The following two examples help illustrate in more detail why automation isn't necessarily productive.

AUTOMATED INEFFICIENCY

Though most computer vendors won't admit it, some activities become *less* efficient when computerized. Take the example of automating data entry, storage, and retrieval in computerized databases, one of the more common business applications. Because the computer can store structured sets of information—such as customer lists and inventory data—very compactly, and retrieve that data much faster and more flexibly than manual filing systems, managers often assume that it's a more efficient solution.

But is it really? *Not if the data's inaccurate!* What's the use of computerizing data if one can't trust the results? Is this productive automation, or "backwards progress"?

Observers who minimize the problem of database inaccuracy ask why more reports and articles don't appear about it if it's so bad. There are at least three reasons. One is embarrassment: What company wants reporters writing about the poor quality of their data? Another is liability; fear of lawsuits from customers, shareholders, perhaps the government. A third is security. Corporations keep their databases under wraps.

It may be true that on-line databases are no *less* reliable than old manual filing systems. However, computer printouts carry an aura of authority that belies their frequent inaccuracy. The neatly organized columns of figures can inspire a false confidence. Only computer professionals and seasoned managers, who know about invisible inefficiency, have learned to doubt computer databases' accuracy and to question the reality of the neatly printed data.

Consider another example: scanning paper documents into computers. The digitized papers can indeed be filed, cataloged, retrieved, and archived more easily and quickly than their paper originals. But optical character recognition isn't usually perfect. It may have a 99 percent accuracy rate, which sounds fine until you start thinking about decimal points in financial reports or product model numbers or phone numbers. This is one reason law firms still hire double-blind teams of data entry clerks to key in data from paper documents.

INFLEXIBLE AUTOMATION

Even in tasks where automation *does* boost efficiency, an improvement in performing a single, narrowly defined task doesn't necessarily translate into productivity gains in the broader business context, where that task may change over time. In a manufacturing plant, for example, automated assembly systems may not be able to switch over to different designs as quickly as human workers, reducing the company's ability to match production to demand in a fluctuating market. Some manufacturers are now "de-automating" their plants for this very reason! Consider the following case, from the May 7, 1993, *Wall Street Journal:*

"Federal-Mogul . . . revamped its Lancaster, Pa. auto-parts plant in 1987 with state-of-the-art automation. . . . But before long, Federal-Mogul found that although the plant turned out parts much faster than before, it couldn't shift gears quickly. To switch from making a small clutch bearing to a larger one, for instance, required a slew of changes. . . . Out went the robots [and] most production-line computers."

Blind faith in the efficiency and productivity of computers prevents managers from even *asking* whether their systems really work. Perhaps that faith has its roots in the extraordinary technological successes of our age, or an admiration for the engineers that can place 3 million transistors onto a square inch of silicon. Whatever its cause, it has certainly added billions of dollars to the computer industry's coffers.

Mission: Invisible

Just as it's difficult to evaluate a human employee with no job description or project assignment, one can't measure the cost-effectiveness of an information system without knowing what it's supposed to be doing. Many business computers have no clear job description. That's part of what makes measuring their productivity so difficult, and the second reason many organizations don't try.

Managers may buy computer systems for the sake of some shadowy vision of efficiency or modernity. They may automate because their competitors are doing so, or because of the blind faith in technology we just discussed. Projects that should never go forward receive approval because no one wants to be seen as impeding the march of progress.

The manager who implements a corporate-wide network so that "everyone in the organization can communicate faster and better with everyone else" has not defined a specific enough goal. Does every individual *need* to communicate with every other individual? Why? Without a clearer goal, the new system might become another vehicle for corporate junk mail and interoffice chitchat, or employees might not even use it at all. A better goal might be "to speed up idea exchange between marketing and engineering during new product design," or "to reduce time employees waste reading irrelevant interoffice memos by using the computer to restrict distribution."

Just as bad, some organizations lay out too many goals for their computer projects. When hiring employees, savvy interviewers grow suspicious when a candidate professes the ability to do anything and everything well. Companies should harbor similar doubts when a project champion or system vendor claims that the new computer will reduce operating costs, improve product quality, shrink development time, and increase customer service levels all at the same time.

Who's Got the Tape Measure?

To really find out whether a given computer system improves business productivity, someone has to *want* to measure it. Who is measuring the effectiveness of automation in your organization? Who is motivated to do so?

It may seem reasonable to expect the Corporate Information Systems (CIS) staff to track productivity impact. However, these are typically the same people who lobbied for the system in the first place. If they demonstrate that their suggestions didn't work, their reputations and, perhaps, careers may suffer. In addition, computer professionals work hard to justify projects with legitimate value; they are not about to undermine those projects by casting doubt in their managers' minds about the value of automation in general. They're also not likely to provide reasons to cut the CIS department budget.

The computer vendors? They stand to gain if they can demonstrate productivity benefits. However, as long as their customers accept those benefits without proof, the vendors are unlikely to probe for the whole truth—especially if it may expose their systems as adding less benefit than their customers already tend to believe is present. As a result, most computer companies advertise only the minority of cases in which their products deliver a very clear, easily measurable efficiency improvement. One should not expect them to evaluate their products objectively; they're trying to sell more of them, after all.

Ignorance in this case is bliss for all the individuals directly involved in automation, except for one group: the end-users. The trouble here is that in many organizations, no one is asking their opinions.

Difficulties of a Scientific Approach

"When you can measure what you are speaking about, and express it in numbers, you know something about it; but when you cannot measure it . . . your knowledge is of a meager and unsatisfactory kind."

—LORD KELVIN,
PIONEERING BRITISH PHYSICIST,
Popular Lectures and Addresses
(1891–1894)

Another reason no one tries to measure computer impact is that measuring productivity is so difficult. A brilliant scientist such as Kelvin may declare that quantification is essential to knowledge, but that doesn't make it easy.

In interviews with chief information executives of thirty companies, Thomas D. Clark, a Florida State professor, reported that "40% felt that the assessment of [computer] systems at the enterprise level was not useful because of the difficulties involved." To measure the extent to which an information system is improving productivity, in the spirit of the scientific method, one would have to operate for a year with the system; shut it down for the following year and do everything manually; and compare the results. Even then, the only way this experiment would work is if business conditions were identical both years. In reality, there is no "control group" against which to compare. The business world makes a poor laboratory.

A more practical approach might be to determine whether the company, or division or department, enjoys greater success after automation than before. However, so many other factors affect success that this approach won't tell us much. Do you get well after a bout of flu because of medication, because you rested in bed for a day or two, or because the virus simply ran its course? Pharmaceutical firms and your doctor would like you to believe the drugs played an important role; the computer industry and your CIS department would like you to believe computers help improve your business. But do they? How do you *know*?

THE TROUBLE WITH COST/BENEFIT

In those cases when someone does make an attempt to measure the impact of computerization, the usual method is *cost-benefit* (or, *price-performance* or *cost-effectiveness*). Automators often use this approach to help justify their projects. Here's how it works in a nutshell:

Assume we could quantify computer performance, representing in dollars the administrative savings and revenue increases over, say, a year's time that we may reasonably attribute to the computer. We could then divide this sum into the system's cost, including the amortized purchase price plus all direct and indirect costs, to yield the cost/benefit ratio. If the quotient is less than 1, then presumably the computer system is improving productivity. Whether it is improving productivity *better* than other alternatives is another question; a barely productive computer system, with a ratio of 0.99, represents a poorer investment than a money-market account paying 3 percent interest.

BENEFITS ARE HARD TO QUANTIFY

Much of this book deals with how to distinguish "good" computer systems from poor ones, and how to manage them intelligently. Assuming for the moment that we have a well-designed system and that we manage it properly, what benefits might it bring?

❑ Reduce operating costs, including personnel, the computer's traditional role.

❑ Help managers make better decisions by providing fast and accurate information on markets, operations, and competitors—Executive Information Systems, or EIS.

❑ Improve customer service (for example, faster order processing, product support).

❑ Speed product development cycles and get products to market faster.

❑ Improve product quality.

❑ Offer new product features or services by analyzing sales trends.

❑ Attract new customers.

❑ Gain repeat business from existing customers.

The first of these might be reasonably easy to quantify. But how does one quantify the value of better executive decision making, or improved customer service? What is the dollar value of getting products designed and built 50 percent faster? How does one attribute new sales or repeat business to automation projects? These questions are so difficult that most managers never really try to answer them. The denominator of the cost/benefit ratio therefore remains shrouded in mystery.

Organizations often try to make up for this uncertainty by devoting considerable effort to estimating and tracking information system costs. They don't realize that the accuracy of cost/ benefit analysis is only as good as the accuracy of *both* ratio components. It's not necessary to go into detailed probability calculations to understand this point. If the cost estimate is accurate to within 5 percent, but the benefit estimate is only correct plus or minus 50 percent, the ratio of the two cannot be accurate to within 5 percent and, in fact, will probably not even be accurate to within 50 percent.

ORGANIZATIONS UNDERESTIMATE COSTS

All companies know much more about computer system costs than benefits because of the ease of totaling up the hardware and software product prices and staff time. However, managers and business owners frequently ignore the many *indirect* and *life-cycle* costs of information systems, leading them to overestimate cost-effectiveness and buy systems that hurt more than help. Even activities that become more efficient when computerized, improving operations and *seeming* to save money, may incur costs that outweigh the efficiency gains.

Management guru Peter F. Drucker recently wrote, "Traditional cost accounting in manufacturing—now 75 years old—does not record the cost of nonproducing, such as the cost of faulty quality, or of a machine being out of order, or of needed parts not being on hand." Replace "manufacturing" with "automation," and "parts" with "data," and the statement is equally true.

Examples of frequently underestimated, or even ignored, costs include physical facilities, insurance, personnel time, training and support, professional and technical services, conversions, upgrades, and downtime. Later in this chapter, we'll take a closer look at these costs and how to estimate them more accurately.

How Hard Do Computers Work?

Are computers working as hard as they could be? Unused computer power is difficult to notice, much less quantify, and this is yet another reason businesses believe Myth #1. There is no obvious way of seeing how hard a computer is working, and its potential productivity depends upon a complex function of hardware, software, and human factors for which no convenient unit of measure exists.

We can evaluate the performance of human beings more easily because we are human beings ourselves, and our awareness of our own capabilities forms a frame of reference. Except for those who spend their professional careers studying information systems and productivity, we have no such frame of reference for computers.

Most organizations have no idea how well or poorly their computers work! It turns out that system inefficiencies lurk invisibly behind every luminescent screen, within every whirring disk drive, along every twisting network cable.

SPECIFICATION CONFUSION

Perhaps *specifications* could help quantify computer power. How do vendors rate computers? Partly because of the wide variety of tasks that general-purpose business systems handle, experts widely acknowledge even the most well-accepted computer specifications to be nearly meaningless.

Processors—computers' electronic brains—may be rated in "Millions of Instructions Per Second" (MIPS), but manufacturers will not guarantee that one 10-MIPS machine will run the same program at the same speed as another 10-MIPS machine. Many other design elements influence performance:

- The speed with which data moves internally through the machine;

- The "intelligence," or processing capabilities, of "peripheral" devices;

- The efficiency with which multiple users (or multiple tasks) work simultaneously;

- The extent to which user programs take advantage of the unique features of that particular machine, and so on.

For these reasons, some computer makers will not even publish MIPS ratings, leading industry pundits to redefine the MIPS acronym as "Meaningless Index to Performance of Systems."

Other ratings, such as *clock speed*—measured in millions of cycles per second, or megahertz—and *word size*—16-bit, 32-bit, etc.—give a general guide to speed but are not definitive. A 16-bit machine might outperform a 32-bit machine, and 33-megahertz processors can outpace 50-megahertz processors. Even a 2,000-megahertz, 128-bit machine will be slow if no one's written appropriate software for it, if no employee knows how to use it, or if the network it's attached to creates a bottleneck.

BENCHMARK BIAS

Another technique for measuring computer power is the *benchmark*, a program that taxes a machine's power, like a treadmill, and measures its speed performing certain tasks. However, benchmarks contain internal biases depending on what they're designed to test. Some focus on a processor's number-crunching power; others on the speed of input and output operations; still others test performance with multiple users working concurrently. Computer and component manufacturers have become adept at optimizing their products for common industry benchmarks, making comparisons all the more difficult.

Often a computer's software blocks the hardware's ability to work well. Partly, this is due to customers who accord software secondary priority, partly to software vendors who create "resource hogs"—inefficient programs that sap hardware power. Finally, the designs of many systems don't reflect enough attention to human factors or ergonomics.

No one number, nor even one combination of numbers, accurately describes the performance of a particular machine, much less a network of interconnected machines. If it is so difficult to rate the maximum performance of a computer using laboratory tests, it's even harder to determine whether the machine is working up to its capacity in a real-world business situation, or if problems or design failures are holding it back from its potential performance. The second half of this chapter addresses this issue, but it's so challenging that most companies don't know where to begin.

Imagine a driver with a new car whose parking brake was set at the dealership. This model has a brake indicator light, but it's under the hood instead of on the dashboard, and the handle is tucked out of sight. Customers would never accept such a design in an automobile, but computer makers somehow get away with designing machines this way. The brake disks silently and invisibly dissipate motor energy into useless heat and friction. The owner has no idea that the car is performing under its capabilities and could drive it for weeks or months without detecting the problem. Similarly, computer users, especially on a new system, have no way of knowing about the silent forces dissipating the power of the computing engine. The computer experts may have tools to measure those forces, but, as we've seen, they may not be talking.

CONSEQUENCES OF MYTH #1

"Though barely out of its infancy, information technology is already one of the most effective ways ever devised to squander corporate assets."

—STRATFORD SHERMAN,
Fortune (Autumn 1993)

Now that it's clear why businesses may believe that computer productivity impact can't be measured, what are some of the consequences of not at least *trying* to measure it?

Unproductive Systems

Problems not easily seen tend not to get solved. This is the main reason so many business computers don't improve productivity. Though spending on information technology now accounts for about 30 percent of U.S. businesses' capital budgets, the *Journal of Systems Management* reports that "the huge investment in IT [Information Technology] has had little impact on productivity. . . . While manufacturing productivity rose 44% during the 1980s, it edged up a scant 1.9% in the service sector, the site of 85% of IT spending . . . the most productive companies spend less on IT than companies with average productivity." And yet, companies continue to buy unproductive information systems when they could be spending those dollars more profitably.

Tool-to-Task Mismatches

In cases where computers do improve productivity, it makes sense to ask if they are working at tasks best suited to their abilities. The cost/benefit ratio may be low in a given situation, but is it as low as it *could* be given the capabilities of the technology? Are we seeing ratios of 0.8 when we should be seeing 0.6 or even 0.3?

The answer, in my experience, is usually yes. Invisible inefficiency cripples the performance of even productive systems when the tool does not well match the task.

Though a secretarial pool made up of Ph.D.'s who are also expert typists might be very efficient in terms of words per minute typed, using such individuals as typists is highly unproductive. The company would receive much greater value if they performed tasks better suited to their abilities. Similar situations abound in business computing: The only employees using computers are administrative assistants with word processing software, and financial analysts with spreadsheets. Companies miss out on the computer's ability to perform "what-if" analysis, to perform statistical correlations and regressions for decision support, to offer multiple views of the organization's performance in real time, to research electronic databases for strategically valuable information on markets and competitors.

Many managers seem proud of their unfamiliarity with computers—"I have people to do that kind of thing for me"—not realizing how those machines could help them manage better. This attitude ensures that the organization won't use its information systems to their potential. In addition, automators don't let their imaginations roam far enough afield when it comes to applying computer technology in new and productive ways.

Underused Systems

Finally, even in cases where businesses computerize productively and use the technology to best advantage by matching tools to tasks, we often see significant overcapacity. Many systems loaf along at 5 percent or 10 percent of their capacity, like the Acura NSX bought to drive around town at 40 mph.

Though companies should not necessarily make maximizing computer use a business goal, and though overcapacity may come in handy later when the organization grows, we'll see later that overcapacity costs a great deal today and is likely to deliver zero return tomorrow. It's cheaper and smarter to buy upgradable systems better matched to today's demand.

THE PROBLEM

What conclusions can we make at this point?

- ☐ Business customers perceive little of the misuse and under-use of their computing resources; they have an unjustified faith in the technology, though a healthy skepticism is far more realistic. Some activities become less productive when computerized; others that *appear* to improve productivity may create hidden costs exceeding the benefits provided.

- ☐ Businesses don't clearly delineate goals for computer systems, or they specify too many goals at once, making it all but impossible to evaluate system performance.

- ☐ Neither customers nor vendors are likely to go out of their way to measure computer impact.

- ☐ Assigning a dollar value to the benefits of automation is difficult, partly because scientific comparisons with manual systems are impractical.

- ☐ Forces that sap computer power often operate without customer knowledge.

The result of all this is:

- ☐ Information system productivity remains far lower than it could be.

- ☐ Companies don't match computer power with appropriate tasks.

- ☐ Systems often tick along at a small percentage of their capacity.

In the chapters that follow, the hidden problems will be discussed so managers can understand and correct them. For now, here's how businesses can do a better job predicting and measuring computer impact.

THE REALITY

Organizations *can* reverse old trends and begin measuring computer productivity impact. The methods include:

- Changing attitudes toward computing;

- Associating computers with specific and creative business goals;

- Involving employees and vendors with monitoring technology impact;

- Doing a better job measuring cost/benefit factors and wasted capacity.

Many companies are starting to embrace these methods and reap the benefits, and it's certain that "the ability to harness extraordinary technological change will define economic winners and losers in the foreseeable future," as Howard Gleckman wrote in a recent *Business Week* article.

The first step to becoming a technology winner is to become more scientific about automation, and begin sketching in the outlines that define both computing's invisible inefficiencies and its equally elusive potentialities. The first step in becoming scientific is to shed inaccurate preconceptions.

Adopt a Healthy Skepticism

In tomorrow's successful organizations, managers and technologists alike will outgrow their blind faith in technology and instead adopt a healthy skepticism toward all claims of improved productivity. Computers are tools that don't automatically make their users good mechanics. The secret is in choosing the right tool for the job and wielding it skillfully.

Our natural tendency to trust technology makes it a surprise to learn that the high-tech laser scanners in the grocery stores have a 5 percent error rate; that a computer-controlled radiation therapy machine could unintentionally deliver lethal X-ray blasts; or that the $15 billion Patriot missile had a software flaw that cost twenty-eight soldiers their lives in Dhahran in 1991, as Leonard Lee describes in *The Day the Phones Stopped*. The appearance of slick efficiency often belies underlying design flaws invisible to all but rational skeptics.

I wish I had $100 for every computer-generated table I've seen in my career that was inaccurate, misleading, incomplete, or all three; for every computer advertisement I've read that has promised increased productivity unconditionally, unequivocally, and without any basis in fact; for every business person I've met with such implicit faith in their PC's reliability that they never made a copy of essential data, only to rue that decision later after frantic wasted days of trying to rebuild a "crashed" hard drive.

The skeptical business person not only guards against technology failure but, more important, questions its contribution to productivity. Does the automated calendar really save time when one must manually reconcile one's laptop and desktop computers after each business trip? Can an electronic document imaging system boost productivity if the scanning software only gets ninety-five out of a hundred characters right on average? Will the automated factory reduce costs when the annual maintenance contract costs more than twenty production workers' salaries? Can the word processing system save time when employees now perform ten times as many rewrites on every document?

The answer is usually maybe, sometimes no, rarely an unambiguous yes. Those who assume productivity benefits from information technology may be the least likely to realize them.

The more managers know about computer systems, the better they will understand their strengths and weaknesses and be able to rationally evaluate which possible advantages are realistic and which aren't. Skepticism without knowledge isn't useful.

Associate Technology with Business Goals

Managers who associate information systems with concrete business goals when evaluating existing systems or considering new ones have a much better chance of being able to evaluate them later on. If companies buy computers to fulfill clearly delineated business functions, they can begin to analyze how well the systems perform by measuring the degree to which they fulfill those functions.

Though many of the examples in this book have to do with medium or large organizations, here's one from a small business—mine. As a consultant, I spend a lot of time reading computer trade journals. At one point, my company subscribed to thirteen different periodicals, some of which ran several hundred pages per issue. I was reading two to three hours a day. To a degree, that's part of the consultant's job, but a few years ago I began looking for ways to reduce that time drain while still staying current in my areas of specialization.

I noticed an ad about a service that provided the text of various periodicals on an optical disk (a CD/ROM). The supplier would provide a new disk each month, and I could scan the contents by key words, such as "wide area network" or "IBM mainframe," saving time. The subscription cost $1,000 and I'd have to buy a $500 CD/ROM drive to connect to my desktop computer. My specific business goal was to cut back my reading time to about one hour a day, freeing one hour.

I made a few reasonable assumptions. If 25 percent of the time savings went to billable consulting, 25 percent to marketing activities, and 50 percent to other activities, such as writing books, then the value in consulting revenues would amount to about $4,800 per year—easily enough to justify the technology expense, even after figuring a day's cost to set up and learn the new system. The decision was easy once I considered the technology in the context of a specific business goal. The need drove the technology, not the other way around!

Goal association is effective whether one is considering an entire information system or, as in my case, add-on hardware and software for an existing system.

CREATIVE GOALS

While saving time is a valid goal, modern businesses can think in terms of newer, more creative goals for today's more flexible computer systems. For example, as Larry Light wrote in *Business Week*, "Chief financial officers long relegated the computer to the back office, where it mindlessly crunched numbers for routine matters such as customer billing. But now it can function as a strategic planning tool and all-around financial adviser." Later in the book we'll explore the role of creativity and imagination in generating new, more productive uses for computers.

LIMITED GOALS

Associating too many business goals with one system is dangerous. Focus on one or two important primary objectives, regardless of the system's size; if it succeeds in those situations, evaluate expanding it later to address other goals. Trying to do too much too fast usually doesn't work and may delay fulfilling the primary goal. Implementing a system that can grow gracefully into new responsibilities presumes a solid planning process, the subject of a future chapter.

Commit Everyone to Monitoring Technology Impact

Many solutions to technology problems don't involve technology, but rather business procedures. This chapter has mentioned that few individuals either within or outside the business have a mandate to measure technology's productivity impact. How can that situation change?

Every organization, large or small, that uses information systems can institutionalize the priority of monitoring technology impact. Many companies already require computer advocates to justify their projects *initially* in productivity terms, but once the system is in place, no one measures its effectiveness in any formal way. Why not require project advocates to provide periodic assessments, quarterly or semiannually, presenting evidence that the projections are coming true? Isn't it equally important to know about productivity impact *after* project implementation as before?

A key benefit of this approach is that marginal automation projects will go forward less often if project champions know they're going to have to demonstrate productivity gains later.

Consider making the same kind of assessments part of system vendor contracts. Computer customers could consider paying vendors at least in part based on demonstrable productivity gains over time. One colleague of mine, a network expert, pitches his projects exactly that way: If he redesigns and improves a customer's network, his compensation is tied to productivity gains measured by criteria agreed upon in advance with the customer. He happens to be good at his job and has done well with these agreements, and so have his customers.

Should the business customer commit to information systems when suppliers and consultants themselves don't have faith in the results?

Measure Cost/Benefit More Accurately

> *"Insights into the meaning of information technology cannot be obtained from an examination of the technology itself. Understanding must begin with meticulous observation of people and organizations under conditions when information technology is or is not applied."*
>
> —PAUL A. STRASSMAN,
> FORMER VICE PRESIDENT OF
> XEROX CORPORATION,
> *Information Payoff* (1985)

HOLISTIC AUTOMATION

Organizations that wish to make consistent and repeated efforts to measure system costs and benefits can do so by observing people and computers in action together. All too often, CIS departments try to measure computer productivity by measuring system "resource usage" statistics alone, ignoring the *qualitative* aspects of how people interact with their machines.

The business that observes, measures, and tests the functioning of its systems of computers, people, and data as a *total system* stands a far greater chance of realizing its business goals, reducing costs, and maximizing benefits than the company that passively allows invisible inefficiencies to sap the organization of its vigor.

One example of how to do this is to perform in-house *usability testing*, in which new users work with systems in development or under consideration for purchase. Small companies can perform usability tests with nothing more expensive or complex than a desk with a terminal or PC where one or more observers can watch over the user's shoulder. Larger organizations might set up more sophisticated facilities complete with conference tables, one-way mirrors, and microphones. In either case, a few hours of usability testing can help an organization buy more productive software, write better programs, and tailor its documentation and training to address problems new users are likely to come across.

How does it work? Observers—who may be managers or consultants in a small company, CIS project managers or technicians in a larger one—watch how quickly the user learns his way around the new program; how many steps common activities require; where the user goes wrong, and how quickly he can recover from mistakes; whether the program catches those mistakes, or allows the user to continue unaware of them; what features the user looks for but aren't there.

The end-user support function offers a valuable perspective into how users work with computers in day-to-day business situations. Larger organizations often set up "help desks" staffed by technicians who handle trouble calls. Companies writing their own software might have their programmers sit in at the help desk for a few days each quarter. By hearing the questions and problems users experience, the programmers should be able to make their applications easier to learn and use. Firms using commercial programs and "outsourcing" support services could analyze detailed trouble log reports from the support contractor for the same kind of information.

Measure the Benefits

Whether a business is evaluating an existing information system, upgrading or expanding it, or considering a new one, it can do better at quantifying the associated benefits. Remember that the cost/benefit ratio is only as accurate as either part of that ratio.

Managers attending my seminars usually furrow their brows doubtfully at first when I talk about quantifying computer system benefits, believing the task to be impossible. Certainly, one can't estimate to the dollar. However, a figure accurate to within

30 percent is better than no figure at all. Once one realizes the importance of this measurement and determines at least to define it within a reasonable *range*, the problem becomes less difficult. Here are a few examples from my own experience that suggest some helpful techniques:

❑ Drexel Properties, a large property management firm, was paying $12,000 a month for data processing fees on a large mainframe computer. By moving this function in-house onto a $240,000 minicomputer, the company projected cumulative cash-flow savings of $390,000 over five years and $1.4 million over ten years. This example illustrates that it's fairly easy to quantify operating cost benefits when one can compare with well-defined alternatives.

❑ A modem manufacturer undergoing rapid growth decided to institute a computer-assisted customer support system to handle problem and question calls. The new system allows the company to reduce time per call because technicians can look up answers to frequent questions on-line by specifying key words and product names.

The improvement in customer service should help generate repeat business. The manufacturer intends to monitor that by asking repeat customers on a product registration card whether the company's prompt technical support influenced their purchase. The cards will show whether the technology is providing a competitive edge and whether the company may attribute some portion of its repeat business to the new hotline system.

This example suggests that if a company intends an information system to improve the product or service its customers buy, it should ask the customer periodically whether he *perceives* any improvement, either formally through written or verbal surveys, or informally through sales representatives.

❏ Northrup Corp. built and sold a component to air conditioner and heat pump manufacturers. It could make the component in over a hundred different sizes, so the design engineers wrote a computer model to predict accurately the size of the component needed to match a specific manufacturer's product. The model also created dimensioning data that plant engineers used to set up production machines.

Benefits here included reduced operating costs and faster product development due to much lower testing requirements and less trial and error during manufacturing. Quantifying benefits involved estimating the time engineers saved writing quotes and the added revenue the company could attribute to reducing the lag time between customer inquiry and product shipment. Some sales would simply never have been made if the company had not been able to act quickly; it could attribute that revenue directly to its technology investment.

Remember that employees typically will use only about 60 to 70 percent of the time savings a computer project may bring for other productive activities.

❏ After automating the process of generating sales contracts for a large car dealership, it became possible to write up contracts in two or three minutes instead of thirty. This allowed salespersons to spend less time writing contracts and more time selling cars. During times of peak consumer demand, the dealership could generate more volume and sign more customers faster than it could have otherwise.

The $15,000 cost of the computer and program paid for itself within two to three months. How to quantify the benefit? Compare sales volume with immediately prior periods when the manual system was in use, and adjust for seasonal variations between months. This example illustrates that it's easier to quantify benefits when a new system replaces an old one during a short changeover period.

There are many ways to attribute business benefits to computer projects. Businesses can, with some time and thought, place those benefits within a reasonable range of dollar values to measure cost/benefit more accurately.

MEASURE THE COSTS

Though most businesses do a much better job measuring costs than benefits, organizations often underestimate or neglect altogether some of the costs computer systems create, such as the following:

❑ *Physical facilities*. Companies with mainframe systems in dedicated computer rooms must supply not only office space but also special round-the-clock air conditioning, air filtering, and electric power. Computers can require substantial amounts of electricity and add to air conditioning costs by generating heat. Systems that must stay running despite power outages need uninterruptible power supplies with auxiliary batteries. Electricians may need to provide separate grounding for computer equipment.

Networks and minicomputers require cabling between offices, expensive both in materials and labor. Companies often buy special furniture to house computers and peripheral devices as well as expensive ergonomic chairs. The extra desk space that terminals and PCs require has an associated rent cost. Companies concerned with security may buy locks for processors, printers, and terminals, card-key systems or combination door locks to prevent unauthorized access, and safes to protect disks and tapes from theft, fire, flood, and sabotage.

❑ *Insurance*. Computers add to the cost of business insurance against fire, theft, and damage. Data insurance often costs much more than policies covering hardware and programs.

❑ *Personnel.* Medium-to-large companies may have an entire CIS staff who maintain the computer, generate new programs, and manage software and hardware purchases. Forrester Research, in Cambridge, Massachusetts, estimates that a five thousand-user PC network requires about one hundred full-time support staff! Even small companies must allocate personnel time to buy, program, use, and maintain the computer system. That cost is part of the life-cycle system cost, including not only direct salaries, but benefits, unemployment insurance, retirement allowances, and bonuses as well.

Employee time costs often greatly exceed projections due to the "fritter factor," discussed below.

TRENDWATCH   *The Fritter Factor.* The ease of making changes to written documents, illustrations, spreadsheets, or database reports on the computer can cause a counterproductive perfectionism. Most people spend far more time writing a letter on a computer than on a typewriter because it is so much easier to reread and improve the wording on the computer, especially with today's computer grammar checkers and dictionary-thesaurus capabilities.

Columnist Dave Barry says, only half in jest, that "I am not the only person who uses his computer mainly for the purpose of diddling with his computer. There are millions of others." It's easy to fritter away valuable time making marginally beneficial improvements to work whose importance does not justify the attention. When an executive spends twenty minutes composing a letter that he could have dictated in two minutes, the productivity impact goes negative even if the letters exhibit somewhat greater polish. When product designs are late because a draftsman is making final cosmetic improvements to the illustration on a CAD (Computer-Aided Design) system, the fritter factor can turn into significant dollars lost. This is what computer pioneer

Adam Osborne meant by his famous statement, "Better is the enemy of good."

Aside from the cosmetic-perfection syndrome, another fritter source is the "what-if–ad-nauseam" trap made possible by the electronic spreadsheet. A friend who works in the oil business complains that before his company will conclude a deal, staff must compile dozens of variations on a spreadsheet theme— many of which have a zero or near-zero probability. It's possible to spend so much time analyzing the sensitivity of individual variables in a business equation that the opportunity to conclude the transaction floats away.

Many computer users fritter away time playing computer *games*, and the software vendors exacerbate this trend by providing them in "bundles" with more serious programs. Gartner Group, Inc., estimates that computer games eat up 26 million hours of employee time a year. Perhaps this is okay as "stress relief," but many organizations have decided that's what weekends are for and ban computer games on company machines. Enforcing such a ban is no easy task.

Others spend hours on computer information services and networks, such as the Internet, wandering around in cyberspace and "chatting" with other participants. (One can even *flirt* online, and some services have created special "forums" just for that purpose!) While some benefits may accrue from cruising the information highway, they have to be weighed against the time spent on-line—an equation often made lopsided, in part, by the labyrinthine structure and slow response time of on-line services.

Some, intrigued by their machine's capabilities, may fritter away time because they enjoy working with it. Insofar as experimentation enhances one's facility with the system, it can pay dividends later. Whatever the cause, users often spend *much* more time with the system than project planners anticipate, raising the effective costs of information systems dramatically.

The trend toward frittering away time with computers is sure to continue.

❏ *Training.* Training and retraining people to use the computer is, or should be, a significant cost, with several components. Instructors must be paid, attendees continue to draw salary and benefits while in class, managers may need to hire temporary help during training sessions, and off-site courses add travel costs. Training costs are recurrent, not one-time. Every time a company hires new employees, transfers existing ones, adds new devices to the system, adopts new programs or modifies old ones, it must educate its users. These costs increase exponentially in a heterogeneous, nonstandard computing environment with many different kinds of hardware and software.

❏ *Professional services.* Companies that hire consultants or programmers to assist in system design, installation, and implementation normally take professional fees into account but may neglect the overhead of contract maintenance and administration, and office space and administrative services for programmers who work on-site.

❏ *Conversions.* Whether converting from manual systems to computerized systems, or from one automated system to another, indirect conversion costs may be large. First-time computerization usually entails loading data into the computer; employees may need extra time up front to check that data for accuracy and completeness. When moving from one computer or program to another, one may need to reorganize, reformat, and transfer data and rewrite or upgrade programs. Conversion costs depend heavily on whether the company's system adheres to industry and corporate standards. Finally, parallel operation, in which both old and new systems run concurrently until the new one proves reliable, incurs additional overhead.

❏ *Upgrades.* Upgrades to hardware and software products can make up a significant component of an information system's life-cycle cost. They may not cost a great deal in direct dollar terms, but when one considers the time required to install and test them, perform any necessary data or program conversions, and train users on new or changed features, it's a significant item.

As businesses become more and more computerized, computer companies rely more on upgrades to generate revenue and will issue them more often. (I sometimes advise my clients to skip every other upgrade to their commercial software packages, unless an upgrade offers a really useful new feature.)

❏ *Downtime.* "Fault-tolerant" computer systems can achieve zero downtime. They have two of everything so that if one component fails, its twin can take over until the failed part can be repaired or replaced. Some fault-tolerant computers can call the manufacturer by modem and order the necessary part automatically. The only way the system manager knows a failure has occurred is by receiving a new part by overnight mail the next morning!

Most modern computers are highly reliable, providing 95 percent uptime or better; customers can only justify spending twice as much for a fault-tolerant system in special cases. Costs do accompany that small percentage of downtime, however. They can be direct (repair and maintenance) or indirect (administrative overhead while people perform tasks manually). A central malfunction could cripple an automated factory, delaying shipments and perhaps losing customers. An accounts receivable system couldn't mail bills on time if shut down for repairs, creating cash flow problems and lost interest income. Opportunity costs can be significant, too; a stock brokerage whose network fails for even five minutes might be unable to execute important transactions. It might also incur significant legal liability.

COST/BENEFIT: CONCLUSIONS

Clearly, businesses should consider all the above costs when trying to assign a cost/benefit ratio to a computer system. Indirect costs tend to be left out of the formula; because many benefits are difficult to predict, the predictions are too optimistic, making the system appear more beneficial than it really is.

Many systems I've worked with would never have been bought if their owners had projected the associated costs more accurately. On the other hand, and just as serious, companies often reject valid computer projects because managers fail to consider the full range of potential benefits.

Measure Unused Computer Capacity

Once a company makes the effort to measure, where possible, the productivity gains (or losses!) attributable to automation, it should next tackle the question of whether it is using its computer systems to their potential. This isn't easy: therefore, the best advice is to . . .

SEEK PROFESSIONAL HELP

It's hard to know how well or poorly a system is running unless one has a frame of reference. Companies can gain access to seasoned professionals who can evaluate a system's performance based on wide experience with similar systems in other companies. Large organizations may have such experts on the payroll; smaller firms can tap the expertise of consultants.

Often I've been able to suggest changes that have improved dramatically client systems' performance without large investments in new hardware or software, simply because I do it for a living and have an experience base my clients do not.

Smaller companies often shy away from consultants unless they get into trouble with their computer systems. This is a shame, for just as with attorneys and accountants, the consultant's best function is to keep clients out of trouble and make sure their systems, whether legal, financial, or technological, are working well to start with.

TEST NEW SYSTEMS

One result of the "blind faith" in technology discussed earlier is that customers don't *test* the computer systems they buy once they're installed. Most computer programs have flaws that prevent them from performing reliably and quickly. Software "bugs" frustrate users, who may not use the program as a result—a major invisible inefficiency. Hardware, too, often fails to measure up to its billing; a printer rated at eight pages per minute may only work at four pages per minute in reality with documents having multiple typefaces and/or graphics. Companies either have to test new systems rigorously, or risk facing reliability and performance problems that inhibit employees from using those systems.

When human lives depend on proper software operation, such as the functioning of a nuclear power plant or the life-support systems of a space station, software engineers use a technique called *formal program verification*. This involves a mathematical specification of what the program should do, and rigorous mathematical proofs that the program really does it. Verification costs about $1,000 per line of program code, and typical application programs contain thousands of lines. In the hardware arena, customers may buy equipment conforming to stringent military specifications. Such equipment is highly reliable, and generally at least twice as costly as hardware designed for office use.

Most organizations can't afford formal program verification for their software systems, or mil-spec hardware components. Nevertheless, a philosophy of testing can help greatly. Before buying a new computer or program, put it through its paces in the field for a reasonable period to make sure it all works. If it doesn't, ask the vendor to explain why.

Many firms feel rigorous testing takes too much time. However, if the customer doesn't find the bugs promptly, they will be ten times harder to find later. Working *around* the bugs may consume far more time than identifying them through testing and having suppliers fix them. Easily corrected problems can persist for years, keeping computer systems from working at their normal, proper speeds.

Businesses can apply the testing philosophy to custom software projects as well as off-the-shelf commercial programs. If your company has hired a programming firm to do a project, reserve 10 percent of the payment until the program has operated successfully for a reasonable period. In this way, you have some leverage to get problems fixed even if they don't surface immediately.

> *"The single true method of philosophizing . . . consists either in the application of mathematical analysis to experiments, or in observation alone, enlightened by the spirit of method."*
>
> —JEAN D'ALEMBERT,
> FRENCH MATHEMATICIAN,
> PHILOSOPHER, AND LEADER
> OF THE ENLIGHTENMENT,
> *Preliminary Discourse to the Encyclopedia of Diderot* (1751)

PERFORM ROUTINE PERFORMANCE MONITORING

Though one can't measure how hard a computer is working by its specifications alone, in-house experts or outside consultants can measure various "vital signs" using specialized software monitoring tools. These tools provide clues as to whether the system is straining to meet workloads or breezing along at 5 percent of capacity. The goals are to find bottlenecks that may be limiting performance, and to identify excess capacity that the company could use in other ways.

This is admittedly an after-the-fact technique, and it might be better to model proposed computer systems before installing them. However, the industry doesn't yet offer adequate tools for modeling networks of PCs and workstations. As Janet Butler points out in *Software Magazine*, "With today's new technologies, IS [Information Services] shops do not have the information base of 20 years of experience gained using large mainframe systems." Monitoring may be the next best thing in the meantime.

Companies can perform system monitoring as a regular routine to answer such questions as:

- Who is using what computer resources, and when?

- How does the system's workload vary through the day? Week? Month?

- How many people are using the system?

- How often does the system sit idle?

- What is system uptime?

- How much data is moving through the system in a given period?

- What is the system's response time—how long do users have to wait on it?

- What bottlenecks limit system performance?

- What changes in system usage become apparent over time?

- What kind of expansion will be needed to meet future demand? When?

Another class of software monitor is really more of an alert system that watches vital signs and proactively warns network or mainframe administrators about common problems. These programs look for overcapacity situations. It would be an interesting experiment to reprogram these alert systems to report *under-capacity* situations as well—to identify unused computer resources!

PRESSURE VENDORS TO PROVIDE MEASURING TOOLS

I was shopping recently for some high-speed storage devices for a client. After having narrowed the field to three suppliers, I called their technical experts and asked them to provide real-world test results for their products. While each company was glad to supply raw technical specifications, which (as we've seen) are often meaningless, none would provide data on how their products performed in typical hardware and software environments. When I asked the suppliers to provide test or monitoring utilities so I could run some tests myself, none could do so, suggesting I rely on magazine reviews for speed comparisons.

How can one measure even basic performance statistics without tools? Computer builders can, and occasionally do, put visual indicators on equipment showing how busy that particular device is at a given moment, but they usually do this only on large systems in rooms where no one ever sees the indicators. Visual performance gauges (LEDs, LCD displays) would be a boon for nontechnical users, who could then readily see whether a machine or component is overloaded.

If dials labeled "CPU Busy" or "Network Traffic" peg out at 100 percent for long intervals, such as during certain program operations, it might alert users to call the hardware experts and see if they could alleviate the problem. If they hover near 0 percent most of the time, there is reason to suspect overcapacity (*that* could explain why most computer makers don't provide these indicators!).

A printer might run slowly due to either insufficient memory or a slow connection; visual indicators would help users know which. Most computers and devices don't have such gauges. Their blank façades hide performance problems.

Performance gauges might not provide detailed quantitative analysis, but they could help users see how their systems respond to different demands and activities. Customers should press vendors to include such indicators in their designs. Where indicators already exist, technologists should find ways to make them available to system users.

THE SOLUTION

Organizations that automate successfully never take productivity for granted when evaluating existing computer systems or considering new ones. Associating technology with specific business goals at the outset makes it easier to measure productivity impact, and involving vendors and project leaders in ongoing monitoring ensures that someone will be there to measure it. Careful consideration of the full range of benefits and life-cycle costs, in the context of people and machines working together in a *system*, will help organizations choose projects that hold the greatest promise for improving operations. Routine testing and performance monitoring of information systems will help identify speed bottlenecks and unused capacity.

Organizations that take a more scientific approach to evaluating and measuring technology productivity impact, even approximately, stand a much better chance of dispelling invisible inefficiency—and using computers productively. The technologists can provide some of the measuring tools, but the business managers are best equipped to provide the evaluation criteria. This approach suggests that those two groups should learn each other's language and talk to each other—a radical concept that the next chapter explores.

MYTH 2

Leave Technology to the "Experts"

"An expert is one who knows more and more about less and less."

—NICHOLAS MURRAY BUTLER,
PRESIDENT, COLUMBIA UNIVERSITY
(1862–1948)

THE MYTH

The time is early 1992. When the City and County of Denver want a state-of-the-art baggage-handling system for the $3.2 billion Denver International Airport, they naturally turn to a firm with unique expertise in the area. Denver taps BAE Automated Systems, Inc., of Carrollton, Texas, to design the software and install the system. The firm agrees to do the

95

project for about $200 million, and starts work in mid-1992 against a deadline of October 31, 1993 (the new airport's opening date).

The baggage system is to be a highly automated one. High-end PCs running complex database programs communicate with a central network server. The computers connect with over ninety track switch controllers that are supposed to guide four thousand baggage carts over twenty-two miles of underground track. The system also uses five thousand photocells and four hundred radio receivers to monitor the baggage carts' position.

Can it really be done in under two years? The experts say yes. The Denver Public Works Department hears what it wants to hear, and believes them. Nobody seems bothered by the fact that the only other similar system in the world—in Frankfurt, Germany—took *eight years* to bring on-line.

As the deadline nears and testing for the system is due to begin, Gene diFonso, senior VP for BAE, is quoted in the September 1993 issue of *Denver Business Journal* as saying, "We can't lose a lot of days at all . . . a week tops, and not even really that."

The initial opening date gets postponed to December 19, 1993, but the baggage system still isn't working, so DIA's opening is again pushed back, to March 9, 1994. Wags in the press start referring to DIA as "Delay It Again." A third rescheduling sets the date for May 15, but that also comes and goes. Denver mayor Wellington Webb refuses to set a fifth "opening date" until the baggage system passes at least one test run without spilling and mangling suitcases, dumping luggage in equipment rooms, ramming carts into each other, and routing empty cars to waiting areas instead of where they're needed. By July 1994, nine months after the rest of the airport was finished, the baggage system has not even passed one full-scale test run without problems, and no one believes the system will be working by the end of 1994.

The delays prompt Standard & Poor's to downgrade the airport bonds to "junk" status. Five hundred thousand dollars in interest costs accumulate each *day* on the money borrowed to build the airport. Desperate, the city calls in the German consulting firm Logplan to assess the situation and recommend a plan of action. In August, Logplan suggests building a traditional system using tugs and carts; debugging the automated system is going to take months. Probable cost: another $200 million, to be funded by more airport bonds. The interest rate on those bonds has to be pretty high to attract investors, who at this point don't have the utmost confidence in Denver's project management abilities.

Hindsight's always perfect, and there's no doubt that factors beyond BAE's control have contributed to the delay: labor problems, change orders, not enough involvement by the Public Works Department, among others. However, it remains that some of the best experts in the country missed a deadline on a two-year project by over a year and were so far off in their understanding of the project's problems that they were talking about delays of mere days just a month before the system was originally intended to go on-line. What was supposed to be a $193 million project is turning out to cost nearer to $500 million—probably more than that when all is said and done. The City and County of Denver trusted the experts, and is paying the price.

DIA is not a particularly unusual example. Big computer projects rarely come in on time and usually have serious quality control problems. The FAA's new automated air-traffic control system is, at last report, $2.6 billion over budget and about twelve years behind schedule. These problems aren't unique to government bodies, either. Though bureaucratic inefficiency exacerbates computer project mismanagement, it doesn't completely account for it. In early 1992, Blue Cross & Blue Shield of Massachusetts scrapped a six-year, $120 million computer project plagued with delays and cost overruns. As Geoffrey Smith reports in *Business Week*, "Blue Cross erred . . . in leaving technology too much to the technologists. After funding the huge project and approving an independent contractor to develop software, top management let nature take its course."

Even small computer projects often miss deadlines or don't perform up to expectations. Small business managers claim they're too busy to get involved with computer projects; they have a business to run. Trouble is, before long they're depending on the computers to help them run it. Alan Farnham's article in *Fortune*'s June 14, 1993, issue chronicled the story of a California tea company that hired consultants to improve their small network, which handled shipping, billing, inventory, and accounting. The expert consultants "improved" the network so much it became incompatible with the shipping software, which the company had to set up on a separate computer. The fifteen-person company now has three consultants for its accounting network.

One reason computer projects, large and small, often fail is that business managers are all too willing to believe the second in our series of computer myths: *computer decisions are best left to technical "experts."*

When it comes to managing a business, leaving technology projects to the experts can be costly. While botched projects don't usually cost a half-million dollars a day, they can have a tremendous negative impact on productivity. Why do businesses trust computer "experts" over and over again, when their on-time, on-budget performance throughout automation's brief history has so often come up short? Why don't the customers of automation projects get more *involved* in them, instead of signing off on the specification document and saying, "See you in six months when it's all done?" Let's see.

ROOTS OF MYTH #2

The roots of Myth #2 lie in naïve customer attitudes, overly optimistic and insulated experts, and a traditional communication barrier between the two groups. Once these causes are understood, approaches to a more productive reality will become clear.

Here are the naïve customer attitudes in a nutshell:

- Many business managers aren't familiar enough with the high-tech industry to understand its problems.

- They don't understand the technology well enough to perceive its limits.

- They disdain getting involved with details of implementation.

- They don't appreciate how heavily they'll be relying on their automated systems in the future.

- They believe the hype from an industry that has a long history—no, let's call it a *tradition*—of overselling its products and abilities.

On the other side of the coin:

- Computer experts, whether within the customer organization or outside it, tend toward overconfidence by temperament.

- They often agree to impossible projects out of perceived economic necessity.

- They may not fully appreciate business goals or business realities.

Finally, few business people or IT experts would deny the existence of a language barrier that impedes communication. That barrier is so strong that even a nontechnical book such as this one must include a chapter on computer technology basics. Let's take a closer look at each of these factors.

Customer Naïveté

IGNORANCE, I: INDUSTRY PROBLEMS

Business professionals tend to trust the computer marketplace. After all, capitalist economics teaches that free-market competition supplies customers with the products they need at the most reasonable prices. The desire to achieve and maintain market share induces companies to improve the cost-effectiveness of their products, making technological advances in the process that ultimately benefit the customer. Right?

This paradigm of the free market makes several assumptions:

- Suppliers can move in and out of the marketplace quickly.

- Customers can switch suppliers quickly.

- No one supplier can significantly influence the total market.

- Suppliers don't cooperate to protect their collective interests.

- No economic, political, legal, or physical barriers to competition exist.

- Suppliers inform customers accurately about products so customers can make informed decisions.

- An efficient distribution system exists.

None of these assumptions hold true in the computer marketplace. The computer business is no more a truly free and competitive market than the United States is a true democracy. Leaving technology projects to computer companies to manage without close customer involvement is akin to letting Congress run the country without citizen involvement. (If that doesn't make you uncomfortable, nothing will.)

IGNORANCE, II: TECHNOLOGY LIMITATIONS

With high technology, familiarity may not breed contempt, but it does breed a certain realism about technology's real-world limitations. Unfamiliarity, on the other hand, breeds a dangerous kind of naïve faith.

One reason some business managers don't learn about automation and its limitations is *technophobia*. Managers resist becoming too involved in computer issues because they assume that those issues are too difficult for someone with a nontechnical background to understand, and no one wants to look unintelligent. (This is also one reason many managers seldom attend computer classes, though secretly they'd like to gain the knowledge those classes offer.) They may avoid computer terminals because of a fear of typing poorly, or misspelling commands and appearing foolish. They may fear being perceived by peers and superiors as doing "secretary's work" when seated in front of a computer screen (isn't the computer basically a glorified typewriter?).

Those responsible for making decisions regarding computer equipment and programs are often unfamiliar with the technology. They're vulnerable to the recommendations of "experts" whose concerns may not coincide with the overall good of the company and whose vision may be much narrower than their own. They're vulnerable to the sales hype discussed below. Worst of all, they lack a realistic understanding of technology limitations and are vulnerable to overly high expectations.

DISDAINING THE DETAILS

> *"Walk into the office of a typical CFO, and you won't see a computer anywhere."*
>
> —NANCY MARTIN, COOPERS & LYBRAND PARTNER, QUOTED IN *Business Week* (November 2, 1992)

Apart from technophobia, why do many managers disdain getting involved with computer projects?

❑ A good manager spends years learning to delegate detail work to subordinates and focus on larger issues. Because it seems nearly impossible to discuss computer issues without becoming mired in technical details, many managers devote little attention to computer issues and prefer leaving them to the "experts" in the IS department.

❑ Many managers prefer verbal rather than written communications. They spend most of their time on the phone or in meetings. Because the computer's ability to interact verbally is limited, expensive, and not yet in widespread use, its appeal to the manager is reduced.

❑ Managers like their information on paper rather than electronic screens because they need to be able to make marginal notes and comments to themselves and to others. Such commenting is still easier to do on paper than on a computer screen.

❑ Companies have not yet institutionalized the importance of the computer to general management; computers are still very new to the business scene, and organizations change slowly. As a result, aspiring general managers are encouraged to acquire knowledge in finance, manufacturing, and marketing, fields of business experience that have demonstrated their value over decades and centuries, but not in cybernetics.

❑ Seminar companies, universities, and computer firms have not done a good job of providing reasonably priced classes outlining computer fundamentals for nontechnical managers. Many such classes deal almost exclusively with the technologies and not with the organizational and managerial implications of automation.

❑ Few outstanding computer books have been written for the nontechnical business person, and (with scattered exceptions) the ones that exist fail to address the primary concerns of the reader: productivity, effects on the organization and on personnel.

DOWNPLAYING DEPENDENCY

Business professionals often downplay the extent to which their organizations will come to rely on computer technology. When automated systems replace manual ones for managing customer data, credit information, inventory, accounts receivable, and so forth, those systems become crucial to the organization and their failure can be crippling.

"If it breaks, we'll just have to fix it." Okay—what if it takes months to "fix it"? "We'll hire *more* experts if we have to." Okay—will that result in a quicker solution? A little book called *The Mythical Man-Month*, by Frederick P. Brooks, Jr., a senior IBM project engineer, casts doubt. As the author pithily states, "Cost does indeed vary as the product of the number of men and the number of months. Progress does not." Downplaying dependency is dangerous.

BELIEVING THE HYPE

> *"In a world where science is treated as a branch of magic, the rewards often go to those who behave as illusionists, using sleight of hand and distraction to create the impression that difficult problems have easy answers."*
>
> —PROFESSOR DAVID L. PARNAS,
> QUOTED IN *Digital Woes* BY
> LAUREN RUTH WIENER

When it comes to hyperbole and misleading specifications, the computer industry makes the advertising industry look like amateurs. Ever since the 1950s and 1960s, computer companies have been making extravagant and unrealistic promises about what computers could do. Here are examples taken from a pool of thousands.

❑ *Specification hype.* Network cards are printed circuit boards that plug into a computer on one side and a network cable on the other. They're advertised to operate at 10 "megabits" per second, that is, a speed capable of transmitting a two-hundred-page report in about half a second. Unfortunately, because of various real-world factors (such as error checking) that slow transmission, the actual data rate is more like *fifty times slower* than the advertised rate. The two-hundred-page report would actually take about 25 seconds to move rather than 0.5 second. Technically, the device is capable of the higher speed, but in real-world installations, it runs at about 2 percent of that speed. "Your mileage may vary," indeed!

❑ *Benefits hype.* An IBM ad in the July 5, 1994, *Wall Street Journal* runs as follows: "Ellie Frame could view the Mona Lisa, the Grand Canyon, the statue of David, the Great Wall of China—and be back in time for *The Fresh Prince of Bel-Air*—if she had a PS/1 with built-in CD-ROM." To imply, as the ad does, that a computer screen at about 72-dots-per-inch resolution can provide anything like an actual viewing experience, or even substitute for the realism of a photograph in a book (at 2,540 dots per inch), is highly misleading; yet "multimedia" computer vendors make such implications all the time.

❑ *Ease-of-use hype.* An Apple TV commercial showed a tiny pamphlet floating down onto a Macintosh computer as the narrator intoned that "here was all you had to read to learn to use a

Macintosh." The ad conveniently omitted the four-hundred-page books describing how to run any of the popular Macintosh programs, the dozens of voluminous books the tech support people needed in order to answer user questions, or the training classes that, yes, even Macintosh users found necessary. *Caveat emptor*.

My favorite example of ease-of-use hype is a May 8, 1989, *Wall Street Journal* ad for an IBM personal computer. It reads: "I come in one morning, and there it was, big as life. A computer on my desk. IBM, no less. But this is one secretary who didn't have time to learn a computer. My VCR was hard enough. Then I found a note on it saying, 'Just turn it on.' "

Right.

Expert Optimism

The Fighter Pilot Mind-Set

Fighter pilots have to be confident—extremely so. Their job is physically and mentally challenging, and if they doubt their abilities, then failure becomes a self-fulfilling prophecy. Software engineers are a lot like fighter pilots, despite the fact that Tom Cruise isn't likely to make a movie about them (*Top Byte*?). Their job is amazingly complex and difficult; in order to *try* to write a computer program or build a computer network, one must believe one can do it despite the myriad problems that always crop up. The confidence that computer designers muster up before a big project is a prerequisite for the job. They are engaged in a pursuit that is part science, part art, as well as extremely abstract and overwhelmingly detail-oriented. They're cocky, sometimes downright arrogant—but if they weren't, they'd never believe they could do the things they try to do. (For a well-written factual story that illustrates this point, read *The Soul of a New Machine* by Tracy Kidder.)

Nontechnical businesspeople may not understand this attitude fully and therefore may not compensate for it when communicating with computer "experts." The experts' confidence often leads them to say, "Yes, we can do that," when it probably isn't quite true.

BREAD ON THE TABLE

One of the vice presidents of BAE Automated Systems defends the baggage-system fiasco at DIA by saying, "It's a three- to four-year job we were asked to do in two years." The question arises: Why did the company agree to do a three- to four-year job in two years in the first place? The answer is easy. The company wanted the work.

Occasionally, I ask IT managers if they've ever looked a department head straight in the eye and said, "I'm sorry, but what you want can't be done in the time frame you need." Most of them tell me that they feel uncomfortable saying no to company bigwigs, and some have admitted that to do so might put their job at risk. It's true of consultants, too; many's the time a consultant will advise a customer, "You know, that just won't work," only to have the client go off and hire another consulting firm willing to say yes to an impossible project.

Though no one likes to see paying work go to the competition, the consultant's lot is easier—first, because most have many clients; second, because they're often hired for the express purpose of providing a reality check. The salaried employee has a much harder time saying no. Organizations are sometimes much more charitable with employees who say yes and then don't quite deliver—at least they had a positive attitude—than with those who sound a cautionary note and gain a reputation as a naysayer.

Perhaps this is partly a cultural matter, too: Americans are can-do people, and even if we don't really *believe* the promises of the technocrats and politicians, we like their positive outlook! I overheard a phone company executive on a plane flight recently describing his job to his neighbor. "We just won a three-year multi-million-dollar contract; now it's my job to see if we can actually do what we said we'd do in that time frame." I wondered if the customer had any idea that the project manager was so unsure of their contract's feasibility. Employees and contractors often say yes because they have to put bread on the table—if they don't say yes, someone else will, whether they believe it deep down or not.

Just as much at fault as those who promise the moon are those on the business side who believe them. We believe what we want to believe. If it sounds too good to be true—don't ask questions, it won't be *our* fault if it never happens that way. We can always blame the programmers.

Unfamiliarity with Business Goals and Realities

Computer experts may lack a deep understanding of certain realities of business life, such as these:

◻ One wrong punctuation mark in a software program can become a million-dollar error. (Ask the programmer who made the mistake in *one line* of the *Mariner 18* spacecraft's programming that caused NASA to lose the probe.) Computer professionals, therefore, learn to be incredibly meticulous. The world of business does not require an extremely high level of exactitude in every project. Sometimes, an approximate but quick answer is better than an exact answer that takes a long time to provide; the educated guess must occur in time to take appropriate action. Those, however, are not the types of answers that computer experts have been trained to provide.

◻ Sometimes, the experts (particularly if they haven't worked on too many big projects) tend to assume an unrealistic set of circumstances. For example, programmers often say "Yes, we can do that" when they mean "Yes, we can do that as long as you tell us *exactly* what you want up front and don't ever change your mind." The world of business doesn't usually work that way. Today's irrelevancies are tomorrow's change orders. Computer system integrators and application programmers begin to think the business managers can't ever make up their minds, when those managers are often just trying to keep pace with changes in the marketplace.

In many organizations, IT staff have never worked in direct contact with the organization's customers. How can these experts understand the business if they've never met the customer base—the business' reason for being?

The Language Barrier

> *"[Bill Gates] is now one of the wealthiest individuals on Earth—wealthier than Queen Elizabeth; wealthier even than some people who fix car transmissions—and do you want to know why? Because he's the only person in the world who understands 'DOS.' "*
>
> —DAVE BARRY, AMERICAN
> HUMORIST, "THE INTERNET ZONE,"
> *Denver Post* (February 6, 1994)

One can look at traditional college and university curricula from the fifties right up to the present to see the origin of the communication barriers that keep customers and experts apart. Computer science programs typically have included little business education, and business administration programs have included little of a practical nature on managing information systems. This is slowly changing, but in many modern organizations the business customers and computer experts produced by our education system don't even speak the same language, much less *communicate*.

Of course, communication presupposes a desire to communicate. Consultant Naomi Leventhal reminds us that "most systems managers were originally trained in programming and analysis, not in behavioral skills. Unlike many other managers, often they did not bring with them a natural inclination toward group behavior or an enthusiasm for solving people problems."

It's no wonder that business customers tend to pass the baton (and the responsibility) for automation projects to technical gurus. That's much easier than having to *talk* with each other. It's also no wonder that projects managed this way usually fail.

CONSEQUENCES OF MYTH #2

Flawed Project Management

THE EMPTY CHAIR AT THE CONFERENCE TABLE

When the Manhattan law firm of Baker & McKenzie converted its word processing system from specialized Wang machines to a Windows-based PC network, the gurus didn't bother testing the new system on a small scale first with its intended users: the secretaries and paralegals that manage the firm's voluminous documentation. The result, according to Deborah Asbrand of *InfoWorld*: "Productivity plummeted. Files were lost. Complaints skyrocketed. Users wanted their old system back."

Projects that don't involve users at all stages are almost guaranteed to fail. The old, traditional model of IT project development doesn't consider the people who will be using the system day in and day out. The old overreliance on "experts" creates a concomitant underreliance on users. After all, the users aren't technology experts.

Or are they? If Boeing laid out a new jumbo jet without in-depth consultations with pilots, would you trust the resulting design? Users *are* experts—not in designing information systems, surely, but in *using* them. And "usability" is often more critical to a system's success than raw speed or technical elegance.

TUNNEL VISION

After a computer project has started, those involved become closely tied with the project's details and run the risk of losing perspective. The DIA baggage system is a classic example: vendor employees were working so hard to get the system working they lost track of how far behind they really were.

The customer's attitude to bringing in outside consultants to provide "reality checks" is sometimes one of reluctance. (In the case of DIA, consultants were brought in *after* the failures instead of *during* the project's development.) After all, the customer is already paying one contractor to get the job done; why pay another in addition? For internal projects, managers may take the position that "we already have people on the payroll to handle this project for us." As a result, tunnel vision persists and the chances for success diminish.

A RACE WITHOUT PIT STOPS

No Formula One car racing team in the world would think of trying to run a Grand Prix without pit stops. Even if they weren't necessary for changing tires and cleaning bugs off the windshield, they'd still be indispensable for making aerodynamic adjustments, troubleshooting unanticipated problems, and adapting to changing track conditions.

Many automation customers trust the experts to such an extent that they don't specify enough checkpoints and milestones to see how the race is progressing. The result is no chance of an "early warning system" if things aren't going well (see figure 2 on page 111).

Figure 2   A Traditional Recipe for Disaster

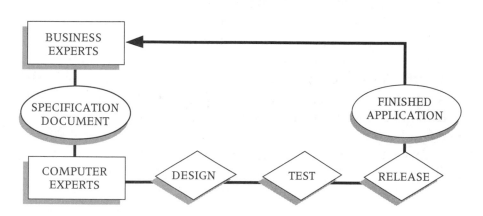

TODAY-ONLY TECHNOLOGY

Without business input all throughout a computer project to alert the design team of all the possible ways the business needs could change in the future, programmers and system integrators may build monolithic systems with built-in rigidities and dependencies that can't adapt to those changes when they occur. The result: information systems that cost a fortune to change in even seemingly minor, cosmetic ways.

Delays, Failures, and Disenchantment

Projects adhering to the old, isolationist school are delayed more often and fail more often than they need to. If managers don't communicate effectively with system designers throughout the project, the designers will be saying, "Oh, *that's* what you wanted?" after the inappropriate system is delivered and management rejects it. If users aren't involved, systems won't match their needs and won't have their support. If outside advisers aren't involved, tunnel vision blinds developers to delays and dead ends. If checkpoints aren't specified, runaway projects occur. And if management insists on getting it done as fast as possible, the system won't hold up over time.

A side effect of botched automation projects is that managers become soured on technology altogether. The early history of "expert systems" technology provides a prime example. The industry touted these systems as being able to encapsulate business expertise in computer code, leading to better decisions and a leaner organization. Implementation of those early systems occurred without much (if any) business involvement; expensive projects went far over budget and way behind schedule; and the predictable result was that business washed its hands of expert systems software for years thereafter and would not even consider meritorious projects based on that stigmatized technology.

THE PROBLEM

Though organizations throughout the world place important computer projects in their hands hundreds of times every day, the "experts" often aren't doing a particularly good job meeting business needs with computers. We need to scrap Myth #2 and replace it with a reality-based action plan for involving business and IT professionals more closely and more productively with computer projects. Fortunately, the broken pieces of Myth #2 suggest exactly the elements of such a plan.

ACTION PLAN

*"Technology is neutral, and all important decisions—
about how to deploy, measure, and adjust it—are
managerial."*

> —ROBERT KRAUT, BELL
> COMMUNICATIONS RESEARCH
> LABORATORY, AS QUOTED IN
> *Enterprise* (July 1993)

Don't trust the technical experts! At least not exclusively, and not
on every aspect of a computer project. The reality that emerges,
now that Myth #2 has been torpedoed, is that *successful automation demands business perspective, management expertise, and user-
community involvement.*

The days of leaving computer decisions to the experts are gone.
In fact, the days of "experts" as we know them may be gone, too:
IT professionals can no longer enjoy the luxury of leaving the
"business side" to the nontechnical managers. Organizations in
which business units and IT units get to know each other are the
ones that will profit from computerizing.

More Informed Customers

THE INDUSTRY'S A MESS

When organizations must deal with computer companies, those
that understand the dynamics of the industry might just get
the system they need. There's not space in this book to go into all
the details of the imperfect high-tech marketplace, but here's a
sampling.

On the supply side, the design and large-scale manufacture of new computers, particularly larger systems, require capital. From research and development to product design to manufacturing and marketing, computer building is expensive. As a result, most computer dollars go to a small number of large companies that can afford the investment.

These large companies make product decisions that would be untenable in a more competitive arena. Some are now so large that they can individually exert great influence upon the market. The giants of the industry can inhibit competition simply by making premature product announcements. Those same companies can, and do, withhold new products in order to maximize profits from old ones. Smaller, more technologically advanced companies face several barriers that tilt the playing field to the advantage of the larger, more conservative firms.

On the demand side, customers can't readily change computer systems because of the substantial investment in programs, data, and training, and because of the general incompatibilities between different systems that make switching over difficult. Inefficient, non-customer-oriented distribution channels inhibit customers' ability to make informed buying decisions.

These deviations from the free-market model of capitalism cost customers money. The profit-motive forces that in theory ensure that customers get the most value for their dollar can become so twisted that they work in the opposite direction. Here are just four examples:

❏ Manufacturers often build several models within a product line in order to increase sales, when, in fact, the high-priced, high-performance models often cost only slightly more to develop and manufacture than the low-performance machines. The market winds up with an excessive number of models with fundamentally similar specifications and artificially created differences—a situation reminiscent of the U.S. automobile industry, which now offers over five hundred different car models to an understandably bewildered public.

Computer companies are careful to limit the performance of new models so that demand for other models within the same product line isn't cannibalized. Sometimes, manufacturers purposely "cripple" new models so they won't reduce overall revenues. A DEC engineering workstation was marketed as a single-user machine; the only impediment to its use as a more flexible multiuser device was the epoxy that the manufacturer poured into expansion slots, preventing the insertion of readily available circuit boards that could connect to multiple terminals. The IBM PS/2 Model 50 used an unusually slow disk drive, a marketing ploy to avoid encroaching on sales of the Model 60 (which cost $1,700 more).

It's disturbing when fine companies purposely hobble otherwise excellent products solely to preserve differentiation within a needlessly broad product line. Any business considering buying a computer system should find out whether its performance has been compromised by the manufacturer to protect the product line—and whether the manufacturer will force the customer to buy a new machine when the time comes for more computing power.

❏ In a business as fraught with obsolescence as computer systems, prudent customers give careful thought to future product directions and trends to reduce the chances of buying quickly outmoded products. A supplier in Microsoft's position of dominance can play upon customer fears about obsolescence, and squelch competitors, by announcing products months and even years before they are scheduled to be delivered—sometimes long before they're completely designed. Customers who can afford to wait will often forgo buying competitive products until Microsoft's offerings become available. This tactic, called "vaporware," was long used by IBM and caused the Justice Department to file a case against them in 1969 that lasted thirteen years. The case didn't have much effect on the practice; IBM announced the "OS/2" operating system software in April 1987 but didn't deliver it until October 1988, eighteen months after the initial announcement.

Customers who are familiar with the vaporware practice won't be taken in by it and will ask the vendor whether an important announced product has even been completely *designed* before deciding to wait for it.

❑ Sometimes even when computer companies have new technology ready to ship, they delay it to make more money from current products. In February 1993, Intel Corporation had its new "Pentium" processor ready to ship to computer makers such as Compaq Computer Corporation. But, probably at Compaq's suggestion, Intel delayed Pentium shipments until May, thereby adding tens of millions of dollars in profit from continued sales of the previous-generation "486" processor. Intel admitted there were no technical or manufacturing reasons for the delay. One computer circuit board maker commented, "What we don't need is for consumers to stop buying 486 machines." When market leaders don't have sufficient competition, they may be motivated to hold back new technology rather than get it into customers' hands as soon as it's ready—truly a perversion of the capitalist ideal.

❑ The small-computer business suffers from competition among different tiers of the distribution chain. Dealers find themselves competing with wholesalers, who in turn compete with mail-order houses; the factory may bypass the entire distribution network in its zeal to garner maximum profits from *Fortune* 500 accounts. Value-Added Resellers, or VARs, who remarket systems with their own custom software, may also compete with the other tiers. Apple Computer, for instance, sells through dealers, mail-order catalogs, VARs, and direct to large accounts—all at the same time.

This chaos instills confusion among customers who do not know where to purchase systems; unhappiness among resellers who find their markets violated with regularity; and cutting back of customer support programs by dealers who must compete with discount houses and wholesalers.

To make matters worse, major computer firms regularly change their policies toward distributors, VARs, and dealers. This is one reason such companies come and go with such startling speed: The rules of the game continually change. The reseller who is doing a fine business today might find his margins cut by 50 percent tomorrow. The resulting impermanence in the distribution network leaves many casualties, not least of which are the customers. Informed customers will explore different distribution channels to get the best deal and to ensure the availability of training and support if needed.

KNOW THE TECHNOLOGY

Business professionals benefit from knowing at least the basics of computer technology. For one reason, savvy managers can avoid overkill—buying more system than they need. Consider the dentist who computerized his office with a system to track patient history and handle scheduling and billing. Because of his unfamiliarity with computers, he fell prey to the sales tactics of an unscrupulous dealer who sold him a $27,000 minicomputer when a $10,000 microcomputer system would have done just fine.

For another reason, managers who understand the myriad ways computer systems can go *wrong* have a better chance of helping them go *right*. In future chapters, we'll examine computer technology limitations in more detail. For now, some key points:

- ❏ No one type of computer is the best choice for all jobs.
- ❏ Few computer systems perform as well as advertised.
- ❏ Computers are not yet easy to use. Training and support are required.

- Computers are not yet well standardized, nor will they ever be.

- Systems designed in a hurry won't wear well as business needs change.

- Computers can be excruciatingly difficult to troubleshoot.

- The more vendors involved, the longer it takes to fix anything.

- "One-off" custom solutions are often horribly expensive and unreliable.

- Systems almost never work right the first time.

YOU BET YOUR LIFE

Business professionals *can* learn enough about the computer industry and its products to collaborate with technicians in designing appropriate systems. Those who read this book will have come a long way toward that goal.

Further, it makes sense to do so. The computer systems that manage an organization's documents, accounts, sales, marketing efforts, and so forth, often have no convenient backup system. If they do their job poorly or fail entirely, the organization's very existence may be at stake.

THE MISSOURI METHOD

There are several ways of combating the computer industry's addiction to hype. The overall philosophy is the "Missouri Method": adopt a "Show me" attitude.

- If a vendor says a system can do X, Y, and Z, ask to see *other* systems that are doing X, Y, and Z today.

❏ If a vendor says an enhancement can speed up the network by 200 percent, agree on a test to measure and verify that improvement before it's paid for in full.

❏ If a vendor claims a new system will have lower maintenance costs than an old system, ask for documentary proof from actual installations.

There's a logical fallacy called the *hasty generalization*. Vendors sometimes present business success stories they claim resulted from using their products. Sometimes, the success story is the result of factors totally irrelevant to the computer system involved; the implied cause-and-effect relationship may not exist. When reviewing case studies, the smart customer says "Show me" that the success story is attributable to the computer system and not to a general economic upturn, a new pricing strategy, or other factors.

Perhaps the best antidote to computer industry hype is to ask a software vendor to warranty their product. *They won't do it*. Photocopy machines, automobiles, and computer hardware all come with guarantees; software comes with disclaimers. To a degree that's the nature of software, but the fact that programming firms can't even guarantee that their products will *work* brings us down to earth in a hurry from the luminous ether of advertising claims.

Maintaining Business Perspective

Tempering Enthusiasm

I've taught thousands of very bright, very confident computer experts that they need to be aware of their gung-ho fighter pilot mentality and temper it with realism—for example, when providing time-to-repair estimates. These individuals believe they can fix anything, and they're often not far wrong; but it's much better to let the manufacturing manager know that it *might* take a day to fix a problem than to proclaim overconfidently that it *should* only take two hours.

Business managers can temper the natural expert overconfidence by asking pointed questions and bringing the experts down to earth occasionally:

- What's the worst-case scenario?

- What's the longest it's ever taken to fix this type of problem?

- What sort of things might get in the way of timely project completion?

A CLIMATE OF CANDOR

The business and technical professionals in any organization all have a responsibility to create a climate of candor when evaluating project feasibility. Managers who make it clear that they value honest answers and technical gurus who insist on providing them will advance the company's best interests.

There's some risk on both sides. Managers risk hearing what they don't want to hear ("The project will take a year instead of six months"), and IT experts risk hearing that if they can't get the job done, someone else will. The essential element is recognizing that the "yes man" syndrome hurts the company in the long run. The only thing riskier than candid project assessments is false project assessments.

Learning Each Other's Language

CROSS-FUNCTIONAL EDUCATION

There is a lot of discussion in management books these days about cross-functional teams. It's useful to remember, as Doug Brockway, with the consulting firm of Nolan, Norton & Company, said in *Datamation*, that "everyone must communicate in business English, not the jargon of their profession. . . . Cross-functional teams . . . are only good if you support and train your staff with the skills they need to succeed as team members."

What are some of the ways IT professionals can learn about the business side of their organizations? Throw them in with other business professionals on specific projects. Give them six-month assignments within other departments or business units. Run them through mini-M.B.A. courses put together by managers or local educational institutions.

What are some of the skills IT professionals need to develop to become productive collaborators? Mark Barmann, CIO (Chief Information Officer) at Charles Schwab & Company, values "long-term thinking over short-term; synthesis versus analysis; and pattern recognition versus straight, linear thinking." Other, more specific skills might include report writing, public speaking and related verbal skills, active listening, conducting meetings, writing memos, building budgets, and understanding financial reports.

"Techno-suits": Experts for a Smarter Era

My name for the new breed of business computer experts is the "techno-suit." This is someone who has one foot in the world of high tech, and another in the world of business: customers, service, sales, budgets, forecasts, and so forth. It's a role that accounting firms and computer consultants have often filled *outside* the computerizing organization; today, it's time for organizations to begin filling that role *internally* (see figure 3 on page 122).

Steve Jobs (former Apple cofounder and president) represents many of the attributes of the techno-suit. He is someone who rides a motorcycle to work and knows the technospeak but can also wear a business suit and talk about earnings forecasts when the need arises. Scott McNeally of Sun Microsystems is another techno-suit. But one doesn't have to be a CEO to fill this role.

The techno-suit may start out either on the IT side or the business side; it doesn't matter. This individual will have spent a great deal of time in cross-functional education programs and multi-

Figure 3   The Techno-suit

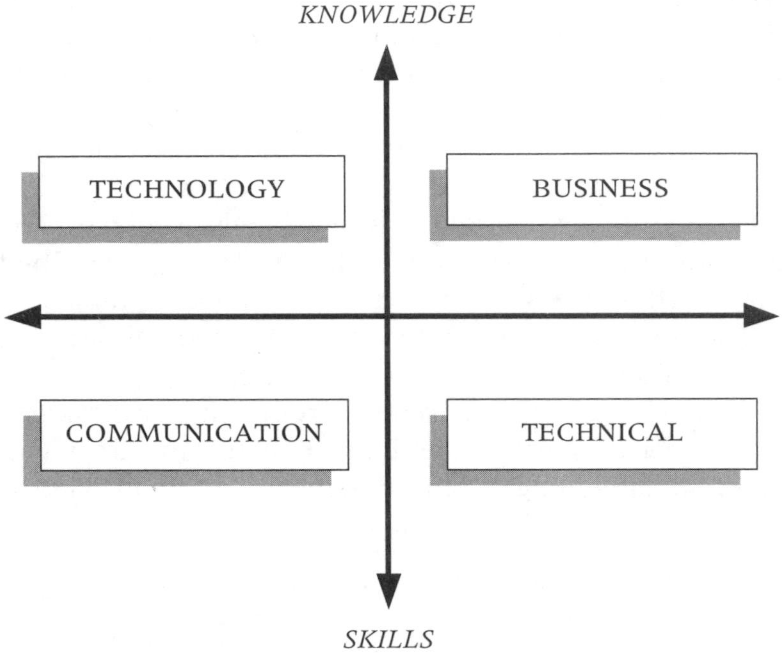

KNOWLEDGE

SKILLS

disciplinary project teams. Techno-suits will initially fulfill a translator's or liaison's role, but before too long they'll be managing big projects and graduating to senior executive levels. Today's CEOs often have backgrounds in finance or marketing; tomorrow's CEOs will just as often have backgrounds in information technology as IT becomes more and more important to organizational success.

Reality-Based Team Project Management

Just as the project management process that derives from an uninvolved business side produces delays, failures, and disenchantment, a process rooted in reality produces on-time, successful systems that help meet concrete goals (see figure 4 on page 123). What are the elements of such a *new* IT project management process?

Figure 4   A Modern Recipe for Success

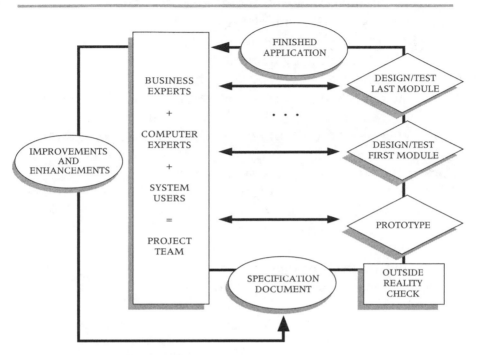

THE RADICAL CONCEPT OF INVOLVING USERS

> *"The project that succeeds is the one that has solid user backing. What's the best way to know what users want? Ask them."*
>
> —DEBORAH ASBRAND,
> *InfoWorld* (February 15, 1993)

Amen to that. Once an organization sheds its counterproductive overreliance on technical gurus and recognizes that system users are "experts" in their own right, it can tap that expertise to design better systems. The organization can often reduce project costs significantly by identifying point-of-use problems early in the project instead of after it's finished.

Even if the user community agrees 100 percent with the technical designers' ideas about how the computer system should look and work, involving users in the process dramatically increases the likelihood that they'll actually *use* the finished systems that result. They'll invest *ownership* in the systems.

While it's true that the users may have no choice about using the systems, any manager would rather have an enthusiastic, supportive user community than a disgruntled and reluctant one. When users are left out of the loop, they'll look for ways to criticize the systems. When the project team includes them, they look for ways to make the systems work.

While merely surveying the user community before a computer project is better than no user involvement at all, it may not go far enough. Projects that include one or more user community representatives on the design team will enjoy the benefit of the users' perspective throughout the entire process: design, prototype, module testing, and (later) modification and enhancement.

An Eye Exam

We've mentioned that one result of leaving projects to IT experts is a loss of perspective, or tunnel vision. Bringing in "wise" outside consultants to perform periodic assessments of computer projects can help maintain perspective and raise red flags when things aren't on track. Here's why:

- ❑ Outside consultants can perceive things differently from project contractors or internal project managers by virtue of being "outside." They're more likely to come up with fresh connections and ideas that might not occur to those absorbed in the project's details.

- ❑ Consultants are less tied to "political" concerns and therefore less burdened by the need to say what the customer wants to hear.

❑ Consultants are free to make recommendations for organizational changes that might affect existing project managers.

❑ Consultants can often communicate with both technical and nontechnical project participants and act as a translator for the two groups, helping to break down communications barriers.

Hiring computer and/or management consultants to help maintain business perspective is no substitute for involvement by nontechnical managers, but it does provide a different viewpoint for such managers to consider as they work with technical project leaders. It also can provide a reality check before a customer presses forward with specific automation plans.

Of course, as we saw in the tea company example at the beginning of this chapter, "unwise" consultants can do far more harm than good. Although there's as yet no formal certification program for consultants like that which exists in each state for professional engineers, the "Trendwatch" section below provides some suggestions for choosing and using computer consulting firms.

Some Guidelines for Using Consultants. Consultants are playing a growing role in helping businesses use computers more effectively. There are a number of reasons, in addition to those listed in the preceding paragraphs:

❑ Large computer companies are concentrating more effort on competing with each other and with foreign companies in the manufacturing area. They have less time to devote to customer education and support.

- The pace of change in the industry continues to increase, making it increasingly difficult for business people to keep up with the state of technology and the direction of technical trends.

- The capabilities of computer systems are increasing, making them more important elements of a company's overall business plan.

- The demand for independent advice is growing, fueled by a continuing dissatisfaction with the distortions of sales hype and the false promises of promotional hyperbole.

- Retaining a consultant for a limited time is less expensive than hiring additional employees who may remain on the payroll indefinitely and who must be paid fringe benefits as well as salaries.

Consultants can enable IT departments to handle programming backlogs or temporary emergencies without hiring new personnel; obtain independent support for beneficial changes in policies or equipment; save the company money, and help avoid runaway computing projects.

There are good consulting firms and bad ones, and, just as with lawyers and accountants, it's not always easy to tell the difference. The following guidelines can help when choosing a computer consultant:

- Find a consulting firm that can offer objective advice. No one computer manufacturer has all the solutions, and the best systems usually combine products from multiple manufacturers. Many self-styled "consultants" are really salespeople in sheep's clothing.

- Hire consultants who will learn your business before trying to make recommendations.

- Look for consultants who can communicate with your people effectively. Brilliant systems analysts may lack the communications skills to interact productively with their clients.

- Look for broad experience with different computer *systems* and different kinds of *businesses*. A firm that's only worked with one kind of machine or one kind of program tends to favor that solution over other, possibly more appropriate solutions. Familiarity with different industries helps spawn creative thinking.

- Find a firm that has a track record of getting things done. Ask your prospective consultants about their projects, and whether they were finished or not! Talk to their clients.

- Hire consultants with competent associates and colleagues. In today's industry, no one can keep up with everything. Consultants who have industry contacts to whom they can turn for help outside their area can be more responsive and effective. Consultants who belong to professional associations may be more likely to know colleagues with complementary expertise.

- Your consultant must be well informed. It's part of the consultant's job to stay up-to-date on products and trends. Ask if members teach and/or attend seminars, or write articles for technical publications.

- Look for consultants who are honest. Personal references will be helpful. The Independent Computer Consultants Association, or ICCA, publishes a code of ethics, as does the Association for Computing Machinery (ACM); ask if the firm subscribes to either.

- Look for incisive, analytical intelligence, but also common sense. Sometimes, the best solution to a computer problem has nothing to do with computers at all.

◻ Finally, look for creativity. Consulting firms that seem hesitant in suggesting their own ideas or approaches may not have the imagination to provide fresh viewpoints.

A good computer consulting firm can be as important to a company's success as a good legal or accounting firm. As more and more businesses realize that, the demand for computer consultants will grow, and computer productivity will rise.

CHECKPOINTS AND MILESTONES

Milestones must be objective and realistic to have any merit. It's not enough to take the project manager's or vendor's word that the milestone has been reached: the project team needs to see it. Nor is a one-way demonstration enough: for completed software modules, team members should be able to interact with the module, use it, play with it, see if it really works. Demonstrations carefully orchestrated to look smooth and complete don't really tell the project team whether the module will work in the "real world." Further, questions that arise during checkpoint meetings can not only reveal deficiencies in the system but also suggest opportunities for improvement or enhancement that might be easier to implement sooner rather than later.

SYSTEMS FOR TODAY *AND* TOMORROW

One of the clearest business realities is that things will change. We've seen that computer professionals are traditionally most happy when told that things won't change, that "Here's the specification document and it's final." Once IT project teams recognize that *nothing's* final, they start designing more modular systems that are easier to improve and enhance later.

The technical reality, which the programmers and system integrators will voice loud and clear, is that designing modular, flexible, well-documented systems takes longer in the short run.

Sometimes it means that programmers must learn new skills: structured programming, Computer Aided Software Engineering, Object-Oriented Programming, and so forth. Business managers must understand this, and plan for it. In the long run, however, flexible systems are easier to fix, expand, change, and improve.

CAVEAT: DEMOCRACY PARALYSIS

Involving business-side professionals with IT professionals sometimes leads to the establishment of project teams that bog down in a paralysis of democracy. As Jessica Lipnack and Jeffrey Stamps state in *The TeamNet Factor*, "Teamnets usually make big decisions by consensus. This does not mean one-member, one-vote where everyone agrees unanimously. This is a potentially deadly practice. Nor does it mean a majority vote with an unhappy minority. In practice, a consensus decision is one without significant opposition, one members can support, or at least tolerate."

THE RESULTS

We've seen several reasons why business professionals are having to get more involved with information technology, and IT professionals are having to become more familiar with business operations. More-informed customers make smarter IT decisions; business perspective can moderate expert optimism; cross-functional education and "techno-suits" can, over time, break down the traditional Berlin Wall between customers and experts; and reality-based project management produces much better information systems for both present and future.

There's one reason we *haven't* mentioned. It's clear that techno-suits and computer-literate managers better understand both the possibilities of technology and the needs of the business.

Such people are much better equipped to create new ways to *apply* IT imaginatively and profitably. The innovative, nontraditional application of IT to business needs is an important result of destroying Myth #2—so important, in fact, that it forms the subject of the next chapter.

MYTH 3

Computers Belong in the Back Office

"So far, most computer users still use the new technology to do faster what they have always done before—'crunch' conventional numbers."

—PETER F. DRUCKER, MANAGEMENT
WRITER AND CONSULTANT,
The New Realities (1989)

THE MYTH

Case 1. A mainframe system in use at Motorola requires three thousand employees around the world to mail monthly financial results to headquarters. There, keypunchers work six days to enter the data, at an error rate of 1.3 percent. Ken J. Johnson, a Motorola VP and controller, decides to move away from that system, switching to a PC network. After the change, employees enter their own financials, bringing the error rate down to 0.04 percent and reducing processing time to two days.

Case 2. At Hyatt Corporation, a new central reservations system comes on-line. When a customer now calls to make a reservation, the clerk can provide descriptions of available rooms, right down to the view, and assign a suitable room on the spot—saving the customer a few precious minutes at check-in.

What's the difference between these two cases?

Both certainly represent valid applications of computer technology. But the first example represents a traditional application, one that streamlines bookkeeping functions and focuses on cost reduction. The second example is an entirely different kind of application: one that directly improves the product or service the company provides, in order to help attract, and keep, customers.

"Crunching conventional numbers" is a valuable function, as is cutting costs and improving accuracy. When I started work in the field, most of the business people using computers were C.P.A.'s, and even today some of the biggest computer consulting companies are the big accounting firms. But too many companies apply information technology to the numbers and stop there. The old view that computer systems belong to the accounting department and *only* to the accounting department has led to our third misconception: *computers belong in the back office.*

ROOTS OF MYTH #3

Why don't businesses think creatively when they think computers? The answer is partly because throughout computing's history, the emphasis has been on mathematical calculation. Also, success stories in the business press have, until quite recently, focused on cost savings and back-office applications. Third, it's easier to think about automating existing functions ("paving the cowpath") than imagining new ones. Finally, it's only been within the last ten years that computer power has grown to the point that "wild" new applications are feasible on inexpensive machines.

Babbage's Legacy

The history of the computer finds its origins in number crunching. From de Colmar's "Arithmometer" (he was an insurance man) to Babbage's "difference engine" (he was a mathematician and banker's son), inventors of the early calculators of the 1800s conceived them solely as mathematical devices. The first modern business computer, UNIVAC, was commissioned by one of the biggest number crunchers of all, the United States Census Bureau, in 1951. It's really only been in the last thirty years that computers have been considered for anything *other* than calculating. So it's no surprise that businesses are most comfortable thinking about computers first and foremost as calculators.

Success Stories

Computer success stories have always concentrated on improving operations and reducing costs:

- DuPont doesn't use purchase orders with some suppliers who can tap into DuPont's own inventory system; the suppliers just deliver new stock whenever it's low.

- A Detroit nursery and craft store uses handheld scanners to check inventory and, if necessary, to order new stock on the spot, reducing inventory replacement time by 75 percent and providing more time for clerks to learn about the products they sell.

- Union Pacific Railroad builds a $50 million consolidated control computer in Omaha and reduces locomotive idle time by 1 percent—which may not sound like much, until you consider that the improvement saves $40 million a year.

These kinds of stories are undeniably impressive but usually send the same message: computers can cut costs, computers can save time. Computers are good at repetitive, well-defined tasks requiring speed and accuracy, and they can store information in an organized way. Receivables, payables, inventory, scheduling. Budgets, sales, payroll, forecasts. Business readers become conditioned to think about IT in these ways to the exclusion of others.

Automating the Present

> *"The fundamental error that most companies commit when they look at technology is to view it through the lens of their existing processes."*
>
> —MICHAEL HAMMER AND JAMES
> CHAMPY, *Reengineering the
> Corporation* (1993)

It's much easier to think about automating current business functions than to think about changing those functions and automating at the same time. Many companies are still allergic to radical change, and too much too soon seems like a bad idea. Computerize the billing system first, as it is, then think about "reengineering" later on. While automating existing processes isn't always (or even most of the time) a *bad* idea, it may not be the *best* idea.

The trouble is, often the best time to think about reengineering business processes is when planning computer systems. Information technology can be an enabler of reengineering because of its ability to open new internal and external communication channels; share data across geographical boundaries; identify new markets; provide "real-time" reporting, etc. If companies don't think about reengineering when they automate, they run the risk that the systems they build won't facilitate reengineering later, *and* they reduce the potential payoff from their investment.

But wait a minute—didn't the chapter on Myth #1 stress the importance of measuring computer impact? How can a company measure an information system's costs and benefits when it's coupled with process reengineering? The answer is that it may be impossible to separate the two, so one tracks the *combined* impact. Atomization can only go so far; how would one evaluate return on investment for computer hardware, for example, as distinct from software? They're inextricable.

The true meaning of the phrase *information system* includes hardware, software, people, *and process*. In the best (and admittedly rarest) systems, these four elements combine synergistically. And when they do, benefits so overwhelm costs that measurement becomes less important than it is with marginal computer systems having exaggerated benefits and hidden costs—that is, the kind most companies still have.

The Very New World

Applications that were the unique province of million-dollar supercomputers or expensive special-purpose machines ten years ago are now possible on small machines costing one hundred times less. *Business Week*, in May, 1994, estimated the cost of computing power was dropping by 30 percent *every year*.

- A $2,500 computer can generate "walk-through" visualizations of home designs based on floor plans the customer specifies, or generate a bill of materials and blueprints for a customized deck in as little as ten minutes.

- A $5,000 computer can now create 3-D product models with lifelike features such as texture, reflectance, and transparency—something that required $100,000 machines only four years ago.

❑ Equipment to create master CD/ROM disks, for such applications as on-line repair manuals and giant parts list databases, used to cost upward of $50,000. Today, a $4,000 device can do the job.

Innovations such as these take time to assimilate into the business culture, however. Voice annotations to business documents; film clips sent by fax line; real-time graphs of stock market conditions—these are now almost passé technologies even on microcomputers, but businesses are only just catching on to their possibilities.

THE PROBLEM

Businesses limit their concept of computer technology to what computer technology has always been in the past: *calculating* technology. They base decisions on computer projects based on what they know the technology can do, which is usually a small subset of what it can *actually* do. They launch programs to automate existing processes, instead of thinking about how IT can help reengineer those processes.

Relegating IT to its historical number-crunching, document-processing, and database management role, and automating current processes instead of redesigned processes, may provide incremental improvements and incremental cost savings. That's certainly nothing to scoff at; many, possibly most, computer systems don't get *that* far. But it will never provide the big changes—or the big payoffs—of which information technology is capable.

ACTION PLAN

"Modern computers can do everything from ruining your credit rating forever to landing a nuclear warhead on your porch."

—DAVE BARRY, *Bad Habits* (1985)

Or, on a more positive note, modern computers can do everything from shortening cycle times to improving marketing effectiveness.

When companies start putting information systems to work *throughout* their business, and push automation strategies beyond the "usual" applications, they start tapping the real power of automation. The rest of this chapter provides some suggestions on how to do just that, beginning with some ideas for creative cost-cutting and then venturing into areas such as enhancing internal communications, providing better customer service, and widening markets.

Creative Cost-Cutting

Computers that reduce costs of doing business are great, but businesses that don't stop with the initial cost savings, and instead take their cost-cutting systems the extra mile, enjoy even greater benefits. Here are some examples:

❏ Ordering supplies directly through an electronic link is a proven way of cutting costs and saving time. Push the system one step farther and it can reduce the likelihood of mistakes, too. At Lockheed's Palo Alto R&D facility, where scientists order materials for experiments on-line, the computer guides the scientists through the process to ensure the proper accounts get charged.

◘ Computer-Aided Design reduces the costs of redesigning a product. At boat builder Chris-Craft, for example, it enabled the company to create a smaller, twenty-four-foot version of a twenty-six-foot boat in just four months by scaling the computerized drawings down by 8 percent and then making the necessary adjustments. The manufacturer takes the system to its next logical step by using it to control the machinery that cuts the pieces, reducing the cost of fitment errors—which are now all but unheard of.

◘ Serial numbers tracked in a computer database help prevent product theft, but sometimes that isn't enough to protect a manufacturer from the costs of crime. A new breed of high-tech thieves can scan cellular phone users' electronic serial numbers and create a "clone phone" with the same numbers. GTE Telecommunications Services took the extra step of installing an "expert system"—software with rudimentary intelligence governed by predefined "rules"—to watch for a "clone phone" situation. The expert system watches for calls closely spaced in time but widely spaced geographically. It also raises an alert when two calls occur at the same time; that can't happen with just one phone.

◘ Customer service centers can reduce the costs of dispatching repair technicians by equipping service reps with "advisory" computers. Such systems guide service reps in helping customers make their own repairs in simple cases. Take the customer service system one step farther, and it can identify problems with new products and forestall costly lawsuits. In the summer of 1993, Whirlpool Corporation detected a pattern with a new washing machine: customers were reporting leaks after a few loads, due to a faulty hose clamp. The company instantly halted production and sent mechanics to fix the clamp on every washer sold—as Whirlpool's director of consumer assistance commented, "Imagine the property-damage liability if there had been a leak in a fifth-floor apartment." In an age when a customer can win $3 million from McDonald's after being scalded by a too-hot cup of coffee, liability has to be a concern. A reputation for reliability is worth a lot, too.

❏ Companies can reduce postage and courier costs by using fax technology; a two-page fax to a U.S. destination is not only faster than "snail mail," it costs less than a stamp. Companies can save even *more* time and money by equipping networks with shared fax-modems that allow computer users to send faxes directly from their workstations instead of printing out a document and then feeding it through a traditional fax machine.

We could go on, but here's a summary of some ways computers can help reduce costs in a nontraditional way:

❏ Reduce redundant data entry.

❏ Reduce the chance of data errors.

❏ Move data entry closer to the point of origination.

❏ Create closer supplier and customer links.

❏ Target prospective customers instead of mailing en masse.

❏ Reduce exposure to fraud and theft.

❏ Reduce exposure to product liability suits.

❏ Move from courier services to electronic transmission.

It's often possible to create new buildings with old bricks. Can you envision some ways to accomplish one or more of the above goals with the systems your business already has? Or with new software running on the same machines?

Digital Dialogue

Once an organization grows beyond a certain size, layers of management often separate entry-level workers from executive decision makers. Bureaucracy, structure, and specialization can stifle the free flow of ideas. Information systems can counteract that negative aspect of growth by providing a new channel of internal communication—one that enables workers to span geographic and departmental boundaries.

Concurrent engineering refers to multiple groups or individuals working on new projects in an environment of ongoing cooperative communication instead of the old sequential model of product development. Manufacturing firms that use computer design tools can develop new products in a process that involves engineering, manufacturing, marketing, and finance all along the way, reducing development time by catching potential problems early and reducing critical-path dependencies.

Another way information systems can help employees cut across organizational layers is the computer suggestion box. A user who logs into a network or mainframe system as a "guest" account can send electronic mail to anyone on the system, and do it anonymously. Using the computer as a suggestion box encourages employees to make candid comments to managers that they might normally have no access to—or that they might hesitate to make in person, especially in autocratic, nonparticipatory organizations. As (and if!) managers respond to the e-mail suggestions, mutual respect grows and the anonymity of the communication channel may become less necessary. This is an example of IT as facilitator of cultural change.

(Companies such as Texas Instruments promote an e-mail or "bulletin board" system as a complaint forum; most organizations would also probably want to encourage *positive* suggestions with the same system.)

In the reverse direction, managers can communicate with workers electronically with a speed and directness impossible through traditional channels. Companies can also allow employees in the field to have electronic access to data they never had before but always needed. For example, sales reps can consult inventory, pricing, delivery schedules, and customer credit information via one point of entry to the company's computer network.

Computers can even ease some of the more mundane internal communications headaches, such as the chore of scheduling meetings. Software is widely available that allows a meeting coordinator to name the individuals that should attend, specify how long the meeting should be, and press a button—the software scans employees' computerized schedules until it finds a time slot of the required duration where everyone's free at the same time. (Of course, this technique relies on everyone using the computer for their personal schedules, and keeping those schedules up to date.)

Cyberservice

One way to begin applying computers creatively is to ask the basic questions: What do customers want? And, Can computers help deliver it? Some typical customer desires are, among others, *convenience; speed; personal attention;* and *rewards* for continued patronage.

CONVENIENCE

Convenience sometimes means going to the customer when, in the past, the customer has always come to the business. Portable computing devices such as laptops enable this change.

❑ When a customer returns a rental car to an Avis airport location, an employee at the drop-off point processes the invoice with a wireless, belt-mounted portable computer and printer. The customer gets his bag out of the trunk and the bill is ready; if there are any discrepancies, the customer can deal with them on the spot instead of weeks later.

❏ ADP developed a portable computer system with CD/ROM storing parts and repair data for most U.S.-market cars. Insurance adjusters can provide immediate repair estimates and, ultimately, payments on-site as a result—no claim forms, no weeks of delay.

❏ Retailers are making ordering products more convenient. Andersen Corporation, a premier window manufacturer, puts PCs in stores so customers can size, price, and order the windows they want, all at one time.

❏ On a larger scale, Electronic Data Interchange, or EDI, is used by Ford Motor Company, GM's Saturn plant, and many other firms to help suppliers, manufacturers, and customers exchange data from computer to computer without a paper intermediary. Customers enter an order on-line, which then automatically goes to the warehouse, accounting, billing, and shipping. Many EDI systems include provisions for electronic payment. Medical supplier Baxter International Inc. estimates that EDI can cut the average cost of a hospital supply order from $28 to $12. There's less paperwork for the customer and the product gets out faster. Which brings us to:

SPEED

Convenience also means speed. We mentioned Avis in the preceding section, but one of its competitors, National Car Rental, has the edge in speed when it comes to filling out paperwork at the rental counter. I recently rented a car from National after not having done so for about three years. When I gave the counter clerk my name, National's computer still had my address and phone numbers from my previous rental. That saved me and the desk clerk two or three minutes—and made me wonder why Avis *still* has to ask me for all that information every time I rent a car, even though my company has an account with them!

Speed can be more than just convenience; it can be a life-or-death issue for medical patients. Data on poisons, for example, is available on CD/ROM, so doctors don't need to flip through books or get a specialist on the phone when they need quick treatment information after little Jimmy drinks the Drano.

Getting Personal

❑ The dealership that works on my car has an inexpensive computer system that shoots out a postcard whenever it thinks I should have an oil change, based on the last time I was in the shop. The postcard is a personalized reminder. It generates business for the shop, too, because when a car's in for an oil change, it gives the mechanics a chance to spot other problems that might need attention.

❑ In medicine, customers *need* individualized care. Computers can help advise doctors ordering prescriptions by computer, warning about side effects, allergic reactions, and dangerous combinations—all tailored to a unique patient profile stored in the computer.

Rewarding Patronage

In catalog retailing, customers tend to reorder from companies that give them rewards for past business. When a customer buys something from Victoria's Secret, one of the more sophisticated catalog outfits, the company's computer system sends out a special "thank you" catalog with a coupon attached for a discount on the next purchase. The computer helps the retailer keep existing customers happy while simultaneously prompting additional sales.

Opening Markets

Computer systems can help creative companies find new markets.

❑ The process of matching entrepreneurs to individual venture capitalists has always been a hit-or-miss proposition. A new electronic information service, American Venture Capital Exchange, provides a vehicle for start-ups and financiers to find each other—in cyberspace. The low cost of managing an electronic database allows AVCE to charge as little as $300 a year to the entrepreneurs and $95 a year to the investors.

❑ Peapod Inc. helps grocery stores in Chicago and San Francisco sell to stay-at-homes by allowing individuals with home PCs to order groceries electronically for home delivery.

❑ High-end print shops, which produce 35-mm slides or photorealistic prints from computer graphics programs, are starting to reach nationwide markets by allowing customers to transmit files by phone instead of in person, and send proofs back by overnight mail.

You may already have the data to do it.

❑ Companies can identify new markets by simply tracking customer service logs. Attachmate Corporation, which provides software to link PCs and mainframes, reviews its 165,000 annual support calls to figure out what customers are doing with its products and what limitations they find. It's a logical next step to design new products that meet those needs. It's the same policy WordPerfect Corporation used to bring its software from nowhere in the mid-eighties to top of the heap in PC word processors in the early nineties: track customer complaints and make sure product upgrades and new offerings address them.

◻ Looking at existing customers' buying patterns can help predict future sales. That's a goal of Dell Computer Corporation's CIO Thomas L. Thomas, who wants to call customers with good deals on the products their profile suggests they're about to buy. Dell already sends catalogs to customers based on recent inquiries to the company—every one of which gets logged into a massive database.

Imagining Innovation

> *"Out walking in the frozen swamp one gray day*
> *I paused and said, 'I will turn back from here.*
> *No, I will go on farther—and we shall see.' "*

—ROBERT FROST (1874–1963),
"THE WOOD-PILE"

One childhood talent that atrophies with age is the willingness to carry ideas to seemingly absurd extremes. When approaching the boundaries of conventional thought, adults tend to say to themselves, "I will turn back from here." But it may be far more rewarding to "go on farther" and let one's imagination roam. It's just possible that you will hit upon a profitable new way of using computers.

The typical way people think about computers is to visualize a known *product* first—PC, mini, mainframe, or network, database, or spreadsheet—and from that starting point to imagine possible uses for the product. This pragmatic approach can beget some good systems, such as Chris-Craft's design computers and GTE's "clone-phone" buster, but it's limited at the outset by the thinker's knowledge of current computer technology, and it fails to describe an ideal computer system to work toward in future years.

I've found it's helpful for business executives to set long-term goals that are unconstrained by the planner's knowledge of technology or the product profile of the current computer marketplace. The manager visualizes an ideal business environment in which computers help solve the business problems particular to that manager's industry or company. This archetypal environment creates an ideal against which companies can evaluate new computer products as they appear.

Sometimes, the "fantasizing" process suggests product ideas that customers can then suggest to vendors, who often focus on incremental rather than fundamental product advances. Without this process, customers don't really know what kinds of products to ask the computer industry to build for them. By stretching their imaginations, businesses begin asking for products and systems that meet practical business needs.

It could be, too, that the wildly futuristic technology your imagination suggests to you might actually be available! Here are a few executive "wish list" items that exist *today:*

- A notebook computer that can link up to the office network just by being in the same room as a network link, with no cables to connect.

- A computer network in which idle machines can automatically pitch in and help out overloaded machines performing intensive jobs.

- A program that taps into electronic information services at night, culls articles from specific periodicals about specific topics, and presents a list of titles ready for browsing each morning.

- A system that simulates what would happen to a manufactured product if dropped from various heights onto a hard surface accurately enough so that building a physical model isn't necessary.

- Software that pays company bills on-line, automatically, and on the last possible day before finance charges start accruing, eliminating the need for some of the 12 billion checks corporations write each year.

□ A network server that looks for possible security "holes" and suggests appropriate action to seal the potential cracks in the armor.

□ A computer so reliable that it gives itself continuous checkups and calls up its manufacturer to order replacements for parts that are starting to fail.

□ A word processor that detects spelling mistakes as they're made and corrects them on the fly.

□ A program that helps separate a good credit risk from a bad one, and learns from experience over time to become more and more accurate.

Could any of this technology benefit your business? It's all out there. It may not be cheap, but it's getting cheaper every day, and it may be inexpensive enough now to put to work in your organization.

Changing the Computer Culture

Watch a child assembling structures from Lego blocks or Tinkertoys or an Erector Set. The possibilities are infinite because the pieces are easy to fit together and can connect in different ways. Imagine the child's frustration if each piece could connect only to one other piece in the whole set. That's how many organizations put together computer systems and software programs.

To apply IT creatively, whether to reduce costs, enhance internal communications, improve customer service, or discover new markets, it's necessary to build modular systems in which the hardware and software pieces can move around and connect in different ways. This means being able to pull data out at different stages in its flow through the system and apply it wherever it makes sense. It means sharing communication links among network users, and placing printers near their users. It means standardizing on data file formats so anyone can use anyone else's data without time-consuming, tedious translation steps. For companies doing their own programming, it means developing software libraries of reusable modules so employees can try new ideas out much more quickly than in the days of monolithic, single-purpose software applications. (This is the idea behind so-called Object-Oriented Programming, and it may be the biggest shift in software engineering in twenty years.)

Creative information systems can't develop in the old environment of specify—code—test—deliver. That process is too cumbersome to encourage experimentation. The new culture of software development is more like building structures from Lego blocks than like building massive and unique cathedrals. This culture fosters creativity.

Organizations might consider creating rotating teams composed of flexible, business-savvy software developers and creative users and managers who can "brainstorm" and try out new automation ideas. The industry provides a number of prototyping tools that can help such a team flesh out its thoughts quickly, without having to actually build the final systems.

Companies that build modular, flexible computer systems will be able to bring prototyped ideas to reality months and years faster than those that don't. They'll also be able to make structural changes faster. Modular information systems can facilitate the organizational changes in companies to move from vertical, departmental, functional structures to horizontal, process-oriented, cross-functional structures.

◼ Example: Some companies embarking on "process re-engineering" have combined credit and order processing functions, formerly two departments, into one. Credit authorization and order processing are two parts of the same process; combining them saves time and reduces overhead. But it's only feasible if the credit department's systems can link up with the order processing systems.

THE REALITY

"Only when your aspirations and desires lie outside your resources does creativity occur."

—C. K. PRAHALAD, PROFESSOR,
UNIVERSITY OF MICHIGAN,
Business Week (August 31, 1992)

Computer technology is incredibly plastic. Customers can form and mold it to perform functions its creators never imagined; this chapter has just scratched the surface of possible innovative computer applications. It has, however, identified six steps to realizing payoffs that leapfrog the incremental improvements automation usually brings:

1. Based on knowledge of current technology, consider creative new ways of cutting costs that go beyond automating bookkeeping tasks.

2. Apply IT to overcoming internal communications barriers and inefficiencies.

3. Direct technology at satisfying customer needs and desires.

4. Reach new markets and provide new products by using on-line information services, customer service data, and sales data.

5. Imagine the ideal computer-assisted business environment, and apply technology to that vision as it becomes available.

6. Encourage experimentation and process reengineering by treating hardware and software as building blocks rather than components of monolithic systems.

All that's well and good; but how can managers apply new technology if even the computer experts barely have time to keep up with it all? The previous chapter outlined some of the pitfalls of leaving technology to the "experts." Creative automation depends on business men and women learning enough about technology, and technologists learning enough about business, to perceive even a few of the myriad connections between business needs and available technology. Management involvement in high tech is therefore a prerequisite for getting computers into the *front* office, where the profit potential explodes.

The next section invites the reader to apply this creative automation philosophy to its greatest resource: employees. The conventional wisdom is to buy whatever technology promises the most benefit, and fit people around it. The *true* wisdom, as we'll see, is to do just the opposite.

MYTH 4

Fit People Around Technology

*"For the Inquisition was less tyrannical
Than the iron rules of an age mechanical."*

—OGDEN NASH (1902–1971) *Look
What You Did, Christopher!*

THE MYTH

It's 1984, and I'm working with a dozen attorneys on a big lawsuit in Washington, D.C. During our first week's work, I notice that it takes up to a week for staff to locate specific documents, holding up work. I suggest to one of the attorneys that it might be worth using optical scanning equipment to digitize the tens of thousands of pages associated with this case. He nods and

151

says, "Come on across the river with me; I want to show you something."

We drive over to Virginia, park, and elevate midway up in a futuristic skyscraper. There, row upon row of secretaries sit, tapping page after page into computer workstations. The setup minimizes errors by having two people keying in the same documents at the same time on two separate workstations; any discrepancies raise an alert to see who'd slipped up so he or she could correct the error. They'd been there for weeks, and would be there weeks more, until they'd transcribed every page.

I looked at a few of the documents waiting in stacks; nearly all of them used Courier, the traditional typeface of the legal profession and its IBM Selectric typewriters. What about leasing some optical scanning equipment that could do the job automatically, and quite accurately, with that standard Courier font? My colleague replied that the firm hadn't looked into that but that the typists were doing an excellent job.

Their eyes were glazed over, like those of the habitual gamblers parked in front of casino slot machines. I knew that most of them would end each day with sore necks and wrists and backs from the constant data entry. The setup may have been productive for the short term, but it was untenable for the long term; fortunately for the law firm, all the typists were temporaries. To me, the scene differed little from the old assembly lines where workers spent their working lives spinning nut "A" onto bolt "B."

Companies everywhere deploy technology without much thought about human factors: I see it every week. Electronic sweatshops are becoming rarer, true, with the advent of lawsuits for carpal tunnel syndrome and related maladies, but companies still think they can automate productively by dropping technology into the workplace and decreeing, "Use This and Be Effective." The next myth we'll expose, therefore, is: businesses should *fit people around technology*.

DEBUNKING MYTH #4

Why won't it work to buy information technology and simply plant it in the human community, where it will automatically flourish? Because information systems are *systems*, and *people* are part of those systems—all too often, an uncomfortable, frustrated, uninvolved, bored, unchallenged, resentful, and exhausted part.

Inhuman Designs

"TERMINAL" ILLNESS

Most people don't like using tools that hurt them. If a company simply plops computer workstations on employee desks, it's only a matter of time before neck strain, back pain, sore eyes, and tense wrists will follow—perhaps, in our litigious culture, along with a few lawsuits for good measure.

Eighty-one percent of all office injuries at DuPont's main office in Wilmington, Delaware from 1992 to 1993 related to computer users' wrists and arms. The *Sacramento Bee* newspaper reported that neck problems were in second place among its seven hundred computer workers. A Canadian furniture company estimates that 4.4 million people in the United States suffer from ergonomics-related problems. Many such complaints fall into the category of Repetitive Strain Injuries, such as carpal tunnel syndrome and tendinitis. Other problems are eye strain and headaches, which usually go unreported.

What causes these conditions? The physical positioning of equipment is one contributor. Chair height and monitor height are frequently all wrong, and workers don't know how to correct them. Sometimes it's the furniture itself: chairs with improper lumbar support and nonadjustable height. Other environmental factors, such as noise from whining disk drives, glare from shiny screens, and excessive office lighting levels can contribute, too. Sometimes it's not just the poor ergonomics of the workstation but the long stretches without breaks that induce or aggravate physical discomfort.

Two things can happen in the workplace of discomfort: workers (whether executives or staff) will find any reason to avoid the technology, or, failing that, they will resent it bitterly. Antagonism between people and their tools reduces productivity, morale, improvement, and learning.

Consider snow skiing, a sport that has made tremendous strides in user-friendly equipment. Skiers with poorly fitted, uncomfortable boots not only ski badly, they also develop a negative attitude about the sport. They don't get any better over time, nor do they want to *learn* how to get better. The season my wife and I bought ski boots that actually *fit*, we started having more fun; our skills improved, and we became more enthusiastic about learning advanced techniques, such as how not to fall down every few minutes. The right equipment makes all the difference, and *right* means *ergonomic* as much as it means *powerful* or *appropriate*.

BRAIN PAIN

There's another kind of pain associated with computer systems: *brain* pain from working with computer programs that are:

- ❑ Counterintuitive;
- ❑ Unresponsive;
- ❑ Unintelligible;
- ❑ Inflexible;

❑ Cluttered or poorly structured;

❑ Hard to control;

❑ Unreliable; and

❑ Hard to navigate.

That brain pain isn't limited to employees, either; it can extend to those customers who bump up against the computer system. Consider the customer service computer system that demands the service rep key in customer data *in a specific order*. If the customer starts to give the data in the "wrong" order, the rep has to ask him to start over and provide the details in the "right" order. Such a system is needlessly frustrating to all involved—all because of poor "human factors," all because the system designers didn't think carefully enough about the *people* who'd be using the system.

The Uninvolved Resist

One reason so many computer systems don't fit well with the people who must use them is that the company never involved the users at any point in deciding what the system should look like. Programmers drive custom software projects; IT experts and senior managers evaluate commercial systems. Project decision criteria are cost, features, and speed. Usability, human factors, supportability? What are those? Companies that don't find out may find they have bought affordable systems with marvelous features and superb performance that employees use grudgingly and resentfully if at all.

Psychology Case Study: E-Mail

"Increasing computer connectivity doesn't necessarily equal increased organizational productivity. Tomorrow's design challenge doesn't revolve around building networks; it revolves around designing worknets."

—MICHAEL SCHRAGE, *The Wall Street Journal* (November 29, 1993)

Human psychology is a key determinant in IT success. Take the example of electronic mail, widely viewed as one of computer networking's greatest benefits. There are at least two psychological aspects of e-mail that can undermine its effectiveness.

One has to do with the atmosphere of a meeting. If e-mail dialogue replaces regular meetings, it enables participants to resolve problems and negotiate agreements on-line—except for the toughest situations, which then call for a special meeting. The result is a higher level of aggressiveness in those rarer face-to-face meetings; every meeting becomes, by definition, a difficult one, and the character of personal interaction turns largely negative. Michael Schrage reports that this precise problem prompted a cutback in e-mail use at one large computer firm until it could devise a better system.

The second aspect has to do with people's basic need to control their environment; specifically, who has access to it. Someone quipped that as soon as you put a telephone on your desk, you're at the mercy of every damn fool who knows how to dial. That aphorism goes double for e-mail because, though one can refuse to take a phone call, there's no way to refuse an e-mail message. Or is there?

New programs called "Bozo filters" can block e-mail access from people users don't want to talk to. But with Bozo filters, managers can insulate themselves from other employees with challenging ideas or different opinions and styles. Electronic mail becomes a selective forum rather than an inclusive one, fully as restrictive as the old layers of middle management and hierarchical reporting structures. The need to manage one's electronic environment is valid, but we'll see that companies can find better ways.

Smith and Taylor versus Productivity

> *"The division of labor, however, so far as it can be introduced, occasions, in every art, a proportionate increase of the productive powers of labor."*

—ADAM SMITH, INFLUENTIAL
SCOTTISH ECONOMIST,
The Wealth of Nations (1776)

Adam Smith's rationalist view, particularly as extended by Frederick W. Taylor (1856–1915), has perhaps done more to undermine human productivity than any other philosophy in history. While the application of reason and science to technology in the eighteenth century proved incredibly fruitful, the de-skilling division of labor into its most minute components was never the best way to run anything, even in the quickly passing era of mass production. After over two centuries, business is beginning to understand that.

SPECIALIZATION PARALYSIS

In the last chapter, we talked about how changing business processes while automating can produce quantum leaps in productivity. Changing, however, requires flexible workers, and many companies still adhere in one form or another to Adam Smith's precept that dividing labor among specialists is the most productive way to manage.

The United States has become a nation in which specialization is so enshrined in the workplace that a trade show exhibitor is forbidden to plug the lights for his booth into an electrical outlet; a licensed union electrician *must* do that, lest some unimaginable catastrophe befall. One United Auto Workers organized plant at Detroit Diesel has 93 different work classifications; one can't get a handrail painted without having five classes of workers involved. Specialization also drives our educational system, which produces electrical engineers who design computers but don't know the first thing about software, and software engineers who don't have a clue about human psychology.

Too-narrow specialization holds back reengineering and productivity. Do your business's information systems reinforce specialization? To the extent they do, changing the business to meet global competition becomes tougher.

PEOPLE AREN'T MACHINES

The other damaging aspect of Adam Smith's view is that it totally excludes any consideration of workers as humans, but treats them as though they were machines. Machines don't get bored, tired, frustrated, or demotivated if asked to do the same operation seven thousand times per day for ten years. People do.

The mechanization and automation that the Industrial Revolution brought about has been much criticized for its dehumanizing effect on human labor. Employers required workers to adapt to the rhythm of the machines rather than vice versa. In truth, human beings are still capable of far more valuable work than can be done by machines; and to treat people like machines and employ them in mechanical and repetitive jobs is not only an inefficient use of human resources, it's also an act of enslavement on the human spirit.

Why is the "keyboard sweatshop" described at the start of this chapter ultimately counterproductive? One reason is that the normal life of an administrative assistant doesn't consist of uninterrupted typing; there are conversations with the boss, with colleagues, meetings, research, and so forth. People enjoy variety. Without it, the brain goes numb. And after enough time being numb, people become convinced they *like* it that way as their brains atrophy.

Another difference between human and machine is that machines don't mind wasting time; they have no "life" outside their assigned work. People obviously do; but the mechanistic view does not consider that employees may have to drive two hours to work and two hours home each day. Machines, when injured, generally are repairable; not always so with people, who may suffer permanent impairment. Machines don't get pregnant and have children, either. If all this seems obvious, as I agree it does, ask if your company takes it into full account. Organizations that recognize these differences and act on them can apply computer systems for the benefit of employees; but they'll have to give up the Smith/Taylor philosophy to do so.

A Matter of Control

MISUSING EXPERT SYSTEMS

Machines must be controlled, and employees viewed as machine components also must be controlled. Senior management often regards computer systems that encapsulate business expertise as more valuable and trustworthy than human employees, in part because they can control the machines to a greater extent.

This attitude has perverted the intent of computerized "expert systems," which should supplement human expertise but which companies try to use in place of it. The financial services consulting director at Ernst & Young, David Shpilberg, recently commented in *Fortune*, "Ideally you'd like to have [for a customer service representative] a renaissance person who can comprehend the complexities of the problems, has the patience of Job, is an effective communicator, and doesn't want to earn over

$30,000 a year. So what do you settle for? A good actor who enjoys interacting with the client and can read scripts."

Wow. Apparently, companies ought not try to *develop* such "renaissance persons"; they should rather put their faith in computers and hire actors to read scripts they don't understand. This is the sort of attitude that is making reengineering such a difficult exercise in corporations today, and it's based on a value system that puts control above trust, machines above employees, and technological Band-Aids above long-term solutions.

It's also based on a certain paranoia: Companies can keep computerized expert systems forever once they're paid for but may lose their investment educating *people* when those people leave the company. It may seem easier for companies to try capturing expertise in computers than to deal with the more fundamental problem of why well-trained employees want to leave the company in the first place. Such companies are fooling themselves, of course; the faster the global economy moves, the greater the advantage educated humans have over computerized expert systems, which work best on small, constant, and well-defined problems. Companies that try misusing expert systems on large, volatile, and ill-defined problems would do better investing in their employees.

MACHINE-CENTERED SECURITY

Another aspect of control is computer security. Organizations that move to a modular, flexible, and more open information architecture have much bigger security headaches than in the days of the central mainframe. As data theft, sabotage, and computer viruses become more prevalent, IT implementers have to protect systems while simultaneously making them available to more people.

The trouble is twofold. First, paranoid system administrators subscribe to a "need-to-know" philosophy rather than a "need-to-withhold" philosophy. Second, today's security systems aren't built around people, they're built around computers. Companies that have linked work group networks, departmental networks, corporate databases, and enterprise-wide e-mail systems may require users to remember a different password for each system—passwords that, by the way, change every ninety days. That's an unreasonable expectation based on a poor understanding of human beings.

BIG DIGITAL BROTHER

Companies concerned with controlling employees may view computer systems as a new tool for monitoring performance, whether in units of computer output per hour or by electronically "eavesdropping" on electronic communications. There's no doubt that electronic monitoring can be a useful tool for training new employees and preventing computer espionage. Without carefully considering the human reaction to such a use, however, computer performance monitoring can blow up in the company's collective face, by sowing mistrust, increasing debilitating stress levels, invading privacy, and fostering an "us versus them" atmosphere between monitors and those being monitored.

Rewarding Information Hogs

A couple of years ago, I was interviewing a computer support technician at a semiconductor plant run by a big, well-regarded company. The support group suffered from low morale, and my job was to find out why. It took about half an hour. "We don't get any credit for doing a good job at our 'formal' day-to-day job," pined the tech. "The only way to advance in this organization is by getting involved in some high-profile project. All of us are too busy supporting computer users in the plant to do anything like that."

The support staff at this company contributes to expertise sharing more than many other groups: Their daily job is to help educate plant-floor personnel in using their automated systems reliably and effectively. But this company, like most, doesn't reward those who share their knowledge: It rewards "stars," individuals and teams who do something dramatic, often outside their regular responsibilities.

If sharing information is one goal of automation—and everyone agrees it's one of its most potentially profitable goals—but employees aren't rewarded for enabling and extending that cross-pollination, the organization is putting its information systems and its employees at cross-purposes.

THE PROBLEM

The centuries-old philosophy of making employees adjust and adapt to the machines they use is alive and well in business computing. Managers still believe they can deploy computers without giving much thought to how they'll work together with their human operators. The consequences of this computer myth are by now a matter of history: billions of dollars invested in information systems that don't work.

ACTION PLAN

"The only way I see to get more productivity is by getting people involved and excited about their jobs."

—JACK WELCH, CEO OF GENERAL
ELECTRIC, QUOTED IN *Fortune*
(January 25, 1993)

Okay. How does one *do* that?

This book can't begin to discuss all aspects of motivation. It can, however, drop a few hints as the subject relates to information technology.

Ergonomics

The first element of people-centered information technology is the easiest to fix: physical ergonomics. It may not even be expensive: Teaching computer users to position their screens slightly below eye level, to adjust chairs so that feet are flat on the floor, to remove every third fluorescent light in overhead fixtures, and to take a break from the computer once an hour doesn't cost money. DuPont's Wilmington ergonomics program incorporates safety training and has reduced repetitive-stress injuries for its seven thousand computer users by half.

Even when new equipment is necessary, it's not usually dear. Tilt-swivel stands for monitors, anti-glare screens, wrist or forearm rests, and articulated keyboards that accommodate the human arm's natural angles don't cost much. Ergonomic chairs can be pricey, but one doesn't need a model that is adjustable seventeen different ways to make an improvement over old, fixed-height chairs. Further, computer workers would rather have a refurbished but adjustable chair than a brand-new, nonadjustable one.

There's no excuse for companies that don't pay attention to these issues when introducing computer equipment. Few things make less sense than managers who will spend lavishly on hardware and software but scrimp on user comfort and health.

Fine; but what can companies do about unergonomic *software?* After all, unless one's designing custom software, one has to use what the industry supplies, right? True, but "the industry" offers a wide variety of choices, some much more ergonomically correct than others. Who's best equipped to evaluate software ergonomics when the company's considering different systems? Usually, those who'll be using them, which leads to the next topic:

User Buy-in

Companies are beginning to include computer users at every step of technology introduction, from concept to implementation.

❑ At the *concept* stage, users can sometimes help the organization avoid the need for an information system at all by suggesting process improvements. The myth is that if you automate a lousy process, it gets better, when it actually produces lousy results quicker.

Also at this stage, users and managers can debate the goals of the computer system. If management's aim is to use computers to cut employment, obviously user buy-in will never occur, and user involvement won't help. If the goal is to improve customer service, explore new markets, teach people new skills, or reduce cycle times, however, system users who understand the goal are more likely to come on board with the project and improve it.

❑ At the *evaluation* stage, computer customers are starting to use a technique the better software vendors have explored: usability testing, in which users work with software prototypes and designers observe their reactions. Businesses can perform usability testing without fancy one-way mirrors and designated test facilities, of course; the point is to watch people interacting with system designs before they're cast in stone, and address usability problems sooner rather than later.

❑ During *implementation*, users can smooth transitions from old systems to new ones and help coordinate technology phase-in. They may have to put in extra work, for example, running old and new systems in parallel, but if they've been involved in the project from the outset, they'll understand the need and make the extra effort to launch the new system successfully.

User buy-in is also necessary if electronic communications are to work without the problems mentioned in the "psychology of e-mail" case study. Here, employees buy into an agreed-upon set of rules called "netiquette."

"Netiquette"

Companies can't simply install electronic mail systems and expect them to work perfectly. Smart companies put a few ground rules in place to deal with human behaviors; users receive a printed copy when they get their e-mail account, and may read the rules on-line at any time. Here are some examples:

- ❏ E-mail will reduce, but not eliminate, regularly scheduled meetings.

- ❏ No "Bozo filters" allowed. If someone's bothering you electronically, sit down with them and resolve the issue personally.

- ❏ E-mail senders will help recipients manage their environment by including brief headings stating subject matter and priority.

- ❏ E-mail users will avoid distributing messages to everyone on the system unless absolutely necessary.

- ❏ When a manager programs an e-mail system to send messages weeks or months later as "reminders," the original date of authorship will appear.

- ❏ E-mail recipients should not "acknowledge" a message electronically without having read it.

Computer networks require management just as personal business meetings require management. Companies that deploy technology hand in hand with policy that considers human psychology, such as the above "netiquette" rules, will be technology winners.

Rediscovering the Renaissance

> *"Companies are rediscovering that people, not machines, are their most valuable resource and that they can best improve their competitive performance by getting humans and technology to work together in harmony. . . . Instead of splitting jobs into innumerable minor tasks, a more human centered approach is to give workers more knowledge of, and responsibility for, the entire work process."*
>
> —TOM FORESTER, SENIOR LECTURER
> AT GRIFFITH UNIVERSITY,
> QUEENSLAND, AND PERRY
> MORRISON, PSYCHOLOGY
> LECTURER AT THE NATIONAL
> UNIVERSITY OF SINGAPORE
> *Computer Ethics* (1994)

MOVING BEYOND SPECIALIZATION

Today's focus on process rather than function, which is driven by heightened competition, demands flexible, well-rounded employees who see and understand all steps in a business process. Taylorism doesn't get us there, overspecialization doesn't get us there, and information systems that reinforce the philosophy of dividing work into little bits don't get us there, either. To quote from the MIT Commission on Industrial Productivity, "A newly graduated American engineer may well arrive at his first job with a more extensive college preparation than a Japanese graduate, but these educational advantages are apparently counterbalanced after a few years by on-the-job training and rotations in

Japan that produce engineers excelling in product development and manufacturing."

Fortunately, computer systems can help organizations move beyond specialization and cultivate employees with a broader view of business activities. This ultimately may prove the most productive application of computer technology to business. Two examples may convey the idea.

Performance support refers to on-line computer "help" systems that don't limit themselves to helping users operate their computers but assist them in performing business processes (of which computer use is just a part). One simple example given in the magazine *Release 1.0* is the credit card service representative who must deal with a customer irate over an overdue-payment notice. The performance support system accesses the bank's database and presents the customer's true payment history and sales volume. It then suggests whether the customer is really worth keeping based on that information, or is, in fact, a habitual deadbeat feigning righteous indignation. The service rep can use that information to decide whether to waive the overdue charge to keep the business. This kind of system encourages administrative employees to consider how their decisions affect the business down the line.

Another way is to encourage information sharing and idea cross-fertilization within project teams or work groups by implementing so-called peer-to-peer networks to supplement the traditional "client/server" networks most companies have favored in the past. In a peer-to-peer network, every participant can share data on his or her workstation with every other participant. (In the client/server model, only information on a central "server" is shareable.) Network administrators have shied away from peer-to-peer networks because of their poor access-control security and decentralized administration. However, a good compromise is to put peer-to-peer networks in place only where the "need-to-withhold" is absent and access control doesn't really matter. These kinds of networks empower teams and encourage idea sharing more effectively than client/server networks.

The imaginative reader will be able to conceive other ways information systems can contribute to a multiskilled and flexible workforce. It's a crucial exercise for people-centered companies.

PEOPLE ARE PEOPLE

Though ergonomics are important, it's clearly not enough to make information technology physically nonharmful; successful automators find ways to make it a productivity booster. One way is by using IT to help implement the "flex office."

For one reason or another—kids, injury, disability, distance—some of the organization's most talented contributors find it difficult to come to the office at all. Management can decide to let them go, or not hire them in the first place if the law permits the latitude. That's a failure, however, especially since computer technology can often enable them to work productively at home. See the "Trendwatch" section following for some ideas, and the notes on some newly available technology.

Homework. In 1994, about 6 percent of the U.S. workforce worked at home at least a few days a month during normal business hours. Home PCs, "groupware," high-speed fax modems, and new connection technology made it possible. But can employees work effectively at home?

American Express Travel Related Services finds that by equipping agents with the necessary home computer equipment, the company could save on rent at the same time employees produce more and better work, without the distractions of the conventional office.

Sometimes, workers can come to the office, but only with a severe time penalty. Many business persons have at one time or another endured a work situation involving excessive travel, whether in cars or airplanes.

Workers can compensate somewhat for wasted time in the air by trying to read or work in those little revenue-optimized people containers the airlines call "seats." Notebook computers can facilitate that effort, especially with today's more legible screens and longer battery life.

But it's tough to work in a car, bus, or train during rush hour. Because the office computer system can always be "on," there's less reason for every employee to show up at precisely the same time, and *flex time* can result in better morale, better attitude, and better health.

Technology can also make it less necessary to come to the workplace *after* hours. At Southern Hills Hospital in Nashville, the on-call radiologist would generally drive to the hospital to see medical images from trauma victims—a twenty-minute delay. With an ISDN link and high-resolution portable PC, the doctor can stay at home and get the images in under thirty seconds.

ISDN is short for Integrated Services Digital Network, which enables transmission over existing phone lines ten times faster than today's highest-speed modems. It costs $200 to $400 for installation and $25 to $50 per month, often plus a per-minute usage charge. Long popular in Europe, it's less expensive than some other newer technologies and is capable of handling voice, video, teleconferencing, high-resolution digital images, and data—unlike today's conventional high-speed modems. It's now available in most major U.S. cities.

ISDN is not the last word in fast home-to-office links, however. There's a good chance that home workers will soon be able to link up to electronic information services through their cable TV link, using "cable modems." Companies that stay on top of developments like ISDN and cable modems can put employees to work at home when it makes sense—benefiting all involved.

Trading Control for Effectiveness

AUGMENTING HUMAN EXPERTISE

Using computer expert systems to replace human expertise rather than to augment it is a good way to systematically bleed away the versatility, competence, loyalty, and enthusiasm of an organization's employees. It's also a good way to make the company vulnerable to the wild mistakes computers by their nature can make but people by *their* nature are unlikely to make.

Much business literature in recent years has discussed the "hollowing out" of an American economy that is shifting production overseas and losing a domestic manufacturing base. Using computers to transform jobs to a lower degree of skill rather than to a higher one represents perhaps an even more dangerous hollowing out: an erosion of workforce competence.

So how can expert systems augment and even magnify human expertise? One example appeared in the previous chapter: detecting patterns in customer complaints that can help identify priorities for new product design. Another is to help free up computer technicians from routine support responsibilities by helping them diagnose common problems based on pattern matching against problem history. A third is to replace that electronic sweatshop with OCR scanners that can perform the drudgery automatically. A fourth is to remind pharmacists of potentially incompatible drugs. And so on.

There's an argument that expert systems, computers, and even technology in general eliminate jobs. I've read dozens of studies on this controversy, and there are many bright people on both sides. There's not space here to fully debate the issue, but it does seem clear that businesses can choose whether they'll emphasize using computers to empower, or eliminate, personnel.

Sensible Security

> *"Left on our own, we security directors can generate solutions until the company is knee deep in controls . . . . That [need-to-know] principle may be appropriate in the military, but it is commercial suicide. To succeed, organizations need to share information within themselves as freely as they possibly can."*
>
> —Paul Dorey, head of information security, Barclays Bank, *Enterprise* (July, 1993)

Mr. Dorey wisely suggests that computer security can be based on a "need-to-withhold" rather than a "need-to-know." Insofar as business improvement depends on employees making new connections, business computers should allow employees access to any data that doesn't have to be confidential. In fact, security gurus are today as concerned with maintaining information *availability*—reducing downtime from hardware failure, software viruses, and so forth—as with protecting information from the wrong sets of eyes.

Human-centered computer security provides a single point of entry to the system, so users don't have to remember fourteen passwords. Clearly, that single gateway must be a secure one. Access techniques fall into three categories: something you *know* (password), something you *have* (portable code device), and something you *are* (fingerprint, voice pattern, retinal scan). While "something you are" is expensive and not too practical for remote users, a combination of a password and a portable "credit-card"-size device can provide excellent security. The device provides a code the host computer will validate, based on date and time, and the user provides a password. If someone steals the device, they probably don't have the password, and if someone gets wind of the password, they probably won't have the device.

Monitoring in Moderation

Electronic monitoring isn't a bad thing per se, but just like electronic mail, it helps to have a few rules to make it work in the human environment. Gary Marx and Sanford Sherizen at MIT suggest the following elements of a monitoring policy:

- Only collect information directly related to the employee's job.

- Provide advance notice of monitoring—be up front about it.

- Provide employees access to data collected during monitoring.

- Establish a mechanism for appealing decisions based on monitoring.

- Put a time limit on how long monitoring data can be used.

I'd suggest another element: Develop a computer privacy policy and publicize it to all employees. Maybe the company will take the attitude that any data on company machines should be business-related and therefore does not enjoy privacy protection; that may be a valid stance, and as long as everyone knows about it and therefore won't use their workstations to send love letters or create résumés or download risqué graphics from the Internet, problems are much less likely.

A New Kind of Star

"Many companies spend big on technology to allow employees to share information, but forget that sharing ideas is an 'unnatural act' in corporate cultures that reward individual achievement. 'If we really cared about information sharing, we would start to evaluate people by how well they share,' says [Thomas H.] Davenport [of Ernst & Young]."

—IRA SAGER, *Business Week*
(May 1, 1994)

In the new "smart company," which prizes information sharing and employee empowerment, the incentive structure reflects those priorities instead of combating them. This may mean a new kind of star: the performance *enabler*, the idea *connector*. It also suggests an entirely new way of employee performance evaluation that values teaching ability on a par with individual productivity and that rewards employees for developing cross-functional skills and venturing outside their individual comfort zones. Modifying the pay system is a necessary (but not necessarily sufficient!) step toward profiting from information sharing.

THE REALITY

Successful automation doesn't start with technology, it starts with employees. If Jack Welch is right, and the best route to productivity is "getting people excited about their jobs," then technology becomes more of a "bottom-up" process than a "top-down" process, for the people doing the work have perhaps the best ideas about how to improve it and are best equipped to evaluate how information systems will work in real-world environments.

Successful people-centered automation includes some or all of these elements:

- An ergonomically correct workplace;

- Human-friendly software;

- A technology development process that includes users from square one;

- Communications systems with rules based on sound psychology;

- Systems that broaden employee vision, competence, and flexibility;

- Technology that helps people work wherever it makes the most sense;

- Computers that augment, rather than replace, human intelligence;

- Sensible security based on a need-to-withhold and on human abilities;

- Employee monitoring in moderation if at all;

- Incentive plans that reward performance enablers and idea connectors.

This chapter discussed information sharing at several points. The value of sharing data is real, but zealous companies may exaggerate it to the point that individuals become washed away in a sea of facts and figures. The last in our list of "big picture" issues goes to the heart of any information system: Is more data always better? And if not, who needs what data when? The next chapter takes on these questions.

MYTH 5

The More Data, The Better

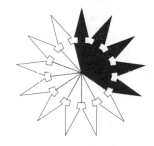

"It is a capital mistake to theorize before one has data."

—Sir Arthur Conan Doyle,
British author and creator of
Sherlock Holmes (1859–1930)

THE MYTH

The Sherlock Holmes–style approach to any problem is to start with data. Observe it, ponder on it, look at it in different ways; then theorize, and finally, act. It's possible to carry this philosophy too far, however; to become so enamored of *data* that one loses any chance for extracting useful *information,* which we'll define simply as data that *means* something. The fifth computer myth, then, is: the more data, the better.

DEBUNKING MYTH #5

Three broadly different kinds of data flow through company computers and employee brains:

- Internal business data, both reported and created, such as sales figures, capital budgets, product designs, and customer profiles;

- Interpersonal communications, such as correspondence, e-mail, and groupware; and

- Data from the outside world, for example, from stock reports, news services, and periodical databases.

All three kinds require management to be really useful. Simply increasing the quantity of any of the three kinds doesn't necessarily help the business, and may hurt. Without sound data management, the sheer volume of data becomes overwhelming; computers can't provide it in a timely and convenient manner, or provide too much too fast; the right people can't get to it, but the wrong people can; it's in an indigestible format; much of it is inaccurate; and it's all but impossible to find connections in it. At the end of the day, data remains *data* rather than becoming *information*.

How Much Is Too Much?

> *"Where is the wisdom we have lost in knowledge?*
> *Where is the knowledge we have lost in information?"*
>
> —T. S. ELIOT, ENGLISH POET,
> *The Rock* (1934)

CREATING A MONSTER

A 1987 television special depicted the manufacture of the Crack-A-Snack British candy bar, produced in a continuous stream, guided onto a conveyor, and cut into four-inch sections by a slicer. During an early test of the production apparatus, the slicer lost power, but the product kept on rolling out of the machine. Soon a huge tangle of unsliced snack bar ribbon accumulated in the output trays and began spilling onto the floor, growing by the second like a horrible mythical serpent. Seeing how many reports some companies generate with their computer systems reminds me of that gooey, useless ribbon of raw dough taking over the room.

The early promise of computer technology was to reduce or even eliminate paper. But the computer has become the best thing that ever happened to the paper industry. The last decade has seen business paper consumption increase 50 percent, in part because the computer can easily generate multiple document drafts and in part because long, detailed reports are as easy to produce as short, summarized ones.

It's also easy to generate lots of scenarios using computers. It's a powerful tool, but the danger—as playwright George Bernard Shaw astutely noted a hundred years ago—is that "the open mind never acts." Too much information can have a numbing, paralyzing effect. Reams of "what-if" scenarios can so muddle a business decision that nothing gets done.

TAKING IT ALL IN

Though much of a computer system's utility derives from its management of internally generated data, businesses are recognizing that data from the outside world can have strategic value. Some databases are too large to maintain in-house; some are too specialized to be cost-justifiable; some are proprietary, copyrighted, or just unavailable for purchase. The information services industry has grown up to provide large, varied databases on all conceivable topics for subscriber access.

All is not sweetness and light on-line, however. The prices charged often range as high as $3 per minute. Copying a single article can cost $40. These can add up very quickly, especially if a user is "browsing" the service or doesn't know all the arcane commands for navigating it. It's no wonder smart companies like Microsoft are aggressively buying up rights to data "content."

Sometimes it costs a lot to access data that ought to be in the public domain. For example, West Publishing Company, a Minnesota publisher of federal and state laws and owner of the on-line database service Westlaw, claims that the numbering system used by the Texas legislature (and by West) is protected by copyright. That is, although the *laws* are in the public domain, the *numbering system* in universal use by Texas lawyers belongs to West, which therefore enjoys a de facto monopoly and prices its data accordingly.

Just *searching* the information superhighway requires skills most computer users don't have and most companies don't teach. A researcher looking for data on *Ford* will capture dozens of journal articles mentioning Linda or Harvey Ford as well as Ford Motor Company. Specify *schools* as a key word, and you'll get a lot of data about fish as well as education.

❏ When searching for articles on a particular topic (for example, 1995 articles about "information overload") using the Dow Jones/News Retrieval on-line service, novices have to view the *entire first page* of every article meeting the search criteria. While convenient for Dow Jones, which bills by the word, this is not at all convenient for the researcher, who can usually determine an article's relevance from the headline. (Advanced customers willing to memorize commands such as "..p hl,dd/doc=1-30" can coerce the system to display headlines and dates only.)

Finally, there may be so much data on-line on a particular subject that there's no convenient way to make sense of it all and separate the relevant from the irrelevant.

COMPUTER CHOLESTEROL

"Information volume has always grown as costs have come down."

—PAUL A. STRASSMAN, FORMER
VICE PRESIDENT OF XEROX
CORPORATION, *Information Payoff*
(1985)

A time-management guru once estimated that 90 percent of all filed documents never get retrieved: File cabinets are more like document graveyards than information storehouses. Computer filing systems are no different. They have an incredible capacity for accumulating junk, especially as it's not immediately *visible* junk.

One network manager I know totally rejects computer "housekeeping," that is, getting rid of old and unnecessary data. He hypothesizes that it costs more in effort to *identify* the old stuff than it does to pay for the extra storage space and keep everything. It's a great theory for those of us with packrat tendencies anyway, but high-tech packrats do more than just add to disk space requirements. They also:

- Slow down the computers that have to keep track of all those files;

- Waste the company's time and money making unneeded "backups";

- Slow down data retrieval tools that have to slog through more chaff;

- Make it harder for users to locate specific files quickly.

Excess data in information systems is computer cholesterol: lining the communications channels, building up slowly and invisibly, restricting flow.

It's All in the Timing

> *"The important thing is not to know more than all men, but to know more at each moment than any particular man."*
>
> —JOHANN WOLFGANG VON GOETHE,
> GERMAN POET, NOVELIST,
> AND SCIENTIST (1749–1832)

Information is a little like money: its *timing* is almost as important as its quantity. The ninety-year-old lottery winner won't be able to enjoy that ski condo in Vail, and the sales manager who responds to an RFP after its deadline won't benefit either.

TOO LATE

"The right time" might be *now* as opposed to five minutes of frustrating searches from now. The computer *interface*—how it looks to the user—can get in the way of extracting information instead of facilitating it. The Internet, a huge network of computers, is the "information superhighway" most often mentioned. But Paul Saffo of the Institute for the Future comments, "The Internet . . . probably has the worst interface of any device in all of human history. It's just way too complicated." Even its fans have renamed it the "information ball of yarn."

Computer interfaces to *internal* company databases matter, too. In an era of high turnover and cross-functional training, the amount of time employees in new positions need to figure out the computer's interface becomes critical. Employees move from one different system to another, facing new and steep learning curves each time that inhibit their ability to get information fast. The nonstandardization of the different systems an organization uses to manage its data makes this problem worse; each departmental database presents a different face to the worker.

It's not just the interface that slows down data access: It can be the lack of tools for making ad hoc queries, too, or the lack of education on how to use those tools. Any system that requires designing a complete report format to get new or different data will be cumbersome and flat-footed compared with systems that permit rapid, one-off, English (or near-English) inquiries.

TOO OFTEN

> *"Who hasn't wanted to escape to some desert island where nobody can phone, E-mail, copy, FAX, or page you? Where you can't get any information at all, whether it travels via satellite, cellular waves, fiber optics, the U.S. Mail, FedEx, or regular old copper telephone wires?"*

> —RICK TETZELI, *Fortune*
> (July 11, 1994)

❏ A senior designer at the British firm Lucas Aerospace comments, "Some computer-aided design systems we have looked at increase the decision-making rate by 1800 or 1900 percent . . . the stress is enormous," as engineers try to handle data unbridled by the intermediate steps of printing blueprints.

❏ The computer support staff at a U.S. pharmaceutical company has to take their cellular phones around with them everywhere—even to the bathroom. If they're unavailable by phone anytime during work hours, it's grounds for dismissal. I wasn't surprised to hear the IT manager confide that turnover in the group was very high. The burnout rate more than offset any productivity gains from increased availability.

There's such a thing as getting information too often. Too much information can push employees past the point of maximum productivity by overwhelming them with decisions and causing job fatigue. It's the nature of some businesses that people have to be available when traveling, for example, or when out of town or at home. But the physical infrastructure the United States has now built, which allows anyone to access information and *be* accessed for information at any moment during their entire life, exacts a certain toll.

A good friend whom I bumped into a few years ago told me all about the latest pager technology his company was developing. I told him that being available at all times to all my clients was perhaps the second most horrifying thing I could imagine, next to not *having* any clients. I think he was a little offended, but it seems to me people need time when they know they *won't* be faxed, paged, or called, so they can daydream—really relax and think. Executives at Xerox Corporation and Computer Associates are reporting positive results from creating "quiet times" and restricting e-mail to certain times of day. Part of the stress of business life derives from the notion that everyone must be available all the time to everyone else.

Route To: Whom?

THE DATA MISERS

Plenty of information may be floating around, but is it floating by the right people? Arno Penzias, Nobel-winning astronomer and head of research at AT&T Bell Labs, describes a typical hospital emergency room where patients pester attendants every few minutes, wanting to know when their turn will come. Why not install a TV monitor with everyone's name on it and their place in line? The ER staff could get a lot more done without the constant interruption, and the patients wouldn't get quite so distraught.

Why hoard information that employees or customers could use? One reason is control. The keeper of the list at the emergency room, the French restaurant, or the Department of Motor Vehicles enjoys a certain bureaucratic power. More seriously, senior managers may resist disseminating data that qualify them uniquely to make decisions based on that data. *Fortune* writer David Kirkpatrick comments that "many who have grown comfortable dwelling near the [organizational] pyramid's apex are understandably distressed by the way groupware disrupts old-style hierarchies." If passing along data is one's sole function, computerized data distribution can threaten a *middle* manager's very livelihood as well.

SECURITY CLEARANCE

Keeping confidential information away from the wrong people is almost as important as getting it to the right people, and that mandate is becoming tougher and tougher in the modern business computer environment. The previous chapter discussed basing computer security on a "need-to-withhold" rather than a "need-to-know" basis to simplify security. But with ever larger data streams rushing through computers, and with EDI systems allowing suppliers and customers, as well as employees, access to a company's computers, the job of constantly reevaluating what data needs to be withheld, and how to protect access to it, becomes exponentially harder.

The more modems, fax modems, and workstations with diskette drives on a network, the more potential security "holes" that ex-employees, competitors, investigative reporters, or (for that matter) government officials can use to access your business's confidential data. Downsizing and distributed computing have created major security headaches for companies that don't want everyone to know everything about them.

Form Defeats Function

Louis Henry Sullivan, the influential American architect, wrote in 1896, "Form ever follows function." Unfortunately, computer systems ignore that dictum blatantly and regularly. In such systems, form *defeats* function.

Information's function is to *inform;* that's where the word comes from, after all. To do so, its presentation must allow rapid and accurate comprehension, not by other computers but by human beings. Two examples:

◾ The more numbers there are on a computer-generated report, the harder it is to separate out significant data. Tables of figures may be precise, but they're hard to assimilate and hard to act on. This was one of the problems with GM's computerized Cadillac plant at Hamtramck, Michigan: operators couldn't see what adjustments they needed to make to robotic welders from the long numeric printouts the system spat forth.

◾ The fancy 3-D bar graphs modern computer programs can print at the touch of a button look impressive but aren't as useful as older-style two-dimensional charts. It's harder to compare values along a perspective line, and there's no grid for reference.

A Crisis of Confidence

Appropriate information amount, timing, distribution, and format mean nothing at all if that information is wrong. The greater the access to a computer information system, the greater the chance of inaccuracy. And data that can't be trusted can't be used.

Dozens of corporate databases I've seen are such a mess that no one trusts them. Why aren't they accurate?

- Human error causes data entry and transcription errors.

- Systems may fail to validate data as it's being keyed in, that is, to test it to make sure it falls within a range of reasonable values, as well as to cross-check it against existing data.

- System users who don't feel *all* the data is important make incomplete entries.

- Database programs don't always alert users of errors or problems.

- It's difficult to find erroneous data among the hundreds, thousands, or even millions of entries.

- Many systems fail to automatically update all relevant data when a user makes one change.

According to *The Wall Street Journal,* "A 1991 survey of 50 large businesses' information chiefs by Massachusetts Institute of Technology researchers found that half of them believed their corporate information was less than 95% accurate, limiting its usefulness; almost all of them said that databases maintained by individual departments weren't good enough to be used for important decisions." And how much do those databases cost?

Filtering Out Connections

> *"A chap in Italy discovers that by kinking a water pipe he can make a spray; that idea gets picked up by a doctor in the 19th century to spray antiseptic; that idea gets jumped on by a German engineer who invents a carburetor from it. It's an accidental, Monty Python view of how history works."* *

> —JAMES BURKE, BRITISH
> JOURNALIST (1994)

* For the curious: The Italian was Giovanni Venturi, and the German was Wilhelm Maybach—who, in 1900, fitted his carburetor invention onto an engine that partner Gottlieb Daimler named after his distributor's daughter, Mercedes.

BBC science journalist James Burke hosted a fascinating PBS series in 1979 titled *Connections,* demonstrating that many of today's most important discoveries trace their roots to connections between seemingly disconnected fields of inquiry—such as medicine and the internal combustion engine. After a few episodes, one suspects that progress depends more on discontinuity and happenstance than on the methodical pursuit of truth.

Burke's ideas come to mind when considering a popular new class of computer technology emerging in reaction to data overload: *filters.* Filters can apply to all types of computer data but most commonly address correspondence and outside information services. They can cull, separate, sort, prioritize, and file data according to criteria the user predefines: key words, sender identity, date, project, etc. Some filters, such as General Magic's Telescript, can roam the network for relevant files and copy them to the user's workstation. But one big problem with data filters is that by specifying in advance which topics and key words one wants information about, one pre-empts the chance of a serendipitous connection between previously unrelated facts or ideas.

A related problem is that predefined document components or "templates," while certainly speeding the design process of a new airplane or a legal contract, might inhibit creativity. As an aerospace company's engineering VP says in *Technology Review,* "We don't want to standardize one landing gear to the extent that we don't give anybody the opportunity of building a better one." Like filters, templates help avoid workers becoming overwhelmed by data; but opportunities are lost in the process. As soon as an organization starts limiting data flow, it may be sacrificing creativity to avoid infoglut. How can one know today what fact or connection might be relevant tomorrow?

THE PROBLEM

Computer systems store and provide access to data, not information. Companies are just learning how to move from one to the other. Christopher Locke, who worked on the Japanese government's Fifth Generation Computer project, says in *Byte* magazine: "Too many companies are drowning in a sea of high technology without insight or content, often producing products and services of abominable quality. . . . The challenge is not to increase efficiency, as in the heyday of mass production, but to deepen vision."

How can a business address that challenge?

ACTION PLAN

The goal for handling business information intelligently is stated in a deceptively simple phrase: to provide the right amount of information, at the right time, to the right people, in the right form—accurately.

The Right Amount

SELECTIVE CREATION

Businesses can begin limiting how much data they generate with their computer systems. For example, those addicted to creating dozens of scenarios with electronic spreadsheets might consider reducing information overload by focusing on the following aspects of any business model:

  ❑ *Assumptions.* Careful review of assumptions often reveals they're unrealistic, and the dozens of scenarios are worthless, so review them first before playing "what-if." As technology author Steven Levy states, "Even the most elegantly crafted spreadsheet is a house of cards, ready to collapse at the first erroneous assumption."

- ❑ *Sensitivity analysis.* Which variables have the greatest impact on the bottom line? Play "what-if" with those, rather than wasting time with less significant variables.

- ❑ *Boundary cases.* What's the worst scenario? What's the best? Defining upside and downside may make further analysis unnecessary, for example, if the downside is too low or the upside not high enough.

SELECTIVE ABSORPTION

Given the sheer volume of information available today to any business manager, there is no way one can "know" all of it. Fortunately, there's no need to know all of it as long as one can *put one's hands on it* with reasonable speed. The astounding factual knowledge some people command is impressive, but when a factually challenged teenager can get to those same facts with a PC and a modem, one wonders whether memorizing a broad array of facts is the highest and best use of one's gray cells.

To the extent that the computer can act as a fast and thorough research tool, it's liberating rather than overwhelming. One way to deal with personal information overload, then, is to ask when confronted with data: Do I need to file this in my brain, or can I get it from the computer when I need it?

Another aspect of selective absorption is *focus:* whether the data has to do with the four or five top priorities one has set for oneself in a particular time frame. Does this data item pertain to those priorities? If not, one bans it from one's brain *and* computer workstation.

GOOD HOUSEKEEPING

The good news is that housekeeping is easier than it used to be. Archiving software can scan a workstation or an entire network, flagging files of a certain age or those that haven't been used for X number of months. Some network administrators have taken to notifying users of old files and destroying them (the files, not the users) if users don't respond within two weeks. Cleaning the electronic house makes all systems faster and reduces infoglut.

At the Right Time

INFORMATION SECURITY

Part of having information available at the right time is having it available at all. That's the province of information security, an essential discipline for the computerizing company. We'll explore reliability and uptime in a future chapter; suffice it to say here that any security plan that isn't documented, up-to-date, tested, and set up to provide 99 percent or better uptime isn't a serious plan.

I NEED IT YESTERDAY

> *"Actions to reduce the human cost and simplify the human interface to computers will have the greatest impact on growth."*
>
> —B. SCHACKEL, *Behaviour and Information Technology* (1985)

Computer interfaces became much easier to use with the arrival of the Graphical User Interface or "GUI," which replaces plain-text screens. Nevertheless, interface designs have been stifled by their designers' perceived need to use metaphors from the everyday office world (desktop, trash can, spiral notebook, etc.) and thereby make systems more approachable. These metaphors succeed only partially at best since they don't match their real-world counterparts exactly. No one would really put twenty manila folders inside another manila folder; and why would one drag an on-screen diskette icon to the "trash" to eject it?

Fortunately, imaginative designers at places such as Xerox and Silicon Graphics are developing new interfaces that promise quicker access to information. Examples are *cone trees*, 3-D labels that move from broad (left) to specific (right) and can be "spun" like a Rolodex, and *Navigator*, seen in the movie *Jurassic Park*, which allows the user to define a data landscape and then fly over it as though in a plane, landing on the area of interest. These new interfaces don't use office metaphors—but so what, if they help people get to information faster?

To the Right People

PUSHING DECISION MAKING DOWN AND OUT

Getting information to the right people may entail a change in who makes decisions. Insurance claims adjusters in the field, with parts and labor data on a CD/ROM, can authorize on-the-spot payments. Suppliers with access to customer inventory computers can see when stock of a given item is low and send new product automatically, without a purchase order. Nurses with access to poison databases can take emergency steps without waiting for a doctor. Sales reps with price and stock data available can write proposals at a customer's office.

Any organization distributing data down and across structural layers will find that moving the data doesn't guarantee the people who have newfound access to it will use it appropriately. They may need education to develop skills to match their new capabilities. Often, they'll assume the responsibilities gracefully. Usually, their morale and performance will increase. Almost always, they'll get things done quicker. But redistributing information also redistributes responsibility and authority. It's a cultural shift and it doesn't happen overnight.

GROUPWARE

An e-mail user can send a message to one specific person, or to many people, at a time. What e-mail can't do is allow communication between many people simultaneously, and that's where *groupware* comes in. Instead of dividing the world up into users, groupware divides it up into electronic *bulletin boards*, where anyone can post messages and anyone can read them.

Lotus Development Corporation's *Notes* product, the preeminent groupware application at this writing, has sold over half a million copies and is changing the way organizations communicate internally. Groupware facilitates cross-functional teams and encourages open comment and discussion—sometimes more than managers are used to, or comfortable with.

It's not inexpensive, however; today's technology costs about $500 per seat, and it usually involves specialized education and programming to get the most out of the system. Also, groupware is subject to some of the same dangers e-mail is: workers using the system for social rather than business purposes, people putting half-baked thoughts and ideas onto the system, too much irrelevant material to wade through. Groupware without guidelines may add to information overload rather than alleviate it.

FOR YOUR EYES ONLY

> *"The only fence against the world is a thorough knowledge of it."*
>
> —JOHN LOCKE, ENGLISH
> PHILOSOPHER, *Some Thoughts
> Concerning Education* (1693)

Distributed databases, e-mail, and groupware tend to make data more available and therefore vulnerable. Here are a few tips to keep company information out of the wrong hands while getting it into the right ones:

- Restrict physical access to network servers, minicomputers, and mainframes.

- In a network environment, consider using workstations that don't have diskette drives or tape drives. Consider removing such drives from machines that have them.

- Secure all modems. Set them to answer only after four or five rings to make "crackers" likely to bypass them. Use call-back modems for users from fixed remote locations. Assign modems to phone lines with different prefixes from other office lines to frustrate intruders looking to target your business.

- If a network area is to be off limits to some employees, customers, or suppliers, make it invisible to them. People don't get curious about what they can't see, and system administrators can hide files with ease.

- When disposing of tapes or diskettes with confidential data, physically destroy them. For an industrial spy, discarded computer tapes are worth more than a mountain of inter-office memos and sales reports. Network guru Patrick Corrigan tells of a Southwest headhunting firm that offered a hospital consultant $40,000 to pilfer a backup tape with personnel files on it.

- Teach employees how to create *good* passwords, defined by Corrigan as "difficult to guess, easy to remember and long enough to be difficult to break." Examples of good passwords are SECOND?GUESS and POWER$TIE, while bad passwords use family names, birthdays, job titles, car model or make, and so forth.

In the Right Form

ORGANIZED

The consequences of poor computer file organization are the same as for poor paper organization: lost documents and time wasted looking for a specific document. The bad news is computer storage systems, much like desks, impose few restraints on those who use them. If a PC user wishes to file all letters in a computer directory called LETTERS, it's possible. It would be much easier to find those letters later on, and archive old correspondence, if they were stored in areas named JULY95, AUG95, and so on. But there's no way to force users to set up an organized directory structure on their workstations.

Data filters, discussed earlier, can place computer data files in electronic folders according to preset criteria. Another interesting technology is the *indexer,* which creates multiple indexes to system files so that users can access them by date, location, or content. With indexing, it doesn't matter so much where files get stored, for the indexer can pull them up wherever they are.

SUMMARIZED

Different employees need different levels of detail from computer reports. Companies that take the time to create different levels of summarization depending on the user's needs take a giant step toward controlling data overload. Bill Kuipers, in *Direct Marketing,* shares some tips:

❏ Define *critical business indicators* and create reports that summarize them. There's an entire field of software called EIS (for Executive Information Systems) dedicated to this goal. It sometimes takes several prototype reports to reach optimum layouts, and it takes a "techno-suit" to create them.

❑ Use *reporting-by-exception* to flag quantities falling outside preestablished norms.

❑ Use *A-B-C analysis* to focus attention on the most important products, services, customers, and markets. "A" items account for 50 percent of total volume, "B" items account for the next 30 percent, and "C" is everything else. The "C" category will have the most items but is least important to manage.

GRAPHICAL

Graphical data is faster for users to understand, but there are graphs and then there are graphs. Scales that don't start at zero can exaggerate slight numerical differences. Three-D charts are almost useless for comparing quantities that don't line up adjacent to each other. Line charts or scatter diagrams without grid lines are similarly tough to read and use. Organizations that take some time to devise meaningful, accurate, and understandable graphs will acquire more knowledge from their databases.

With Accurate Facts

How does so much inaccurate data get into a computer system? We mentioned some key reasons already: Computer programs often aren't programmed to validate, cross-check, and update new information.

❑ *Validation* means that impossible or unreasonable entries get flagged the moment a user tries to enter them. Simple rules might just check for data *type:* A user can't enter a letter where a number should go, for example. Better rules also check for appropriateness: An August sales number that's ten times higher than July's figure might indicate a misplaced decimal point, causing the program to ask for confirmation before allowing the entry.

❏ *Cross-checking* against existing data improves internal consistency. A retailer, for example, maintains a mailing list for sending expensive catalogs to customers. That retailer may waste 5 percent of those catalogs because of duplications. A smart mailing list program would cross-check new entries against existing entries with the same address, to prevent a new entry for "Rob Petrie" when a "Robert Petrie" with the same New Rochelle address is already in the system.

❏ *Updating* means that if the retailer changes Rob's address for mailing list purposes, the system also changes the address for billing purposes so a clerk doesn't have to change it twice—and can't *forget* to change the billing address, introducing inaccuracy.

Another source of data inaccuracy assumes a sinister overtone: *computer viruses.* These programs can alter data at random, sometimes operating for weeks, months, or even years before a business detects the infection. Viruses can gain entry through any modem- or diskette-equipped workstation linked up to a network, and they can spread across geographical boundaries at the speed of electrons.

Organizations relying more and more on computers should examine each point in the system where information can enter, and implement virus protection measures in addition to validation, cross-checking, and auto-update routines. None of this is rocket science, and although antivirus software is growing sophisticated, it's available and 99 percent reliable. Much of virus protection, too, is a matter of policy and user education as much as technology.

Think of the information flowing through the computer system as drinking water. Just as one germ can infect an entire city water supply, such as Milwaukee's, one inaccurate data element can "infect" any report referencing that data, and it can be just as tough to find the source of the problem afterward.

Just Browsing

If an organization succeeds in supplying the right amount of information at the right time to the right people in the right form, it's still short of an optimal system. The optimal system provides for serendipity, for "connections." It allows *browsing*—"Management By Wandering Around Data." (MBWAD: A new jargon acronym? Okay, maybe not.)

Some software vendors are starting to build tools for browsing computer databases. One called *Topic* builds "semantic networks" linking data in complex yet easily navigable ways. Others allow the user to move a pointer around a pictorial representation of the data and "zoom in" on specific areas; for example, a medical program uses a human body as a starting point and provides successively more detailed zoom screens as the user delves deeper into the anatomy.

One problem with browsing data is that computers use so many different file *formats,* or structures. A really useful browser has to be able to roam around all the connected systems and read all the different kinds of files out there. It's a formidable task, made easier by customers who standardize on a limited number of data formats in their software applications.

Data filters have a long way to go before matching the intelligence of the *human* filters that have protected business persons for years from unwanted or irrelevant data: administrative assistants and secretaries. Combining browsing programs with software filters brings us at least somewhat closer to the ideal of an electronic Della Street—an intelligent assistant who keeps out the clearly irrelevant but leaves the door ajar to the unexpected and intriguing fact or individual.

THE REALITY

One short chapter barely begins to address the complexities of converting data into information and, ultimately, knowledge. But if nothing else, this chapter has shown that it's not just how *much* information a business has that matters; it's the *quality* of that information, measured as physical availability, human accessibility, security, and accuracy. Computer data management is a young discipline—certainly younger even than data processing—but it's one of the more important skills a business can develop.

Championship basketball coach Pat Riley is fond of saying that although a team needs a philosophy, "at game time it all comes down to *execution*." With this chapter, we conclude our survey of "big picture" issues and move to eight myths that prevent companies from applying technology successfully today. The philosophy's in place; now it's time to execute.

Part IV

Myths and Truths: Applying Automation Now

MYTH 6

We Don't Have Time for a Plan

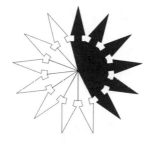

"It is thrifty to prepare today for the wants of tomorrow."

—AESOP, *The Ant and the Grasshopper* (about 550 B.C.)

THE MYTH

A nonprofit organization I worked with uses computers enthusiastically but has never adopted a coherent strategy. The organization added PCs for specific tasks over time (document processing, accounting, membership data, etc.) as seemed appropriate or convenient. Eventually, there were six different brands of computers in use—some for identical purposes. Staff in one department drafted documents that editors rekeyed into a different computer for printing. Employees who understood one kind of machine were unfamiliar with others, creating problems when people were on vacation or ill. Training and support costs were high because of the variety of machines and programs.

In sharp contrast, when a small credit-reporting bureau decided to automate its debtor-tracking database and letter-writing activities, the firm's two managing partners immersed themselves in the decision-making process of what software and hardware environments to use. They asked me literally hundreds of questions about how the different systems we were considering would be able to adapt to changing business conditions and different growth scenarios. We examined the stability and financial health of the vendors, and the different types and costs of support services available locally. We studied what might be involved in moving the simple, stand-alone microcomputer we started with to a network, minicomputer, or mainframe later. We determined to document every stage of the software development process for ease of migration later.

As a result, though that company is now doing twenty times the business it was doing seven years ago; it has been able to expand its computer network to handle the growth while discarding *no* hardware and using the same database software framework. It has incurred almost no retraining costs during that time because every improvement has built on the expandable basic system. The extra time we put into the planning process up front has saved that company hundreds of thousands of dollars as it has grown to its present size. *Planning pays.*

To do anything in business without thinking of the future is foolhardy. Yet, many companies spend significant dollars on computer systems without ever formulating the most rudimentary computer plan. The quick fix, ad hoc approach predominates: Buy something today that seems as if it will work, and if it doesn't work tomorrow, deal with it then. Organizations consider each arising need separately. Management holds no vision of the company's computer resource as an interconnected, evolving whole. Myth #6, then, is simply stated: *we don't have time for computer planning.*

This is the first chapter in part IV, which addresses the implementation and application of computer technology rather than the "big picture" issues considered in part III. Just as planning is the first step in applying information technology, it is the first topic to consider here.

As in part III, we first study the roots of the myth so the solutions will make sense. Please be patient: The magnitude of this problem may seem overwhelming, considering the rapid pace of change in the IT world. However, tried-and-true solutions do exist, but they will be meaningful only if one first understands why ad hoc automation is so often the rule rather than the exception.

ROOTS OF MYTH #6

Four factors that contribute to the ad hoc approach are uncoordinated departmental purchasing, crisis spending, a management orientation toward quick action, and deviating from existing plans midway through a project.

Uncoordinated Departmental Purchasing

I recently spoke with a manager at one of the top five American civil engineering consulting firms. In recent months this firm had adopted a policy of decentralizing computer control and allowing departments and even individuals to make local buying decisions for the hundreds of PCs the company owned. This policy resulted in a hodgepodge of incompatible networks and a practically insupportable variety of hardware and software. The costs to perform even routine administrative tasks, such as making backup copies of key files, had grown prohibitive because of the complex computing environment.

This example illustrates how different departments or divisions within an organization often purchase computer systems independently, without coordination. This practice creates isolated computer systems that, viewed individually, may perform well at their prescribed jobs but which do not communicate or share resources. I've found such isolated systems in accounting, sales, inventory control, product design, advertising, human resources, project management, market research, and plant automation.

Uncoordinated departmental purchasing wastes computer power because:

- ▢ It fosters systems that are redundant and often lightly used;

- ▢ It inhibits coordination and communication between departments;

- ▢ It adds enormously to the expense of linking the systems later;

- ▢ It increases training expenses for employees who move between departments; and

- ▢ It limits the organization's ability to shift computing resources between departments to accommodate changing workloads.

Why do divisions and departments fail to coordinate their computer projects? One reason is the historical barriers between those groups, which have developed their own cultures and traditions and whose goals often conflict. Another is the trend in some firms to push more authority and responsibility down to division and department levels, to make the organization more responsive and less burdened with centralized bureaucracy of the type that is slowly suffocating companies like IBM and DEC.

Another reason involves the dramatic shift in computing architectures from large, monolithic, expensive central systems to small, distributed, inexpensive units. A department that could never afford a mainframe within its spending authority limits certainly can buy much less expensive mini- and microcomputers without consulting upper management for approval. Ironically, the free fall in price/performance ratios and the shift to smaller, cheaper designs have actually made it *more difficult* for organizations to automate productively! Individual departments now have the authority to buy whatever they think they need, whenever they think they need it.

They have jumped at the opportunity. Traditional mainframe bureaucracies have proven notoriously slow in meeting departmental needs. As a result, according to Shannon Gaw in *LAN Magazine,* "these departments were left with no alternative but to attempt to resolve their own needs. LANs [Local Area Networks of PCs] provided a relatively cheap, simple, and flexible solution. . . . Interoperability was not an issue, since LANs were built to be introverted—to fulfill needs internal to one department. . . . Then IS [Information Services] came in to work one morning to find users camped at their doorsteps wanting connectivity, not only to the LAN down the hall, but also to the LAN across the country, and to the corporate IS infrastructure as well. The explosion in PC's and local area networks happened so quickly that it caught many CIS [Corporate Information Systems] departments off guard, and they have not developed policies fast enough to deal with the influx."

Specialized computer systems will always make sense for specific departments, and no one is suggesting that product design engineers should use the same equipment and software that bookkeepers in accounting use. Departments should buy equipment and programs that meet their special needs but which also can connect with other departments' systems where it makes sense. Autonomous and uncoordinated departmental purchasing presents a tall barrier to an effective organizational computer system.

Crisis Spending

Computer systems cost a lot of money. Small computers don't cost as much as large ones, but they're likely to be used by small companies with less to spend. As a result, companies often put off their purchase until business pressures force the issue. At that point, the company has not given itself enough time to evaluate alternative technologies. The pressure is on, and any computer is better than this inefficient manual system—right? *Wrong.*

The organization in a hurry to meet a computer need—be it a total system, a software package, a hardware device, or consulting services—may not obtain multiple bids, or may not review carefully the bids it does receive. It's true that for microcomputer hardware purchases, the dollar savings from comparison shopping don't amount to much in today's market due to intense competition and razor-thin margins. However, large multiuser systems, most software, and most services still vary widely in price and are somewhat negotiable. Shopping around brings a better deal for the customer, but it takes a little time.

Perhaps even more important than the dollar savings that comparison shopping and competitive bidding produce are the life cycle savings companies enjoy when they get the best product for their needs. In an industry of 100,000 products, the first choice is not likely to be the best over the long haul, either in terms of speed, features, compatibility, upgradability, reliability, or price.

Sometimes a crisis pushes managers into creating their own "quick and dirty" computer programs to meet urgent operational needs. I've seen these programs cause many more problems than they solve. One support manager for a California electronics company explained how the exploding demand for help desk services in his firm drove him to assign a staff programmer to create a software tool that would log and track support calls. "We didn't have time to shop around for an off-the-shelf solution," he said.

The programmer completed the work in two weeks—it's fairly easy to write simple, mediocre programs in a short time. But by now the program was six months old and hopelessly inadequate. In-house programmers didn't have time to keep upgrading the original program. Time pressures had not allowed the programmer to document his work, so outside contract help would be prohibitively expensive. The manager had begun evaluating commercial software that could handle the job, but he now faced a conversion headache that involved porting old data to the new system and retraining the help desk staff.

Over time, "quick and dirty" solutions just get dirtier, as we'll see in a later chapter that examines the issue of custom versus off-the-shelf software in more detail.

Crisis spending also surfaces when organizations must *expand* existing computer systems. Companies wait until expansion becomes imperative and then frantically buy tack-on products that provide short-term relief. Months go by, and they repeat the procedure. Managers in crisis mode don't ask the relevant questions: Do we really need to expand the present system, or should we scrap it for a new one? Will the quick-fix expansion create compatibility or support problems later? Is it the best product for the money?

Automating from crisis to crisis is an enormously inefficient practice. Certainly, management's tendency to delay capital expenditures until they are necessary is understandable, but the worst time to buy a computer system is when a company really needs it. It takes time to set up computers properly, to teach employees to use them, and to integrate them into the procedural work flow. The larger the computer system, the longer this takes. During this implementation process, which may take months or years, the computer system is a net *drain* on organizational productivity, just as adding employees is often a net drain until they learn the business.

Ready—Fire—Aim

Quite apart from dealing with crises, American business attaches great importance to speed, not only in delivering goods and services to customers but in making decisions, reacting to changing markets, and implementing new technology. (Many corporations pay only lip service to the latter; the reasons for corporate inertia are examined later.) Some companies adopt a philosophy of quick action that they apply to every circumstance, crisis or not. Tom Peters and Robert Waterman devote a chapter to the "bias for action" in their widely read book *In Search of Excellence.*

Consultants often struggle to persuade executives that this philosophy of quick action can wreak special havoc when it comes to computer systems. Rapid short-term decisions usually cost the company dearly over the long run. Companies dedicated to the quick fix may seem to be moving rapidly forward, when in fact they are merely moving rapidly. The *direction* of motion, and the *results* of quick action, ultimately determine success or failure. Here's one of a litany of examples from my own experience:

The research and development manager of a Dallas engineering firm where I once worked bought a microcomputer database program after a day or two of research. He instructed his employees to build a database of lab tests for a product under development. The system began operating in short order; other managers in the company marveled at the speed with which the R&D group was computerizing its work.

When the time came to *modify* the database to reflect changes in test procedures, however, the engineers discovered that their software did not permit such changes. They would have to create a *new* database structure, and reenter all the old data by hand into the new program. The R&D group limped along, performing periodic rewrites and rekeying all the historical data each time so they could use it for comparative analysis. The productivity gains from computerizing the lab tests were great at first, minimal after one rewrite, and *negative* after several rewrites—but at least that computer was up and running quickly!

Changing Horses in Midstream

"No one would ask a bridge builder to change his design from a suspension to an arch-supported bridge after the bridge was half-built. But the equivalent is often demanded of software builders."

> —U.S. CONGRESSIONAL OFFICE OF
> TECHNOLOGY ASSESSMENT,
> quoted in *The Day the Phones
> Stopped,* by Leonard Lee (1992)

Large automation projects run over budget and behind schedule more often than not. The automated baggage system at Denver International Airport is over a year late at this writing, costing the city of Denver about a million dollars a day in lost revenue. A 1988 study by the accounting firm of Peat Marwick Mitchell & Company revealed that of its six hundred largest clients, 35 percent had encountered "major runaways" among their computerization projects.

A key reason so many of these projects spin out of control is that businesses make design changes midway through implementation as it becomes painfully apparent that the system isn't working as intended.

Why do companies deviate from project plans? *Lack of user involvement* during the planning process is one reason. When the project is half done, users see it for the first time and point out serious deficiencies that never occurred to the system designers. The designers then try to correct those problems without abandoning the work they've already done and without making major structural changes. "Patches" and "workarounds" start proliferating like measles spots.

In addition, nontechnical managers often keep themselves too far removed from computer projects during planning and development. A *Business Week* article by Jeffrey Rothfeder puts it this way: "One problem with giving data processing professionals and outside suppliers free rein over a new computer system is that they tend to be overly optimistic . . . [they] feel they have to keep the executives happy by promising even what they can't deliver. And suppliers are out for sales." Furthermore, in-house systems professionals probably won't suggest products or approaches that could reduce the importance or size of the CIS department.

Managers who learn the fundamentals of computer systems can articulate their goals to systems professionals, understand the impacts of different design decisions, make planning decisions that work to the overall company's benefit, and apply their management skills to automation projects. Lack of management involvement ensures unrealistic goals, budgets, and timetables, and designs that don't meet management objectives—again requiring ad hoc fixes that distort original plans, drive costs skyward, and create a far less reliable and manageable system.

The third reason companies deviate from project plans, especially in software projects, is that they *think* it's easy to do so. Because it's so easy to change software—it just takes a little typing at a PC or terminal, right?—managers mistakenly believe that they can "edit" their new idea for the half-finished program into the program as easily as a newspaper editor can add words to a reporter's article at a computer keyboard. In reality, each part of a program affects dozens or even hundreds of other parts. Change orders increase the likelihood of errors and may even require the redesign of major parts of the program.

CONSEQUENCES OF MYTH #6

Consultants like myself harbor a fondness for planning, and large accounting and consulting firms have built enormous planning methodologies that customers understandably shy away from.

The business reader may therefore ask whether the results of unplanned automation are really so bad. They're worse. Consequences of the ad hoc approach include painful expansion, excessive support costs, low flexibility, poor organizational communications, disorganized data, inefficient resource use, slipped timetables, and busted budgets. Let's look at each in turn.

Painful Expansion

CONVERSIONS

The ideal business computer meets the information processing needs of the business today and can be upgraded and expanded as necessary tomorrow with no loss of investment in systems or training. The ideal business computer does not exist.

Technological obsolescence is a fact of life in the frenetic computer world. It often makes economic and competitive sense to upgrade computer systems; many companies delay too long to do so, as we'll see later. However, converting from one computer and set of programs to a newer system can devour tremendous amounts of time and effort. If repeated regularly, conversion inefficiencies negate most of the productivity gains that automation was supposed to bring in the first place. Technicians must discard old components; programmers must rewrite programs; instructors must retrain employees. After the conversion, productivity suffers while users learn their way around the new machine and programs.

Companies can make conversions much less disruptive if they plan them in advance and select the original equipment and software with future upgrades in mind. One can plan for product interchangeability and upgradability, making conversions much simpler and faster. Such foresight is, however, uncharacteristic of ad hoc automators.

If the company takes care to buy mainstream computer products that will have some resale value when the company upgrades, it can limit the cost of conversion. Five years ago, my company arranged the sale of a computer system that originally cost $23,000. To the president's chagrin, it brought $500, but we were very lucky to find a buyer at all. The system was an "orphan," an offshoot of IBM's main product line that IBM never developed or enhanced. Though such a decline in market value is part of the risk of buying any high-technology product, and though it's not easy to predict which product lines will stand the rigors of time and intense competition, careful planning can minimize the risk. The ad hoc buyer worries more about whether the system can do the job *now* than whether it will be able to grow with the company. Products purchased without a plan are more likely to end up as orphans that neither expand with the firm nor bring back any salvage value when sold.

The frequency of conversions is an important variable that ad hoc automators often do not control. Because of the drain on the organization that even the best-planned conversion entails, it's undesirable to undergo conversions more often than once every two or three years. Designers should put a certain amount of reserve capacity into place after every conversion, without going overboard and risking overkill. But crisis computerizers buy only as much computer horsepower as is necessary to meet immediate needs. So another crisis occurs in four to six months, requiring another conversion.

Upgrades

Companies can improve upgradable hardware and software and bring it up to the latest quality and performance levels without discarding entire systems. Ad hoc automators don't pay much attention to upgradability when buying products; they may pay a steep price later.

In fact, many hardware vendors don't build upgradable systems. By hard-wiring the Central Processing Unit (CPU) and other vital circuitry on an irreplaceable circuit board, or "motherboard," these vendors ensure that customers who wish to move to a newer or more powerful system must buy an entirely new central computer. The variety of nonstandard cabinetry and cabling manufacturers use also stands in the way of convenient upgrades. Though this certainly contributes to manufacturers' sales volume, it leaves the user with a substantial cost obstacle to upgrading. As a result, many companies that didn't look for upgradability first will continue using outmoded computers.

Microcomputer makers in particular have been slow to consider upgradability important. Apple Computer provides a case history:

Year	Old Computer	New Computer	Upgrade Method
1980	Apple II	Apple / / /	None
1982	Apple / / /	Lisa	None
1984	Lisa	Macintosh	None
1987	Macintosh	Macintosh II	None
1989	Macintosh II	Macintosh IIci	None
1990	Macintosh IIci	Macintosh IIfx	None
1991	Macintosh IIfx	Quadra 700	None
1992	Quadra 700	Quadra 950	None

A few of Apple's computers are upgradable—the IIcx and Quadra 650, for example—but those units are the exception. Brand loyalty often provided no rewards when it came to moving up to new technology.

Computer makers may argue that they can't provide the latest features without fundamentally changing the machine; this is usually just a smoke screen, however. Many of the changes that preclude upgrading (such as box size and shape) aren't necessary, and a few manufacturers have been building upgradable systems for years. Companies like DEC have often made significant upgrades possible with their minicomputers using the same cabinetry. In today's marketplace, many PC makers advertise upgradability to CPUs that aren't even in production yet. Dell, for example, advertised Pentium upgradability for its "486" computers before the Pentium CPU was even in production. The customer must hunt for such systems, however, as part of a carefully considered automation plan.

Excessive Support Costs

TRAINING

Ill-planned computing facilities, such as the one described at the start of this chapter, require greater training costs than well-planned facilities. The wide variety of machines and programs—many of which perform similar if not identical functions—implies a more diverse training schedule than would be necessary in a more homogeneous environment.

Some companies reason that it costs too much to train personnel in a hodgepodge computing environment, so they don't do it; or they provide training for only the most popular products, and ignore the others. Therefore, one problem leads to another, and organizations with unplanned computer growth provide less training than other companies. Ironically, those firms needing training most urgently supply it least often.

DOCUMENTATION

Though most organizations do a miserable job of documenting their computer systems, the ones that try have a special challenge when trying to write user and technical manuals for the hodgepodge situation. Perhaps the technical writers will produce documentation for the most widely used hardware and software, but individual departments and work groups must usually document their own systems. The result? They don't. This compounds the usability problem and renders those systems even more difficult to maintain and expand over time.

User Support

Much of my work has dealt with end-user support, especially in "help desks"—CIS groups that answer user questions and troubleshoot problems, primarily over the phone. These groups struggle valiantly to keep up with the support challenges posed by ad hoc automation, but it becomes next to impossible to deal with the variety of user needs these unplanned environments generate. The result is poor service to the users in the form of slow response time and slow solution time.

Low Flexibility

Employee Mobility

Companies with flexible staffs can deal with changing conditions, whether in the marketplace or within the organization. Changing business conditions may require moving personnel from one department to another. A company may need to move employees from engineering into sales to increase demand for its products. On a smaller level, illness and time off may require horizontal micro-movements of personnel to keep key activities functioning smoothly.

Such flexibility is difficult in the ad hoc computing environment for the same reason that training is expensive: There's too much unnecessary variety in equipment and software. When lateral movement of employees requires them to master new machines and programs, the lag time before the employees become productive in their new positions increases. Substitutes become less effective at temporarily filling key positions, and customer service may suffer as a result. The variety of hardware and software in the unplanned but automated office inhibits employee mobility and, therefore, the flexibility of the organization.

EQUIPMENT INTERCHANGEABILITY

Imagine a world in which only one manufacturer made tires that could fit your car; where a single company built an answering machine that would work with your phone; and where you had to own a separate corkscrew for every different kind of wine you drink. Products such as tires, answering machines, and corkscrews are *interchangeable:* made in standard sizes and shapes to work with a variety of other products (wheels, phones, wine bottles). Without design consistency, what happens?

- Interchangeability becomes impossible.

- Customers become hostages of sole-source suppliers.

- Systems grow inflexible.

- Redundancy reigns.

- Downtime soars.

- Product value declines.

Computers are admittedly more complex than corkscrews, though perhaps not so elegantly effective. However, hardware interchangeability *is* achievable with complex devices. Consider telephones: Standard phones have a modular plug that works with standard phone jacks. Consider also stereo systems: Nearly any compact disc player connects easily to any preamplifier or receiver.

Ask a network administrator how difficult it would be to move a shared printer from one floor to another. How many steps would it take? Now ask what would be involved to take that network printer and connect it to a stand-alone PC. Would it even be possible to connect it to a central mainframe? The answers will most likely appall you; no one ever thought of planning for moving components around easily. Ad hoc automators have little hope of achieving any semblance of equipment inter-changeability, again making the organization less able to react internally to external market changes.

Poor Organizational Communications

Connecting disparate and randomly purchased computing com-ponents into an effective, company-wide electronic network is difficult and expensive. Unplanned computer growth results in isolated computer systems with limited usefulness. These iso-lated systems also tend to block personal interaction between departments. One of the more important intangible benefits of sharing computer resources between departments is the infor-mal conversations that result—using electronic mail, for in-stance.

Disorganized Data

Do you know where your data is? In an unplanned computer environment, the answer is usually no.

The advent of *distributed processing*—using many CPUs in a company or department instead of just one—has created a se-rious problem for computer administrators: keeping track of what data resides where. Often, in an ill-planned system, several copies of important operating data are scattered around the orga-nization. Simply ensuring that every employee is working with the most up-to-date information can prove a nightmare in a highly distributed system having many small computers. Provid-ing special reports to managers is a difficult chore when adminis-trators must hunt through dozens of poorly labeled floppy-disk files or tape racks to find the required information. The chore is even more burdensome when each worker has his own files stored in his own computer.

The recent explosion in portable computers—laptops, note-books, subnotebooks, and "personal digital assistants"—scatters data even further afield. Every portable computer user has had to deal with the problem of *reconciling* data: making sure both the portable system and the desktop system have the latest files.

The problem of disorganized data does not usually occur to the ad hoc automators. They may buy one small computer after another, not realizing that with every new data storage device, the ability to rapidly retrieve specific data diminishes. Insofar as computers use different kinds of disks, tapes, networks, and operating systems, the problem worsens because it becomes difficult to move data from one machine to another once one (eventually) locates it.

It's clear, then, that the computer's ability to store vast quantities of information compactly is a two-edged sword. Distributed processing can hold great benefits for companies that plan carefully where information will reside and how they will maintain, update, and archive it. Distributed processing can make life very difficult for companies that do not.

Inefficient Resource Use

Unconnected computing systems often make poor use of expensive equipment resources. A busy minicomputer in market research cannot easily use an idle printer connected to a minicomputer in accounting. As a result, both departments buy their own printer, even though each unit may be busy no more than 5 percent of the time each day. The problem may become more acute with more expensive devices such as disk drives or tape units.

Slipped Timetables and Busted Budgets

Larger computer projects plagued by large numbers of change orders or even radical redesigns never finish on time and always cost more than projected. While it's possible, and even desirable, to restructure the entire software design process so that engineers, managers, and users are involved throughout and projects are completed in modules rather than as a monolithic system, many companies still use the traditional approach of specifying a design up front in a detailed, formal document—which is then modified so often that any hope of an on-time, under-budget delivery is quashed.

THE PROBLEM

Uncoordinated departmental purchasing, crisis spending, an uncompromising dedication to quick action, and deviating from project plans in mid-implementation all contribute to a situational approach to automation. The price of this approach is severe: inconvenient and expensive expansion, high support costs, low flexibility, poor communications, chaotic data management, low resource utilization, and runaway projects. Ad hoc automation looms as one of the largest problems companies must overcome to computerize productively. What can be done about it?

THE REALITY

"For wars are won by skillful strategy, and victory is the fruit of long planning."

—SOLOMON *et al., Proverbs 24:6*
(about 800 B.C.)

A good plan requires time, money, and effort to prepare, whether you are building a manufacturing plant or installing a computer system. Is computer system planning worth it?

Benefits of Planning

The primary benefits of computer planning are simply avoiding all the problem consequences just examined. While no panacea, good planning renders most of those consequences much less severe. In addition:

- ❏ Creating a written computer plan forces managers to consider their *goals* for the computer system, and to discuss those goals with upper management and end-users alike in a concrete way. Ultimately, this should help CIS managers understand the business mission that they must serve.

- ❏ The plan provides a convenient *frame of reference* for discussing and evaluating a computer environment that otherwise might be too sprawling and abstract to grasp easily. The organization can evaluate proposed changes to automated systems more intelligently within the context of the plan.

- ❏ The plan helps bring *continuity* to automation strategies in organizations where reorganizations and restructuring are the order of the day, and managers move from position to position with increasing frequency.

- ❏ A plan document facilitates discussions and negotiations with hardware and software vendors and consultants, giving them a thorough picture of your company's present system as well as your business goals and views of the future.

- ❏ Computer plans help identify deficiencies in underlying policies and procedures. Often, this is the primary benefit of automation planning!

The only thing more expensive than a good computer plan is no computer plan. A prerequisite, however, is a solid *information* plan, which has little to do with automation but everything to do with organizational procedures.

Information Planning

The best computer plan will not compensate for a poor (or non-existent) information plan. The computer system comprises merely one component of an information system. Other components include:

❑ The timing of data entry, modification, reporting, and archiving;

❑ Responsibility for data accuracy at those various stages;

❑ Which groups need access to what data, at what point, and to what extent;

❑ How to ensure adequate security.

Computerization magnifies inefficiencies in the underlying information flows. Companies considering automation should therefore first concentrate on streamlining information flows. The return on investment from data flow planning often far exceeds that from computerization.

Some of my consultant colleagues admire the impressive and labyrinthine methodologies that large accounting firms produce for mapping information flows. I have found those methodologies needlessly detailed and complex for all but the largest projects, though they do ensure hefty consulting fees. Nevertheless, making a high-level chart of information flow usually reduces the cost of subsequent automation because simpler information systems beget simpler and more successful computer systems.

How strange that companies rarely map out *information,* so vital to business success! A company that treats information as its most valuable resource will monitor its flow as closely and carefully as the flow of cash through its bank account or raw materials through its plant.

Elements of a Computer Plan

Consider for a moment the manufacturing VP charged with outfitting a plant to manufacture a new air conditioning unit. Merely buying an assortment of presses, machine tools, fixtures, conveyor racks, and paint booths, placing them haphazardly on the plant floor, and plugging them in will not provide an efficient facility. The first thing the VP of manufacturing will do is assemble a plan that considers the following:

- The goals of the business in building the plant;
- The nature of the products to be manufactured;
- How and when raw materials will move from one station to the next;
- Which operations the plant will perform in-house and which it will outsource;
- Which machines the plant requires, using the best appropriate technology;
- Whether outside vendors should custom-build some of the machines;
- What procedure to adopt for acquiring equipment, such as bid requests;
- Whether existing machines can be used or should be replaced;
- The order in which to deploy machines and the timing of that deployment;
- How much machines will cost (a budget);
- Where they will be placed;

- What support resources they will need (light, power, heat);

- What provisions the company will make to keep them running;

- A disaster plan in case they stop running;

- How people can use the equipment safely and efficiently;

- What kind of people should be hired, and what training they will need;

- How to implement quality control, and at what stages of production;

- How managers can monitor plant performance;

- How the plant will communicate with other company departments, such as marketing, finance, accounting, engineering; and

- How to expand, improve, or modify the plant in the future with maximum use of existing equipment and minimum downtime.

The manufacturing VP will consult with machinists and managers alike during the planning process to ensure that the plant will work without extensive ad hoc changes along the way and to ensure that its budgets and timetables are realistic. He or she will also think in terms of a modular, phased implementation with specified checkpoints along the way and with penalties for suppliers who don't deliver components on time or on spec. Finally, the VP will make sure that the organization commits to the plan so that it will be executed all the way through.

These are exactly the elements of a good computer plan.

Here are a few typical considerations to give a flavor of the process, and to illustrate how good planning can save thousands or even millions of dollars while ensuring successful computer installations. Most of the following sections correspond to the planning checklist given above.

WHO DOES IT?

The manufacturing VP would never think of constructing a plant without consulting with the machinists and experts who will run its day-to-day operations. Similarly, smart computer systems planners solicit advice and comment from future system users to avoid disastrous oversights and misjudgments. Such a policy brings a crucial side benefit: Users will try much harder to make the system work if they offer some design input at the outset. Designers and planners often believe they already know what user concerns will be, and to their credit, they're right perhaps 75 percent of the time. But that's not nearly enough to ensure success.

CIS professionals occasionally display a fondness for technological elegance at the expense of practicality. Corporate planners and managers may opt for the least expensive solution without fully considering life cycle cost issues, and they may undervalue technological concerns through failure to understand them. End-users may not appreciate completely the importance of connectivity, compatibility, and security. All three groups, therefore, should participate in computer plans to ensure a balanced vision. In cases where the automation project will affect an organization's customers, they constitute a fourth group.

GOAL SETTING

The first step of a good information systems plan is goal definition. Many firms adopt inappropriate, technology oriented goals:

- Eliminate paper in the office.

- Put a computer on every desk.

- Build a totally roboticized factory.

Such goals rarely make sense. Why make eliminating paper a top priority, when reducing its use by 50 percent in the most time-critical processes—such as processing customer orders—will give you 90 percent of the potential efficiency improvement? Why place computers on the desks of people who don't need them (not everyone does)? Why strive for 100 percent plant automation when the result might suffer in flexibility and maintenance cost?

Here's a sampling of more appropriate goals for automated systems:

- To reduce product shipment delays by integrating order processing, credit approval, inventory, and billing into a single computerized system;

- To improve customer service by maintaining a database of customer questions and problems, searchable by key words and phrases;

- To reduce legal costs by creating a system to generate draft contracts using approved "boilerplate" modules for forwarding to counsel;

- To reduce product development time by setting up small networks for project teams to share ideas and coordinate schedules;

- To improve the quality of management information by building a program to automatically scan on-line news wires and trade journals for key topics.

Businesses succeed by orienting their strategies around customers and profits, not technology. If technology can help provide a competitive advantage, reduce operating costs, provide better customer service, reduce cycle times, improve product quality, or increase revenues, great; a company should use it. If not, it has no place: *Technology for its own sake is an inappropriate business goal.*

OUTSOURCING DECISIONS

An organization may choose to outsource one or several aspects of an automation project, including the following:

- Technical design;

- Market surveys;

- Plan review;

- Custom programming;

- System integration;

- Project management;

- Service and maintenance;

- User training and support;

- Disaster recovery services.

Many third-party service companies provide these services on a contract basis. The larger computer companies are now jumping into this market, as profits from their traditional products dwindle. John W. Venty's article in *Business Week* reports: "Solving complex information-handling problems for corporations is an obvious way of . . . replenishing profits for old-line makers. IBM, for instance, is pursuing a variety of professional services, including writing custom software, outsourcing, and most recently, management consulting."

Perhaps the most important outsourcing assignment is plan

review. Outside consultants can review your computer plan and make suggestions based on wide experience with many companies. Strangely, many firms balk at bringing in consulting assistance during the plan review phase, when it is most valuable and cost-effective. While it's easy to pay too much for consulting, many reputable firms can save the organization many times the consulting fee by pointing out pitfalls and recommending proven solutions.

Outsourcing decisions depend on various factors:

- How quickly the project must take shape;

- The availability and cost of in-house expertise;

- Security concerns; and

- The cost of outside contractors.

One danger when outsourcing is to share responsibility for the project too broadly. The most successful computer projects may involve a number of contractors but one overall manager. Another danger is not specifying very clearly the scope of each contractor's work, in writing and in advance, to minimize surprises and misunderstandings. Specification documents should set forth criteria for determining contractor performance, and a schedule with clear checkpoints all along the way.

ACQUISITION

Any complete computer plan must include procedures for acquiring the systems chosen in the technology assessment phase. Companies often plan for competitive procurement through a Request for Proposal (RFP). Several caveats come to mind in this connection:

- It's very difficult to compare computer systems line by line using a bid document. Different computers run different programs, and software will influence the buying decision greatly.

Going into too much detail about the "how" of the project in the RFP will disqualify products that might meet 90 percent of the requirements. Giving the vendors some leeway in choosing technology helps avoid ruling out good candidates.

❏ Having said that, the RFP should go into *great* detail about the "what" of the project. In interviews with top CIS executives, Thomas D. Clark reports in *Communications of the ACM* that "the key to production cost control was felt to be a very detailed systems requirements specification . . . one would expect to find a well-developed process to specify requirements and plan projects prior to requesting proposals . . . this, however, was not the case. In several instances, outside vendors or consultants actually developed system specifications as part of the project." It's fine for vendors to produce the technical details, but the *customer* produces the requirements document!

❏ The integrity of the bidding process can be maintained by keeping politics out of it to the extent possible. It's smart to lay out criteria in advance for determining bidder eligibility and for evaluating proposals.

❏ Automatically choosing the low bidder on a computer system may prove a serious mistake. Large computer systems are not commodities; an excellent one can save a company thousands or even millions of dollars, while an inappropriate system can be more trouble than it is worth. Life cycle costs far exceed purchase prices; low-ball bids can end up being very expensive in terms of repairs, downtime, and poor connectivity.

❏ Smart planners listen carefully if a vendor expresses concerns with an RFP. It's just possible the vendor has an idea that can save the customer time and money. No RFP is perfect, despite the considerable time and effort that may have gone into it.

❏ Give maximum weight to software issues, particularly in projects using commercial programs. Customers should always review the available software, select the program or programs best suited for their needs, and then and *only* then focus on hardware, asking for bids on different machines if the software can run on more than one kind of computer.

PHASED IMPLEMENTATION

Which parts of the plan should the organization implement first? Trying to "switch on" a new, large system overnight usually invites disaster. Users must learn a great deal in a short time, support staff face a sharp spike in demand for troubleshooting services, and system acceptance may take longer (or never happen at all) because of the initial confusion, relearning, and fire fighting. Quality testing and performance verification are more manageable if the customer *phases in* project implementation.

The technology planning timeline depends on both business and technical considerations. From the business standpoint, what functions of the new system stand to provide the greatest benefit? Will employees be able to use part of the system before the whole project is complete? When my company developed a new inventory system for a Texas lumber company, we finished the data entry module first so employees could key in item descriptions and codes while the programmer completed other modules. What restrictions do budget cycles impose on the timing of component purchases? To ensure ongoing management commitment to the project, how can the project demonstrate some results fairly soon?

From the technology standpoint, some modules must exist before others. The hardware is often the first prerequisite, although it's often possible to perform software design on time-sharing services or by renting equipment until the actual hardware arrives. Installers must lay network cabling before designers can create and test workstation links. Someone must enter at least a sampling of "live" data before programmers can customize reports; and so on.

Project managers can code these key technical dependencies and business considerations into project management software programs. These tools can greatly facilitate the phase-in by providing continuously updated progress reports and by identifying critical paths and opportunities for parallel, simultaneous work.

BUDGETING

Informed budgeting for computer systems can go a long way toward ensuring that those systems work in the first place and improve productivity over their lifetime. Many budgets, however, guarantee poor computer resource utilization. They underfund system integration, user training, and on-site service; overspend on hardware and underspend on software; make no provisions for outside consultants, and so on. One reason is that most organizations operate on an annual budget cycle, while proper computer system budgeting should take a longer view, typically, at least three to five years.

Long-view budgets recognize that incremental improvements in a computer system can improve its performance substantially. It's unwise to allocate $100,000 for buying a new computer system this year and allocate nothing for next year. It's far better to spend $80,000 now, and budget $20,000 for new products or improvements over the next two years, even in a no-growth scenario. One can only determine which aspects of the system need enhancing after the computer has been running for several months. It's impossible to design a perfect computer system on paper and buy all the needed products at once. Organizations that try will either overspecify the initial system or suffer poor performance later without being able to correct it by modest follow-on expenditures.

Often, planners authorize large amounts for capital equipment (hardware) but very little for software, training, or support. Software has an intangible, abstract quality, which may help explain why I've run into resistance from clients who can understand paying $50,000 for a computer but don't see why the programs it runs should cost even one-tenth as much. The reality is that a well-designed computer system usually includes *twice as much* software cost as hardware cost, or more, over its lifetime.

Budgeters should also allocate typically up to 25 percent of the hardware cost for system integration: putting the pieces together and making them work properly. User training and support costs vary widely, but budgeters generally should plan for 10 to 20 percent of the total system cost, *per year of operation*. These figures often well exceed budget plans assembled by managers unfamiliar with computer projects and what makes them succeed. It may help to have someone with project experience review the proposed budget before casting it in stone.

MAINTENANCE

Any machine deteriorates over time, but the gradual nature of that deterioration may prevent its being noticed until disaster strikes. Regular maintenance "tune-ups" and diagnostic tests can identify developing problems before they become crippling or catastrophic. They also can prevent other types of problems from ever occurring at all.

Further, as time passes, the computer may perform different jobs, run different programs, and handle more users. These changes can create new bottlenecks that limit performance. Regular computer tune-ups can help locate these bottlenecks and correct them so that systems work at maximum speed. These examinations should focus not only on the electromechanical components of the computer system but also on more abstract areas, such as memory and network use. Here are two brief but typical examples:

❑ Computers are rapidly making their way out of "clean rooms" and into the office environment as today's downsizing trend races forward. As a result, office dust collects on logic and memory chips and traps heat, driving temperatures beyond design limits and causing chips to fail intermittently. Simply blowing dust off circuit boards with compressed air once a year can extend a computer's life by several years, avoiding the costly downtime and difficult troubleshooting that intermittent chip failure causes.

❏ Computer networks and minicomputers use high-speed machines to provide centralized file and print access to workstation users. These *servers* store frequently accessed data in fast memory caches to fulfill user requests quickly. The cache sizes may be appropriate at installation time, but they quickly become inadequate when the network grows and disk storage is added. Adding to these memory caches can sometimes *double* server file access speeds.

DISASTER PLANNING

Large, critical systems in which downtime costs thousands of dollars per second usually have disaster plans in place. Smaller systems often don't, and the small computer is just as important to the small business as the large ones are to the multinational banks and financial services firms.

Any good computer plan should deal with contingencies such as theft, vandalism, fire, floods, earthquakes, computer viruses, power outages, and equipment failure. Planners should weigh the cost of downtime against the cost of quick recovery to develop appropriate plans for their organizations' business environment.

The first component of any disaster plan is *notification:* How do you know there's a problem? The answer is fairly obvious if an earthquake or flood occurs, but equipment problems may not make themselves felt immediately. Software monitoring tools may help alert operators of incipient failures on the system.

The second component is *response procedures*. Since the 1970s, larger companies have been setting up "hot sites" with duplicate equipment where operations may continue while technicians fix problems at primary sites. Organizations that can't afford their own exclusive hot site may share a site with other firms using similar equipment, or contract with a disaster-recovery service company. In any case, off-site storage for key programs and data files may be the only way to recover from a disaster. Even if equipment withstands a physical disaster, authorities may forbid access to the building, as happened after the 1993 World Trade Center bombing in New York City.

Third is *prioritization*. Some computerized activities are crucial to operations and some less so. The disaster plan provides for bringing up the crucial programs first. Management helps decide what "crucial" means and therefore participates in creating the disaster plan. Government regulations—in banking, for example—and customer contracts may help the organization decide which programs and functions must be up and running, and how fast, to avoid fines, lawsuits, or lost customers.

Finally, the disaster plan should consider not just how to get the system back up, but how to get people using it again! Using the World Trade Center example once more, some firms had their data secure long before they could find alternative office space for their employees to use it.

Disaster planning is not a one-time exercise; plans must be kept up-to-date if they're going to work. Nor is it a purely academic exercise; good plans get tested to make sure they're going to work.

SUPPORT

Computer systems support encompasses three areas: *documentation, training,* and *troubleshooting*. These demonstrate some synergy in that well-documented systems are easier to teach and troubleshoot, and well-trained users create fewer problems for support staff to track down. Therefore, a good computer plan addresses each area.

Documentation may be the best example of how planning can reduce system costs over time. Systems designers and programmers who document their technical work make future expansion or modification much easier. Perhaps 10 percent of the computer networks and programs that clients have asked my company to improve or expand have been adequately documented. Whatever time consultants have to spend "figuring out" the system comes out of the customer's pocketbook. Troubleshooting poorly documented systems takes easily twice as long, too, as any network technician will attest.

Even the best-designed computer systems can be complex to learn and use. Operators' manuals are often very poorly written, and most people do not learn as well from books as from structured classes, anyway. Budgeters must set aside reasonable funds for education to make the best use of the computer system. Training is no less important for PC or LAN users than for users of multi-million-dollar mainframes. And it is not a one-time expense. New employees need introductory training, competent beginners need more advanced courses, experts benefit from refresher courses, and all users need to keep abreast of software improvements and upgrades as they occur.

Finally, what resources will the organization put into place for handling the day-to-day problems and questions that arise? Whether the company contracts out this function or provides it in-house, goals for response time, resolution time, and accuracy will make up part of the plan. What steps will the organization take to track user questions and problems? What feedback mechanism will ensure that recurring problems in the field don't continue indefinitely but will receive the attention of technicians who can fix them?

COMMUNICATION AND CONNECTIVITY

A good plan considers industry standards, where they exist as well as internal, corporate standards to ensure compatibility and connectivity.

- ❑ Which information should the system share, and with whom?

- ❑ Which programs and functions should be available to other departments or groups?

- ❑ Will the organization's customers need access to the system, and if so, to what extent and how?

The answers to these questions will help determine connectivity and standardization requirements.

EXPANSION

One of the most important benefits of planning is the opportunity to combat rapid obsolescence by specifying products with a *growth path:* hardware and software that can grow as the company grows, with minimal waste and disruption.

Many machines and programs impose built-in performance ceilings; customers should give great weight to products designed with growth in mind. It's important to plan for expansion because of the high costs of conversions and retraining, the low salvage value of hardware, and the high speed of technological advancement.

HARDWARE EXPANSION

System hardware can expand in various ways, illustrated here by a freight train analogy. An organization adds *storage capacity* in the form of memory, disk, and tape drives, to handle more data (adding more boxcars). One adds *throughput* by improving the system's ability to move data in and out (modernize boxcar loading and unloading facilities). It's possible to add *speed* by three methods: adding CPUs in a network or cluster (putting another locomotive at the front of the train), replacing existing CPUs and servers with faster units (replacing the locomotive with one having more horsepower), and dividing the system into groups that handle different tasks (putting fewer cars on each train). Finally, one can increase *availability* of computer resources by adding terminals, workstations, or printers on a Local or Wide Area Network (LAN/WAN), analogous to adding more stops along the route to serve more people.

While this analogy isn't perfect, it provides a useful way to think of the many techniques an organization may use to expand its hardware resources. For example, adding horsepower by up-grading CPUs and servers (*vertical* expansion) is one way to make the system able to run more demanding applications than it could before, just as a stronger engine allows a train to negotiate routes with steeper grades. Vertical growth paths are frequent in the minicomputer and mainframe marketplace, where a central CPU serves many users and may become the limiting factor on system speed.

Expanding in one way may require expanding in other ways. Increasing availability may, in turn, create a need for more horse-power, and increasing speed may require improving network communications, or improving the track, in the analogy. On the other hand, sometimes off-loading computing tasks to new sys-tems can ease the burden on existing systems, delaying the need for a vertical upgrade.

SOFTWARE EXPANSION

The growth path for software matters just as much as for hard-ware. Many programs run on a spectrum of machines ranging from PCs to million-dollar mainframes. Vertical growth means obtaining a version of the same software that will run on a more powerful CPU; planners ask how easy it will be to migrate their programs and data over to larger systems. One achieves *horizontal* growth by upgrading licenses to allow more employees to use existing programs, and by adding new programs. Project planners should concern themselves with ease of software expansion both vertically and horizontally before launching projects.

It's clear from all this that system designers must make educated guesses not only about *how much* the business may grow over the system's life, but also *how* it will grow. Only then can planners specify hardware and software products that can expand as necessary in capacity, throughput, speed, and availability. *Business projections drive technology decisions*—one more reason management can't leave computer system planning to the technocrats.

Executing the Plan

The world is full of excellent plans that gather dust on shelves; some of my own planning documents have met this fate, and it is the consultant's nightmare. Why does this happen?

- ❏ Plan complexity: If no one can understand the plan, how can it succeed?

- ❏ The lack of clearly defined checkpoints or milestones that implementers can use to track the plan's progress and monitor vendor performance.

- ❏ The absence of follow-up provisions: How often will we review the plan and compare it against reality? Who will do it?

- ❏ Lack of management support. If senior management doesn't endorse the plan with vigor and promote it within their organization, it won't succeed.

THE SOLUTION

Smart, thorough computer planning works; uncoordinated purchasing, crisis-to-crisis computing, and "point solutions" don't. The extent and quality of an organization's planning reflect on its maturity and its likelihood of automating productively.

A successful plan involves management, technical experts, support persons, and end-users. It begins with a careful examination and streamlining of information flows.

From that point, it addresses the system's business purpose; "buy versus build" questions; technology alternatives; use of existing systems; phases of implementation; realistic budgets; diagnostics and maintenance; a disaster plan; human factors; support and training plans; how to monitor and control information quality; communication with other systems; and future expansion.

The organization's management then *promotes* and *uses* the plan as a real working document. Thorough automation strategies incorporating these key elements dramatically reduce business computing costs and improve the performance of the computer systems they bring forth.

One key aspect of planning mentioned above is future expansion. It's just as important to avoid "overkill" as it is to build expandability into a computer system, because excess capacity today may not be usable tomorrow. The fallacy of "getting the most powerful system we can afford" is therefore the topic of the next chapter.

MYTH 7

Get the Most Computer Power We Can

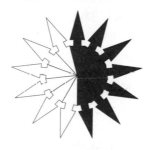

"For years, computer buyers based their decisions on the speed and the number of features in a system—without determining whether those things helped people work faster. . . . But 'the next real boost in productivity will come from fitting the technology to the task—not the faster MIPS and bigger chips,' says Judith Olson, who heads the computer studies department at the University of Michigan's business school."

—WILLIAM M. BULKELEY,
"SYSTEM BUYERS FINALLY
VALUE PRODUCTIVITY,"
The Wall Street Journal
(April 19, 1993)

THE MYTH

Once, I was asked to take a look at the computer setup at the regional headquarters of a nonprofit agency. After a few days studying the systems and listening to their users, I suggested to the agency's director that she get rid of the largest system, a fairly large and expensive word processing minicomputer. The director was surprised: She had expected to hear that she needed *more* computers, not fewer. How could the agency become more efficient by *de*automating?

It was much more difficult to persuade her to abandon the old system than to suggest spending tens of thousands on new systems to augment it. But her employees were wasting a lot of time trying to make the newer computers work with the old one. The organization would have been better off with fewer, but more compatible, systems. (My argument, it turned out, wasn't persuasive enough; the agency ultimately agreed with it, though— two years later!)

It's difficult to persuade business people that they may need *less* computer power rather than more. Try this: Next time you're visiting with a manager who's going through the painful process of laying off employees, ask him if he's considered getting rid of some of the department's *computers*. Chances are the manager will look at you as if you've lost your mind.

But why? No experienced manager would claim that hiring more employees automatically makes a business better. Managers often try to make their businesses better by reducing staff to cut overhead in lean times. But suggesting that they reduce the number of their computers borders on heresy.

There are two forms of overkill. The first is using chainsaws to cut butter: applying technology substantially more powerful than the job at hand requires. The chainsaw may do the job, but the butter won't be too appealing afterward. The second is giving everyone at a table their own butter knife when one would do: using more computers (or computer systems) than necessary.

Examples of overkill pepper the world of business computing:

❏ Many small businesses or departments invest in "client/ server" Local Area Networks (LANs) in order to share a few printers and files, when a simpler "peer-to-peer" network could perform the same function for thousands of dollars less in both initial and ongoing costs. Peer-to-peer LANs offer many capabilities of their more powerful client/server relatives: electronic mail, program and data file sharing, and group scheduling, for example. They don't have ironclad security, but many applications don't need that. They don't require a "dedicated" computer to act as the central "server," and they allow every workstation to share any files or printers with any other workstation—a level of flexibility the more expensive client/server systems can't easily match.

❏ Businesses are still buying minicomputers and small mainframes when, in many cases, they could be accomplishing their automation goals far less expensively with coordinated networks of microcomputers and workstations. One large company in Chicago recently purchased hundreds of IBM AS/400 minicomputers despite the fact that most software development work in the company is now being done on PCs.

❏ Sophisticated, programmable "relational" database programs provide powerful tools for managing complex sets of data. However, many organizations use such programs to manage *all* data, structurally complex or not, with the result that getting a small program written to manage a simple data set is all but impossible. Information Systems departments are so backlogged with programming requests partly because they use complex tools to solve the simplest problems, thus rendering *all* problems complex.

The seventh Computer Myth, then, is: *get the most computer we can.*

Because it's so difficult to see evidence of overkill in computer systems, as explained earlier (Myth #1), it's unlikely to be corrected; where it exists, it persists. The key question then becomes: How does it get started in the first place? Why is inappropriate technology prevalent? The answers are overspecifying, overselling, overbuying, and overusing.

DEBUNKING MYTH #7

Overspecifying

Most companies designate certain employees as responsible for designing and purchasing computers. These people know that management will hold them accountable if the new system can't perform as required. They also know that if the new system *over*performs, probably no one will ever notice. (Similar political considerations influence vendor selection; remember the cliché "No one ever got fired for buying IBM.")

Even independent consultants, who should be free from both the biasing effects of sales commission structures and the political pressures of the corporate hierarchy, may be motivated to recommend more-advanced technology than is really needed. The consultant knows that equipment that is adequate today may be inadequate tomorrow because of changing business directions, at which time the client may want to know why the consultant recommended an "inappropriate" system.

Businesses can make provisions for growth without overkill when designing systems. It requires more thought and foresight, and the willingness to reject or moderate the sales representative's suggestions. It also can become politically dangerous if the system turns out to be *under*designed. And, finally, it's unlikely to be appreciated, because overkill usually goes unnoticed anyway;

why worry about a problem if it is unlikely to be detected? All things considered, it's easier to specify the more expensive technology and not worry about whether it represents the best way to spend the boss's (or client's) money.

Specifiers therefore represent overdesigned systems to management as "what we need" rather than "what we might need" or "possibly more than we need." Such distortion makes it more difficult for managers to make responsible decisions about allocating capital resources. Managers who've never educated themselves on high tech (see Myth #2) have little choice but to believe the gurus.

Overselling

Overselling occurs at two levels. Computer manufacturers keep building systems bigger than customers need because they have higher profit margins. Computer sales representatives keep selling systems bigger than customers need because they profit by doing so.

THE VENDORS

Many of the largest computer companies, which offer a complete range of products from desktop to mainframe, have been trying to convince customers for years to keep buying their older, more profitable, bigger systems. They have poured their development resources into improving those systems, convincing many customers to stay with those product lines even though they represented tremendous overkill in many cases.

Eventually, those computer companies have paid a painful price for this form of overselling. IBM lost its leadership in the computer industry largely due to its reluctance to move from its profitable mainframe product line. Fujitsu, another mainframe maker, practiced a similar form of denial and tried to keep its focus on mainframes, posting its first net loss ever in 1993 as a result. DEC ignored the PC revolution for years, tossing out half-baked PC designs such as the Rainbow and VAXMate while continuing to recommend its large VAX systems to customers that didn't always need it. Digital is now going through wave after wave of massive layoffs and wrenching reorganizations.

Had these companies devoted their resources much earlier to building the kinds of systems customers wanted and needed, they would not be in such trouble today, and thousands of customers would have systems better matched to their needs.

THE SALES REPS

Most computer systems and components are sold on commission, and the salesperson earns higher commissions on higher-performing and more expensive devices (although admirable exceptions to the rule may be found). The sales representative has a fundamental economic interest in overkill.

The computer business differs little from any other business in this respect. A few computer companies have tried to reduce the pressure to oversell by putting their salespeople totally on salary. However, even when salespeople feel no direct economic incentive to oversell, they feel a career incentive to do so. Their superiors evaluate them and nominate them for promotion primarily based on sales volume.

The most notorious oversellers are the salespeople who are least informed about the product. No salesperson wants the customer to return after the sale and complain that the product does not do what the salesperson said it would. If a customer returns a product, the salesperson loses a commission. If the product over-performs, the customer's far less likely to complain. (When was the last time you returned a product—any product—because it worked *better* than necessary?)

The well-informed salesperson can recommend a product to do the job without overkill and not fret about losing his commission or angering the customer; the underinformed salesperson feels less sure of the product's features and specifications and is more prone to suggest a bigger, faster, better model that he *knows* will do the job.

As systems have grown exponentially more complex, under-informed salespersons have become the rule rather than the exception. When I have acted as project manager on clients' automation projects, I've frequently been shocked at how little sales reps know about individual products. In fairness, their job has become nearly impossible as those products have become far more complex and far less expensive. At the same time, their employers encourage them to spend *less* time in training and more time selling.

A minicomputer salesman was asked to put together a quotation for a ten-person construction company wishing to automate bookkeeping. He came back with a recommendation calling for a high-speed mainframe with giant disk drives, sophisticated database software, and custom programming services, for a grand total of $1.2 million. The construction company president took one look at the handsomely bound quotation and politely told the salesman to leave and never come back. But if one out of ten customers takes the bait, that salesperson can afford braces for the kids that year.

Overbuying

COMPUTER ONE-UPMANSHIP

> *"Never buy what you do not want, because it is cheap; it will be dear to you."*
>
> —THOMAS JEFFERSON,
> "A DECALOGUE OF CANONS
> FOR OBSERVATION IN PRACTICAL
> LIFE" (1825)

Another cause of overkill is the desire to have the latest and greatest hardware and software, appropriate or not. The steep decline in price/performance has made it possible to fulfill this desire without straining IT capital budgets. Some managers feel a need to "keep up with the Joneses" and impress colleagues, customers, and competitors with the technological sophistication of the computer system. This can be an expensive need to satisfy, though, in the long run—especially considering that the fancy equipment may add little to productivity despite impressive specifications.

Specifications mean nothing out of context. The condo dweller who buys a four-hundred watt stereo amplifier, but who can never turn up the volume lest he disturb his neighbors, may take pride in the capabilities of his hardware, but he should actually feel somewhat silly pouring money into equipment whose capabilities he can't enjoy.

The desire to be up-to-date seems to be more prevalent in the microcomputer world, perhaps because desktop micros evolve more rapidly and have higher visibility than the monolithic, faceless cabinets hidden in the computer room. "Technolust" also targets hardware more often than software: The latest version of a computer's operating system software has far less sex appeal than a sleek new high-speed laser printer. The manager who orders superfast PCs as technological status symbols rather than as machines necessary to serve a demonstrable business need contributes to the distorted view computer makers often hold of business requirements.

It's easy to be impressed by powerful computer products. Computer magazines abound with statements extolling the virtues of the latest, greatest devices while disparaging last month's "obsolete technology." Computer companies pressure customers to buy new and improved equipment, and new technology can be intriguing and showy. But smart businesses resist new technology unless they see a need for it, except perhaps to experiment with it on a small scale. Buying today's hot systems is often more an expression of management's *desire* to progress than of a well-thought-out *plan* to progress. And it can backfire because of the "release zero" syndrome.

RELEASE ZERO

Software companies give numerical version numbers to their products. Sometimes they get carried away, using ridiculously confusing designations such as 2.01a or 1.5.5, but usually they use "*X*-point-zero" to indicate a major new upgrade as opposed to a minor maintenance release. MS-DOS 6.0, Windows 3.0, WordPerfect 6.0, all represented significant feature advances over previous versions. They were also all fairly dangerous, having more than their share of problems. (The products named above were quickly superseded by DOS 6.2, Windows 3.1, and WordPerfect 6.0a to fix the more egregious of those problems.)

Companies that have to have the latest and greatest software risk the "release zero" syndrome: *Any major new version of anything is likely to be buggy.* Increasingly, software firms are testing their products in the marketplace instead of in the lab. Getting the most possible power at any given time therefore also means putting up with excessive defects. Early software adopters pay for their head start advantage with greater troubleshooting and support expenses, as the "leading edge" becomes the "bleeding edge."

THE FATWARE PHENOMENON

Software overbuying has created "fatware," bloated programs with far more features than 99 percent of users need. Customers have (often unwisely) rejected "lite" versions of programs in favor of full-featured, industrial-strength versions, sending the software industry a powerful message that a long feature list matters more than speed or efficiency. Because software upgrades have grown to account for up to 50 percent of software supplier revenues these days, according to market researcher InfoCorp, new program versions are laden with new functions to attract corporate buyers and have more fat as a result. Swiss software pioneer Niklaus Wirth, inventor of the "Pascal" programming language, believes today's software has become "grossly oversized and inefficient." Examples:

- Lotus 1-2-3 for DOS grew 700 percent in size from 1983 to 1993.

- Microsoft's Word for Windows 2.0c, a word processing program, has 121 main menu commands and 476 separate on-line "help" topics. A newer version, 6.0, has an 829-page user manual.

- Corel Draw!, an illustration program, is now so huge that it ships on two CD/ROM disks—enough space for several *Encyclopedia Britannicas*.

- A 1994 PC needs *160 times* more memory than a 1983 PC to be able to run basic business applications. Does it do these things 16,000 percent better? In some ways, it does things *worse* from the productivity standpoint, because the slower performance of fat software reduces user productivity, as we'll see.

To some extent, fatware is the result of non-modular programs that can't use each other's features. (On my office PC, for example, there are four separate, and large, spelling dictionaries used by four different programs. When I tried to get rid of the spelling dictionary in my illustration software, it wouldn't run anymore!) It's also partly because of a variant of Parkinson's law: As memory and disk space become less expensive, software expands to fill the available space, because it's easier and cheaper to write fat software than lean software. But it's mostly the result of business customers who buy more than they need, and software companies that respond accordingly.

BUT MORE POWER REDUCES OBSOLESCENCE—DOESN'T IT?

Usually not! One problem with relying on excess power to prevent obsolescence is that the *kinds* of computer power are always changing on us:

- ❏ Yesterday, computer power to perform *text* processing may have been prodigious, but today's systems need power to perform *graphics* processing, too.

- ❏ Yesterday, extremely powerful but proprietary *central* systems may have been in tune with the times, but today's more *distributed* computing environments need open systems that can network easily with PCs.

- ❏ Yesterday, paying big bucks for expensive "leased lines" was the way to ensure reliable, high-speed communications across geographical regions, but today, high-speed error-correcting modems enable such links over ordinary lines.

Equipping a department or small business with a lot of the wrong kind of computer power does no good in reducing obsolescence. Ironically, it may do just the opposite and retard the organization from moving to new, more productive technologies by sinking capital into technology that organizations won't readily abandon.

Furthermore, companies may grow unpredictably, and it becomes difficult to allocate overcapacity to those parts of the computer system that will need it. Bigger minicomputers or wider networks? More notebooks or more desktops? Additional engineering workstations or more PCs in accounting? Predicting how a business will grow is risky; allocating overcapacity in advance can be wasteful.

PLANNING AROUND PURCHASING

A final cause of overbuying is antiquated purchasing policies more oriented to million-dollar machine tools than thousand-dollar computers. An aerospace executive told me recently that although he had the authority to authorize million-dollar purchases in most areas, to get a new personal computer required over twenty signatures and typically took several months. When department heads look at that kind of delay, they're naturally inclined to buy more than they need in the hope it will tide them over through the next authorization cycle.

Overusing

Finally, computer customers resist getting rid of old systems, using them long after their practical life is over and creating a large machine population without boosting productivity. We'll discuss organizational inertia in depth later in the book.

CONSEQUENCES OF MYTH #7

If one assumes for the moment that too much power is better than too little, why guard against overdesigned and overspecified computer systems? Two reasons: Overkill makes poor use of capital resources, and it pushes ongoing support costs through the roof.

Wasting Capital

Dollars spent today are worth more than dollars spent tomorrow; overcapacity costs today but doesn't benefit the company until tomorrow—if then.

Computer products depreciate rapidly; new technology is faster and cheaper than old technology. In such an environment, there's no benefit to buying capacity before it is needed, unless one expects the need to arise so rapidly that there won't be time to upgrade later. Extra power bought today will cost half as much next year, half as much as that year after next. Further, if a company replaces a system before putting its overcapacity to use, then the overcapacity was paid for and *never* used.

Skyrocketing Support

Remember the medallion that homebuilders used to display proudly during the fifties and sixties, proclaiming "All-Electric Home" as a badge of distinction? It took a decade or two for the public to realize that all-electric homes weren't as efficient as homes using gas heat. Electricity was certainly the most versatile and "powerful" fuel, but the cost of generating that high-quality fuel, transmitting it, and then using it for the mundane purpose of providing heat turned out to be enormously inefficient. It also proved very expensive in terms of operating costs. We can say the same for overly powerful computer systems.

❑ A simple database program request becomes a major effort because of the complex and powerful tool IS uses. The program may work fine eventually, but it will take too long and cost too much to create, and the cost of maintaining and modifying that program will increase.

❑ The more powerful and complex the software, the more confusing it is to users and the greater the expense of training them.

❑ The more powerful and complex the system, the more difficult it is to troubleshoot and the more time technical gurus will spend fixing problems. That time is not only expensive in dollars per hour, it has an opportunity cost as well in that the technicians can't be designing new systems if they're spending a lot of time fixing old ones.

THE PROBLEM

Riding lawn mowers aren't needed for small suburban lawns, and the latest and greatest computers aren't needed for many business applications. Overkill creates computer systems that cost too much for what they produce. Because so many systems and components are overspecified, oversold, and overbought, businesses pay for computer power they don't really need, lowering the performance/cost ratio and impairing the ability of computer systems to perform useful functions at a reasonable cost. The addiction to "more power" contributes greatly to the poor productivity record of business computers. It doesn't protect against obsolescence because systems usually become obsolete for reasons other than being underpowered.

ACTION PLAN

"Less is more."

—ROBERT BROWNING, ENGLISH
POET, *Andrea del Sarto* (1855)

Phil Croucher, a British computer consultant I know, holds executive briefings periodically for managers who want to automate their departments. The first question he asks is, "What kind and number of computers do you think you need in your business?" Typical responses are: "A network of fast PCs," "One on every desk," "A minicomputer," and so forth.

By the end of the two-day briefing, after the pros and cons of automation have been explored in some depth, my colleague asks the same question. The perceptions of need have typically become much more modest by that point. Sometimes, the managers decide they don't need computers at all—at least not right away. They rarely feel they need as much computer horsepower as they thought at first.

Processes First, Processors Later

Businesses should always look to *simplify processes before automating*. It's usually cheaper and often provides a greater performance boost than buying computers. A brief example:

❏ Workers at Northern Telecom were packing hardware into boxes, sealing them and sending them to shipping, where the boxes were unpacked for QC and repacked for shipping. The simplification step was to have the parts inspected by QC *before* they were originally boxed up. Automating the old process would not have brought the same productivity gains.

Michael Hammer and James Champy, in *Reengineering the Corporation*, identify several common themes in process reengineering: combine several jobs into one, let workers make more decisions, perform work where it makes the most sense (the Northern Telecom example), minimize reconciliation chores, etc. While IT can be an enabler of such process change, it's not always needed to effect it. Sometimes, *existing* information systems can be redeployed to facilitate process change without requiring new investment.

Pay for Performance

The only way, ultimately, to restrain vendors from overselling their products is to rethink how computer customers pay for technology. The typical project contract results in a completion of payments before the system is even put into use. Organizations that tie a significant bonus payment to the system's cost/benefit ratio after a period of time will give vendors an incentive to specify more appropriate technology. Customers and vendors agree on performance and cost measurement criteria during contract negotiation. This approach gives vendors a stake in controlling system costs, both up front and ongoing.

Appropriate Automation

Technology is appropriate for a particular job if it is adequate to do the job as well as necessary, but no better than necessary. This doesn't imply a cavalier disdain for quality; in many cases, "good enough" may be very good indeed. The point is to use resources wisely and minimize waste.

A business that's gone through the exercise of planning its computer system knows what's expected of each component of the system, and can buy hardware and software that will perform up to expectations without paying for unneeded power. A good design team can save a company thousands or millions of dollars if dedicated to the principle of appropriateness.

The designers must have a clear overall picture of the components of the system, as well as of company business goals, to know what's appropriate.

Appropriateness does *not* mean that one specifies products that will meet present needs without regard to future expansion requirements. What's appropriate today must be readily expandable so it can be made appropriate for tomorrow. Unfortunately, the computer industry doesn't always provide for such modular growth; it is, in fact, the exception rather than the rule; and so one weighs the cost of buying overcapacity now against the cost of having to replace components outright tomorrow when they no longer meet the organization's needs. System designers therefore need to understand something of the organization's growth projections—yet another argument for management involvement in technology projects.

TARGETED AUTOMATION

To minimize computer one-upmanship and "technolust," organizations may implement policies requiring linkage between technology investments and strategic goals. We discussed in the previous chapter the fact that computers should target articulated business goals, that they are means rather than ends.

The risk here is that organizations might not know *how* to apply new and powerful technology if it doesn't bring it in-house first. One can't prove a new product will target a specific business goal if one doesn't really know what the new product can do! So companies might consider a "technology lab," where they can try new products on a small scale in an experimental environment. And we refine a suggestion from the previous chapter: Companies should associate *large-scale* automation with defined business goals while allowing small-scale experimentation with promising new technology to proceed without such prior justification.

RELEASE POINT-ONE

Industry-aware computer customers know that they *don't* want to be first on the block with the latest software. Rather than get version 4.0 of a new product, they wait until version 4.1 (or 4.01, or 4.0a) is out; it might actually work the way it's supposed to. I call this the "Release Point-One" approach, and it pays off.

More and more, the world is the laboratory for software vendors. They're under such time and price pressure these days that they don't do the kind of expensive, rigorous testing that used to be expected. Their attitude is, get it out into the marketplace; if there are problems, the customers will let us know, and we'll fix them with a (fairly) prompt "maintenance release" (also called an "in-line" release). Meanwhile, the early adopters pay in long hours of troubleshooting and debugging.

Here's an incidental tip for technology implementers: most

software companies don't tell you when they issue maintenance releases. Frankly, they're a little embarrassed. You'll never get a postcard saying, "We fixed the worst bugs in version 4.0 and the new version is 4.01, which is free if you ask for it." Savvy customers make a regular practice (for example, once a quarter) of calling all their software vendors to ask about maintenance releases and bug fixes. The cost is usually nominal (most vendors feel badly charging customers a lot for fixing defects) and the benefit in more reliable, and sometimes faster, program operation is worthwhile.

SPEED WHERE IT COUNTS

Contrary to conventional wisdom, *speed doesn't always matter.*

Businesses often work on a nine-to-five schedule. Things that computers can do after hours don't have to be done quickly, they just have to be done in time for the next day:

- Optimizing computer disks is a process that rearranges files so that the computer can retrieve them faster. It can be done at night, and it doesn't have to be done quickly.

- "Backing up" computer files from hard drives to tape is an essential protection against hard drive failure, but it usually doesn't have to be done quickly, either. When buying a tape drive for a PC, for example, one can spend $200 on a slow device or $2,000 on a fast one. If backups are performed at night, the $200 device might be just fine. Similarly, network servers that call each other up at night to back up their files to each other don't necessarily need the very fastest modem or satellite links; they just need to get everything done in one evening or weekend.

- Many small businesses use computers to print checks. This, too, can be done at night, allowing the business to use inexpensive, slow printers that are just fast enough to get the job done by morning.

Speed doesn't matter where it doesn't help overall performance, either:

❑ Workstations for employees doing word processing and e-mail don't need superfast network connections; the employees won't notice any difference.

❑ Computers that act as "print servers" that funnel print jobs to attached printers don't have to be fast because they're limited by the much slower speed of the printer they're attached to. This is an excellent application, therefore, for some of those old, slow boxes that can't handle today's more demanding user software.

❑ Clerks doing data entry don't need the fastest PCs or terminals. They can't keyboard the data fast enough to keep the system busy.

❑ Employees doing on-line research don't need the fastest PCs or terminals. The speed of telecommunication links to electronic information services is a bottleneck for even the slowest machines.

Speed *does* count, and in a big way, when human beings have to interact in real time with computer programs that aren't limited by slow communication links. Here, appropriate technology means spending money to improve system response in such user applications.

Faster system response can mean *much* more productive users. A study by IBM researcher Arvind Thadhani found that human productivity increases significantly when computer response time is shortened, even as little as from one second to half a second. The reason is that veteran computer users don't think in terms of doing one thing at a time. They have several steps in mind to start with, and delays of even fractions of a second can disrupt that flow—causing frustration, distraction, and errors.

The issue of system response becomes more important as computers move from being text-based to being graphics-based. Old text-mode applications responded almost instantaneously because the computer didn't have to worry about displaying different type styles or sizes. Characters were stored in a chip on the computer's main circuit board, and they always looked the same on screen. The computer had to keep track of eighty columns and twenty-five lines, or two thousand discrete items, at a time. There was only two colors to worry about, too: white or black (though "white" often meant green or amber on the display).

Today's graphics programs treat every tiny dot, or pixel, as a discrete element. On a typical 800-by-600 display, that's 480,000 things to keep track of—meaning 240 times more work for the computer, and much slower response times. When you consider that modern computers also have to keep track of hundreds or even millions of possible colors for each dot, the "overhead" of graphical computing becomes staggering, and the need for faster systems grows accordingly to maintain productive response times.

Features When They Matter

Full-strength, feature-laden programs carry hidden costs. They almost never run at an acceptable speed when installed according to vendors' "minimum hardware requirements." So customers wind up buying more memory, faster disks, and faster processors than they'd counted on to run their fatware. The other hidden cost, as discussed above, is productivity loss due to slower performance. Smaller programs often run faster than programs with hundreds of features no one uses. These smaller-scale programs, therefore, could improve productivity at the point of end use much more than their fatter counterparts.

So what can the customer do?

❑ First, look for commercial software that does what users need, and little more. (Take the time to survey users, and they'll tell you what they need.) Don't be totally swayed by the popularity of fatware programs, or the fact that they may not cost much more in up-front dollars. Compare speed in real-world tests, remembering that fast response could be worth fifty "bells and whistles."

❑ Second, when using fatware, if the program provides an option for a "custom" installation, use it. That way, the installer can select only those modules that are appropriate and necessary. Some vendors provide for a "minimal" installation that just provides core functionality; try it and see if it's able to do what you need to do. (You can always come back later and add a module or a feature if it turns out you need it more than you thought at first.)

❑ Third, locate fatware on network servers where users can share it. Thirty megabytes of storage on one server is better than thirty megabytes on each of a hundred PCs.

NONTRADITIONAL MACHINES

Sometimes, appropriate technology means breaking from tradition when it comes to office systems and computers. Nontraditional systems carry risks, as we'll see in our discussion of standardization, but sometimes the quantum leap in appropriateness they offer can justify the risks.

❑ An office I recently visited had a laser printer, a small photo-copier, a flatbed document scanner, and a fax machine. All four devices share much of the same technology "under the hood." Wouldn't it be cheaper to have one device that does all those functions? Of course it would, and companies such as Digital Design Inc., Okidata, and Canon USA, Inc., are starting to build them. The Canon GP55 copier, for example, introduced in 1994, can also function as a network printer, fax machine, and digital scanner—and it's not limited to doing just one job at a time.

❑ More radical still are nontraditional machines based on neu-ral networks of parallel processors running "fuzzy logic" soft-ware. These systems excel at tasks ordinary computers aren't good at, such as providing quick-and-dirty answers where three decimal places aren't needed. See the following "Trendwatch" section for more on this promising field.

TRENDWATCH *Neurocomputing.* Computer customers should urge the industry to develop devices, systems, and programs that are appropriate for business needs. One par-ticularly promising example is the *neural-network* computer, or *neurocomputer.*

Many business situations require that an approximate answer to a question be generated quickly; speed is more important than accuracy to the *n*th decimal place. For example:

❑ A credit manager doesn't need to know *exactly* how much credit a customer has, just whether that credit is adequate to cover the current order the customer's trying to place.

❑ Defining the absolute best route for a truck with stops in several cities can take a conventional computer hours (depend-ing on the number of cities), but a neurocomputer can provide a good answer—say, in the top 1 percent of all answers—in a few seconds.

Traditional computers are designed to follow a well-defined and deterministic series of steps that lead to completely accurate answers. Such "von Neumann" computers (named after mathematician John von Neumann in the forties) have a single central processor and a physically separate memory area. It's generally impossible to instruct a conventional von Neumann computer to "hurry up and give me a ballpark figure."

The neurocomputer, modeled loosely on the neural structure of the human brain, excels at giving fast and nearly right answers. It uses dozens, thousands, or even millions of small processors linked together in a complex lattice of interconnections. This is much more like the way the human brain works, getting thousands of neurons or nerve cells working at once on a given problem.

Neurocomputers seem also to be better at pattern-matching chores, such as identifying human faces or reading blurry characters off a faxed page using Optical Character Recognition (OCR). This is big news for companies moving to document imaging technology. Nestor, an OCR developer, claims Intel's neural-network chip, which has 1,024 "neurons," can recognize forty thousand characters per second as opposed to about one hundred characters per second using traditional technology. It's also potentially important for handwriting recognition, long a limitation of conventional computers (fatally so for Apple's Newton).

Neural networks are also finding applications in stock performance prediction (Fidelity Disciplined Equity Fund in Boston), more accurate credit-card fraud detection (Mellon Bank's Visa and Mastercard operations in Delaware), and power-plant operation (Ontario Hydro in Canada).

Not only can neurocomputers outrace von Neumann computers in quick-and-dirty answers, they're less vulnerable to failure, too. Neurocomputers can keep working even if 5 percent or even 10 percent of their processors fail. They have demonstrated an ability to "learn" on their own through a series of trial-and-error sequences. OCR neurocomputers, for example, can learn a new typeface by scanning pages that use it and then comparing their guesses against the actual text.

Machines of the future may have dual architectures: a neural-net processor array for quick-and-rough approximations, and a traditional von Neumann CPU for precise answers. Certainly, neurocomputing has great promise as a new and newly appropriate business technology—not because it mimics how the human brain works, but because it meets a new range of business needs that emphasizes "pretty good and fast" over "exact and slow."

FAST-TRACK AUTHORIZATION

Getting approval for new PCs, software, or even networks shouldn't take six months. The next chapter reinforces the need for new systems to conform to industry and corporate standards, but planning committee approval needn't take more than a week or two. Glacial purchasing procedures were designed to protect the organization from massive mistakes when buying big-ticket items. A fast-track authorization scheme for IT purchases will take some pressure off managers to buy overpowered products, and let them choose systems more appropriate for their present needs. This way, managers will have confidence that if they need to expand in a few weeks or months, they'll be able do so without having to wait for twenty signatures. Making automators go through the same procedures for a $10,000 network server as for a $250,000 sheet metal press makes no sense and encourages computer overspecification.

Trimming the Computer Payroll

Organizations finding themselves overstaffed often lay off personnel who don't add value in proportion to their cost. Organizations might be better off first directing their attention to "legacy" information systems that meet that same criterion.

Getting rid of old, unproductive, and incompatible systems

(such as the one discussed at the beginning of this chapter) reduces the cost of maintaining, supporting, networking, programming, documenting, and insuring a company's computer resource. The short-term write-off can have quick results in lower operating costs. Sometimes, it's better to have those systems carted off to the junkyard rather than keep them on the "computer payroll."

THE REALITY

Companies that focus first on streamlining processes and second on automation stand to reap greater productivity rewards sooner. When companies do automate, project contracts that pay bonuses based on performance and cost targets can help reduce overselling. Appropriate automation means investing technology dollars where they'll pay off: in systems that meet business goals, that work reliably and aren't on the "bleeding edge," that respond quickly to users, and that offer only the features those users need. It also means considering nontraditional systems that make sense. Quick purchasing procedures can reduce the motivation for overbuying. Finally, getting rid of obsolete machines helps reduce computer populations and their associated costs. More computers aren't necessarily a guarantee of efficiency any more than larger staffs are.

English economist E. F. Schumacher (1911-1977) wrote that "small is beautiful." Contrary to conventional wisdom, with information systems more power isn't always more powerful; it's often just more expensive.

Appropriateness, important though it is, is only one concern when laying out a plan for implementing IT. Organizations also have to think about standardization and compatibility—the subject of the next chapter.

MYTH 8

Computers Are Becoming Standardized

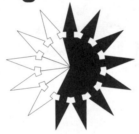

"Computer Integrated Manufacturing (CIM) has traditionally meant equipment from different vendors residing in isolated 'islands of automation' because the proprietary components used by the various vendors could not communicate with each other. In many cases, they could not even share the same cable. . . . Training for these different networks was difficult to provide . . . and the cost of the various kinds of test equipment to keep it all running was also high . . . centralized management and control of the network became virtually impossible."

—COLLIN PARK AND BRUCE TALLEY, "HP MANUFACTURING AUTOMATION PROTOCOL 3.0," *Hewlett-Packard Journal* (August 1990)

THE MYTH

The IBM PC is hailed as a "standard" microcomputer platform in countless books and magazine articles because programs that run on one IBM-compatible PC usually also run on other IBM-compatibles. While that feature has been a big part of the PC's success, the PC-compatible market is hardly standardized. For example, a technician installing Microsoft's Windows-for-Workgroups software on a networked IBM-compatible PC with multimedia hardware must choose from among the following variations:

❏ Sixteen machine types;

❏ Nineteen basic video types;

❏ Eleven keyboard types;

❏ Seven types of pointing device;

❏ Eleven types of sound/multimedia device;

❏ One hundred fifty-eight different network adapters;

❏ Ten different network schemes.

Each of these choices is independent from the others, so according to my college statistics textbook, there are over *400 million* different ways to install Windows-for-Workgroups on an "IBM-compatible" networked PC—and each of those configurations may exhibit its own unique limitations, incompatibilities, and quirks. I wonder why computer support technicians are overworked?

Computer standardization turns out to be one of the field's biggest myths. The industry has done a shockingly poor job developing and adhering to consistent standards that allow computers to work together easily and expand inexpensively. This holds true for office automation as well as manufacturing automation. Business customers, for their part, have been slow to create and implement their own in-house standards for automation. This lack of industry and corporate standards for information systems costs countless millions of dollars every year, driving a massive wedge between computers and their productive use.

In the previous chapter, we illustrated the importance of choosing appropriate technology when automating the workplace. Once system implementers determine the appropriate power system for the job at hand, the next big concern is resistance to obsolescence. An appropriate system won't be much good if it's obsolete in a year. Can adherence to accepted standards help stave off obsolescence and reduce operating costs? Possibly, but not if organizations continue to believe our next myth: *computers are becoming standardized.*

It's just not happening, folks.

Incompatible, nonstandard systems aren't always undesirable. Companies, divisions, departments, and individuals have varying computing needs. Abandoning adherence to industry and/or company standards allows one the freedom to select faster or more functional products from a broader pool. Specialized computers and programs may fill business needs no "standard" products fill.

However, businesses spend large sums buying products and paying staff to overcome the incompatibilities nonstandard systems create. A lack of standardization raises hardware and software upgrade costs; raises training costs by lengthening the learning curve; reduces the flexibility of the computing resource; and either prevents computer-to-computer communications altogether, or renders it vastly more expensive. The decision becomes whether incompatible products can benefit one's company more than they harm it, or whether they're likely to prove needless and expensive hindrances. Managers alert to the many ways in which incompatibilities can create performance and cost problems will make this decision more confidently.

Double Standards

Industry standards are specifications for hardware and software products that different vendors adopt in common. Organizations such as the Institute of Electrical and Electronic Engineers (IEEE) sponsor formal, published standards, and de facto standards result from a consensus of industry leaders, or, in the case of IBM or Microsoft, a consensus of *one* industry leader! The industry has defined a few standards completely and precisely, but most remain incomplete and subject to varying interpretation.

Corporate standards govern or guide the individual business's purchasing decisions. A customer may standardize on particular products, such as IBM AS/400 minicomputers, for example, or Novell NetWare, as the software to run PC networks. Customers may also adopt multivendor standards that span many products: Structured Query Language (SQL) for accessing databases, TCP/IP for networking UNIX machines, and so on.

To thoroughly destroy Myth #8, it's necessary to examine both of the above areas.

DEBUNKING MYTH #8: INDUSTRY INCOMPATIBILITY

> " 'Standards' and 'open systems' have become perhaps the most overworked and meaningless words in the computer industry."
>
> —BARBARA BUELL AND DEIDRE DEPKE, "COMPUTER CONFUSION," *Business Week* (June 10, 1991)

Why has the computer industry done such a dismal job of writing and agreeing on standards for its products? Most other industries would never dream of operating in such a chaotic environment. In fact, most could not. The fast pace of change in the computer industry, the historical diversity of computer products, and vendor marketing strategies all mitigate against the enactment of industry standards. These forces will not change rapidly or soon: they're facts of life to which the business customer tries to adapt.

A Fast-Lane Pothole

> *"The technical work . . . is often difficult. Reaching a consensus can also be time-consuming . . . standards work is frequently a lengthy process."*
>
> —MARY LYNNE NIELSEN, SENIOR
> PROJECT EDITOR AT THE IEEE,
> QUOTED IN *Software Magazine*
> (March 1994)

Probably no industry in the world changes as much and as fast from year to year as the computer industry. Rapid advances in micro-manufacturing and electronics design have created an industry in which ten thousand new products appear each year (that's almost thirty new products a day!). This incredible pace has frustrated industry attempts at standardization.

Hardware advances occur so quickly that slow-moving, bureaucratic industry consortiums and international standards committees don't have a prayer of keeping up, try though they might. Even powerful vendors, who can set de facto standards without the blessing of industry committees, abandon those standards when new technology offers the prospect of better performance. Further, new uses for existing technology often render standards obsolete within months of their adoption. Examples:

   ❑ In telecommunications technology, modem speeds have increased 4,800 percent over the past few years, and modem makers have now begun integrating fax technology with their products. The standards organizations have always lagged well behind the modem manufacturers so that customers wanting the fastest speeds have consistently had to buy products before standards even existed for them, putting themselves at risk of future incompatibility. Even today, there's no one accepted standard for how software should communicate with a fax modem.

❑ The world of optical disk storage shows how new uses can quickly make existing standards obsolete. During its painful evolution from a very nonstandard device in the early eighties, the CD/ROM (Compact Disk Read-Only Memory) had finally become a near-standard: Most CD/ROM drives could read most CD/ROM disks. Then came Kodak, which decided to adapt the technology for storing consumer photographs ("Photo-CD"). Suddenly, thousands of CD/ROM drives became nonstandard in that they couldn't read Photo-CD disks, and drive vendors scurried to bring their new models into compliance with this new, unforeseen use.

Kodak could have made Photo-CD compatible with existing standards, but that would have added months to development time and Kodak is big enough to set their own standard. The recent advent of "multimedia" products that interleave audio and digital video with CD/ROM data has added to the problem: Drives that can read older, data-only CD/ROM disks, and even Photo-CD disks, may not be compatible with multimedia disks.

A Forty-five-Year Patchwork Quilt

Today's computer marketplace, the result of decades of product and company evolution, exhibits extraordinary diversity— as you might expect from an industry consisting of fifty thousand companies in 1993. That diversity is good for customers who want a breadth of products to choose from, but not so good for customers who must make them *work!* Incompatible operating systems, burdensome requirements for connecting new devices, inconsistent user interfaces, differing "macro languages," and incompatible networks all contribute to industry nonstandardization.

OPERATING SYSTEMS

The operating system is the fundamental software that enables a computer to perform any useful task, such as creating a disk file, sending a message to a terminal, or deleting old data. It translates user program commands into language the underlying hardware can understand. Although users may never "see" the operating system, it's always there, managing disks, displays, and printers.

Because this software interacts very closely with computer hardware, one finds very different operating systems on different hardware platforms: VMS on minicomputers, UNIX on engineering workstations, MS-DOS on PCs, Apple OS on Macintoshes. The variety of operating systems in the marketplace has created a serious nonstandard, for an applications program written for one operating system will usually not run on a different operating system. Attempts to bridge this gap with "operating system emulators" rarely succeed; these programs run slowly and often impose unacceptable constraints.

(Example: Apple's high-end 1994 Macintosh systems advertise the ability to run DOS and Windows software with an "operating system emulator," but it can only emulate a PC design [the 286] that's *ten years old*. Why did Apple bother? Perhaps so the ad people could say, "It runs Windows"?)

Even among computers of the same size and type, different operating systems exist. In the microcomputer world, the preponderant operating system is Microsoft's MS-DOS, with 89 percent of the PC market, but several more-or-less compatible versions of this operating system drive the army of compatible machines called "clones." MS-DOS itself exists in several different versions (3.3, 4.0, 5.0, 6.0, 6.2, 6.22) and IBM has its own versions (6.1, 6.3), all of which create a number of both minor and major incompatibility problems. Other operating systems, such as XENIX, OS/2, and Windows, also run on PCs. Apple's Macintosh uses a highly proprietary operating system used by no other computer.

In the multiuser minicomputer and mainframe world, the variety of operating systems is overwhelming. Even one manufacturer's minicomputers do not necessarily run the same operating system. The differences between minicomputer and microcomputer operating systems are even more pronounced. Finally, in the esoteric world of supercomputers, Russell Mitchell in *Business Week* finds "a profusion of alternatives, each with a unique design."

Some variety in operating system software is desirable; an operating system written for a stand-alone personal computer need not concern itself with balancing the activities of multiple users, for example. Nevertheless, the existence and persistence of incompatible operating systems restrict software portability, inhibit companies considering upgrades, raise networking costs, and raise user software costs by forcing programmers to essentially rewrite programs for different operating systems.

DEVICE DRIVERS

The number and variety of computer devices—printers, terminals, modems, disks, tape drives, and so on—have reached staggering proportions. The number of different printers alone is in the thousands. The lack of standards for computer-to-device communication means that special software and hardware may be necessary whenever one connects a different device to a computer. As a result, data processing staff and computer consultants spend a great deal of time and customer money merely connecting devices to computers and making sure that existing software can use the new devices.

Operating systems and user programs communicate with

devices through highly specialized programs called *device drivers*. These programs are a terrific boon in that they help fight obsolescence; but they may not work properly with devices newer than they are, in which case technicians must install new or modified drivers, if they exist. User programs must have their own set of device drivers to take advantage of specific device capabilities. For example, a word processing program must "know" the command that makes a specific printer underline text, for the commands vary from printer to printer. Some programs ship with drivers for over two hundred printers!

Obviously, this raises the price of software and diverts programmers' attention from design and performance issues. Products such as Microsoft Windows attempt to remedy this situation by allowing all programs to use the same drivers, but the problem persists on many computer platforms.

USER INTERFACES

The user interface is how a program *appears* to the user. It encompasses screen design, keyboard layout, commands, menus, help facilities, and error messages. Every interactive business program has a user interface, and many are radically different.

Every software company has its own ideas about how a program should look to the user, and, once again, even products from the same company may not demonstrate consistent interfaces. Because so many programs exhibit such design differences, users undergo far more training to learn new programs, and operate less efficiently when switching between programs.

MACRO LANGUAGES

Many application programs have built-in, miniature programming languages called *macro languages* that customers may use to automate repetitive actions. Macros can record and play back a series of keystrokes or mouse movements in the same way that a player piano can play back a song coded onto a paper roll. They allow users to record a sequence of actions within a running program, save the sequence under a single name, and replay the sequence using that name alone. A typical macro within a word processing program might reset margins for envelope addressing, print an envelope, and then restore the margin settings for letter writing. Macros can save time for users who perform the same activities at the keyboard fairly often.

The problem is that different user programs have different macro languages. Learning one macro language may be fine for improving productivity with that specific program; it won't help much, if at all, with other programs. Even different versions of the same program may present significant differences in macro languages. A macro written in one program will not work in a different program. As Bill Gates, CEO of Microsoft, admits in *Byte* magazine, "When you can run several programs simultaneously, you'll have a difficult time remembering the unique macro language for every application."

NETWORKS

Consider a hypothetical orbiting space station, funded jointly by the United States, Russia, and China to learn about zero-gravity manufacturing techniques. Ten top engineers from each country occupy the station, but none are fluently bilingual. Two interpreters complete the crew, but neither speaks all three languages; one knows English and Russian, the other English and Chinese. If a Russian engineer wants to speak with a Chinese engineer, one interpreter must translate from Russian to English and the other from English to Chinese.

The space station has an expensive computerized language translator, but it only works about half the time and the crew members soon grow frustrated with it. The Americans try to persuade everyone to speak only in English, without success. The engineers try to communicate using basic sign language, which they all understand but which can't convey their complex thoughts and ideas. The engineers are completing few experiments, morale is low, confusion high, and the sponsoring governments grow highly dissatisfied, as they have spent huge sums with little result.

You now have an accurate impression of the state of computer networking in business today. Many different network "languages" exist. Some specialized products can translate between one language and another, but not between all of them, and these translation products often slow down the network. Many vendors have tried to get companies to adopt their network language as the standard language, but so far without success. While users can normally shuttle data across a network from point A to point B, it's often impossible to move whole programs across networks to different systems.

A 1993 Denver TV ad for a regional communications firm shows serious-faced executives mulling over their company's problems and concluding, in profound tones, that "What we need is a network." If it were only that simple. While network vendors extol their products' ability to link different computers into a harmonious system, reality is something else again. Many different and incompatible network standards exist; most multi-vendor networks require great effort to install and manage, and even then don't usually work very well; and coercing different computers into exchanging data at even a basic level can prove a Herculean task. Networking computers costs a lot of money and may provide a small or even negative productivity gain over the system's life. Why?

- Many vendors never *designed* their computer systems (or the programs they run) to communicate in mixed-vendor environments. It can be expensive to retrofit networking capability onto these machines.

❏ Different network designs work better with different hardware platforms. Over time, individual hardware vendors developed their own ideas of what a network should be, creating different *traditions*.

❏ Networks must work with existing operating systems and user programs, but no network can work with *all* software, so designers choose software environments with which their products can coexist and ignore others.

❏ Network *standards*, such as the Open Systems Interconnect model put forth by the International Standards Organization, have been slow in coming and allow a fair amount of latitude in interpretation.

❏ Because networks are *combination* products involving both hardware and software, the rampant nonstandardization in those areas makes the network's job difficult if not impossible.

❏ Few companies offer *one-stop shopping* for networks. Customers typically buy software and hardware products from several vendors, making project planning, implementation, and testing very time consuming and expensive.

❏ Network vendors have not concentrated on *ease-of-use* until very recently. Installers and administrators therefore spend inordinate amounts of time reading manuals and memorizing commands. It's common for network manuals to fill an entire row of a bookshelf.

❏ *Troubleshooting* networks is more difficult than troubleshooting stand-alone computers because they're much more complex and can fail in many more ways.

If networks act as the glue that connects computers, take a look during your next visit to the hardware store at just how many different kinds of glue there are. Then consider that even with all those specialized kinds, half the time the glue doesn't really work.

REASONS FOR DIVERSITY

One reason such diversity exists in today's computer marketplace is the many different applications for which designers have created products. A good example is office networks versus factory networks.

Office networks link computers running accounting, word processing, and electronic mail programs. These aren't time-critical tasks; it doesn't matter whether an electronic mail user sends a message in one second or two. *Ethernet* technology, which allows any computer to access the network at any time, varies in speed depending on network traffic but does well in office networks. Factory networks which link robots, conveyors, and other computer-controlled machinery must respond with predictable speed. *Token-ring* technology, in which computers access the network one at a time in round-robin fashion, has a very predictable maximum response time and is therefore better suited for time-critical applications than Ethernet.

Another reason for computer diversity is computer companies' need to protect the trade secrets and innovations they work hard to create. If Manufacturer A publishes the full specifications of its machine so that Manufacturer B can communicate effectively with it, and so Manufacturer C can build printers and networks that connect to it, Manufacturer A might reveal a great deal of intellectual property and open itself to copycat competition. Company A cannot rely wholly on legal protection (though some try) because computer copyright and trade secret law is poorly developed and inconsistent.

Historically, manufacturer arrogance has played a certain role in creating nonstandard products. Many computer firms refused for a long time to admit that a customer would ever need or want to purchase products from another firm. As a result, they don't design their products with connectivity to other vendors' equipment in mind. In the manual for Apple's original LaserWriter printer, only three short pages discuss connecting it to a non-Apple computer!

Manufacturer myopia is another factor. Some large computer makers still surround themselves with only their own products in manufacturing plants, distribution centers, and sales offices, partly because it's cheaper, partly because these facilities showcase the products to visiting customers and demonstrate the manufacturer's faith in its computers. Unfortunately, customers rarely have such single-vendor shops. The manufacturer doesn't experience firsthand the problems of connecting different brands of computer systems. If the IBMs and DECs of the computer industry used each other's equipment more often, they would concern themselves more with the standardization issue. This practice is starting to change, but it's contributed to the way the industry is today.

The practice of internal competition within major computer companies also helps explain diversity. IBM (*especially* IBM), DEC, and other large computer firms have encouraged competition between design teams within their organizations. These groups design radically different systems independently of each other and compete for top management's approval. The theory is that the cream will rise to the top. The crippling side effect: incompatibilities between products from different design teams.

Computer firm mergers create incompatibilities. When computer companies merge, their product lines may not. Unisys resulted from the merger of Burroughs and Sperry. In the words of a *Mini-Micro Systems* writer, "The mishmash of preponderantly incompatible microcomputers, minicomputers, mainframes and other related processors that Unisys offers is confusing to say the least."

Finally, computer companies, like human societies, develop their own particular customs and traditions. These traditions may include how the machines represent data elements, such as the letter *A*, internally; how they organize information on the disk; and how they communicate with the outside world. Larger IBM systems use one code for representing letters and numbers as sequences of ones and zeros, while most other manufacturers use a different code. IBM's code uses eight digits (*A* is 11000001), the other code only seven (*A* is 1000001). Is one better than the other? It's a moot point as both are popular; the problem is that computers using the two codes can't understand each other without a special translator.

Selling Silicon: Vendor Marketing Strategies

THE DRIVE TO DIFFERENTIATE

All companies try to prove their products superior to the competition. In a market overcrowded with products, manufacturers inevitably introduce nonstandard features and advertise them heavily in an attempt to attract customer attention. It's also easier to claim that your products are better if they're nonstandard enough to make fair comparisons difficult!

The computer company built on products with proprietary features, such as operating systems, microprocessors, and networks, may enjoy a short-term advantage over the firm making more standard products. If a customer wants a VAX computer, he must buy it from Digital Equipment Corporation; if he wants a Macintosh, he must go to Apple. Companies with a monopoly on desirable products can charge high prices and make high profits as long as no one else offers products with similar benefits *and* adherence to industry standards.

Computer makers often use noninterchangeable designs because deviating from the standard can increase a device's performance. For example, a system's back panel may have a series of plugs for connecting terminals. A formal standard calls for twenty-five-pin plugs, but the terminals only use three of those twenty-five wires. The computer maker might use smaller nine-pin plugs to fit more plugs on the back of the computer. The cable manufacturer might offer cables having nine-pin connectors but only the three required wires, to reduce weight and cost. These improvements depart from the published standard but seem to add value for the customer.

Designers often improve on standards in ways that render their products difficult to connect with other products not similarly "improved." A good example is the UNIX operating system program developed originally by AT&T in the early 1970s. UNIX became popular; many computer firms adopted and modified it. By the mid-1980s, there were three major variants, or dialects. By the early 1990s, there were about two dozen UNIX "flavors": XENIX, AIX, DYNIX, A/UX, MACH, SunOS, ULTRIX, OSx, OSF/1, DG/UX, HP/UX, and so on. These variants differ enough to limit the portability of software between UNIX environments.

LOCKING IN THE CUSTOMER, I: RELATED EQUIPMENT

Proprietary designs might deviate from standards, not necessarily in order to improve performance but to capture a larger share of a particular market and maintain higher profit margins.

❑ *Business Week* states, "Standards threaten to eliminate the advantages that proprietary systems have given market leaders such as IBM and DEC. Their designs have delivered healthy profits largely because they've made switching from one proprietary brand to another prohibitively costly."

❑ *Fortune* reports that "as one [Hewlett-Packard] senior manager says, 'Open systems don't necessarily make much business sense because they ultimately drive down prices and margins even faster.' "

Sometimes, manufacturers build closed designs to increase future sales of related products, though they may thinly disguise their strategy as technical advancement.

❑ Example: Digital Equipment Corporation developed a proprietary bus—the internal communications channel—for many of its VAX 8000 series computers. The "BI" bus was not exceptionally better than other industry standard buses, but it did help DEC sell a large number of its own plug-in expansion boards. Customers had no alternative because industry-standard boards would not plug into DEC's bus.

LOCKING IN THE CUSTOMER, II: UPGRADES

Many computer systems provide no convenient upgrade path. Sometimes, vendors that *do* offer expansion capability do it in a nonstandard way, restricting the customer to one vendor and driving up the cost.

Adding memory to a PC might, for no good technical reason, require a unique component only sold by that PC's manufacturer. Naturally, the unique part costs four times as much as the standard part. Until recently, customers wishing to upgrade a laptop computer by adding a modem or network card often faced the same situation. One can hear the marketing executives in product planning meetings saying, "Let's make the base unit price-competitive but build in a few hidden incompatibilities so we can make big profits later with overpriced upgrades to both hardware and software." This is a polite book, so we won't mention any names, such as Toshiba or NEC.

It's the car business all over again; the parts department always provides the biggest profit margin.

The industry is awash with systems that can't accept standard components because of a single cable, bracket, or connector designed expressly to force the customer into paying too much for a part only one company makes. This technique is prevalent in the software marketplace, too. Many commercial software firms sell reasonably priced programs, only to charge exorbitant fees later for upgrades to new versions. If these programs use unique and nonstandard data formats, it becomes very difficult for customers to switch programs instead of paying the upgrade fees. (Of course, customers don't *have* to upgrade; but if they don't, they usually sacrifice access to technical support.)

The effectiveness of this marketing approach derives from the fact that the customer only learns of the pitfalls after using the system long enough to need to upgrade it. The trade journals are remiss in that they rarely consider upgrade costs when reviewing systems. Over the long term, of course, manufacturers whose marketing tactics lock customers into overpriced upgrades will alienate buyers and lose repeat business. Meanwhile, the drive to maximize profits remains a primary reason computer companies don't embrace industry standards when they could certainly do so.

DEBUNKING MYTH #8: CORPORATE INCOMPATIBILITY

The computer industry has failed miserably to solve the compatibility problem and is likely to continue failing to do so. Why don't businesses make up for it by creating and adhering to internal standards of their own design?

As discussed in the chapter on Myth #6, some of the reasons include decentralized purchasing, crisis spending, an orientation to the quick fix, and not following through on existing project plans without radically modifying them. Three other reasons help explain the situation: frequent changes in management and organizational structure; widespread use of custom software; and organizational reluctance to change from old systems.

This Month's Org Chart

The 1980s and 1990s brought a multitude of mergers, acquisitions, and reorganizations. American companies in particular metamorphose so frequently and drastically that information system plans and strategies seemingly change with the wind.

One senior manager wants to run the company's information systems from centralized mainframes for better security and easier administration; that manager's successor wants to move *away* from the mainframes and press forward with networks of smaller systems for lower cost and greater flexibility. Though it's fashionable these days to knock mainframes, the fact is that both approaches have their merits; but such rapid management changes ensure that those merits will never materialize.

A large multinational telecommunications firm I work with reorganized so often in 1992 that the IS staff grew cynical and lethargic about implementing *any* automation plans. A new manager would change those plans anyway in a few weeks!

Changes in organizational structure create even bigger problems for companies trying to automate. In 1993, I spoke with an IS manager of a large New York bank that had just merged with another big bank. He admitted he'd be spending the next two years just trying to integrate the computers from the other bank into his bank's existing computer system. That megachore would dominate the attention of all the automation experts in both banks to the exclusion of any new projects.

Custom Software

Many customers opt for custom software solutions to their programming needs: programs crafted from the ground up, as distinguished from commercial off-the-shelf software. We'll see in the next chapter that custom software can move organizations away from standard environments and introduce significant life cycle costs that may overwhelm the benefits.

It's Working; Leave It Be

It's difficult for a business to discard its investment in old systems to achieve adherence to internal standards. Once nonstandard systems establish themselves in an organization, it's tough to justify abandoning that investment for the sake of a seeming abstraction like "compatibility." The more those older systems cost and the larger the support organization that has grown up around them, the harder it is. Examples:

❑ Most businesses use a hodgepodge of network interface cards (NICs) to link their mini- and microcomputers. While it would cost less over the long run to replace NICs that don't meet corporate standards, few businesses do so, ensuring that network administrators will continue devoting substantial time to troubleshooting and upgrading the patchwork quilt of devices.

❑ Some mainframe systems are being used primarily as "disk farms" to store centralized databases. The maintenance cost alone on these old mainframes often approaches the cost of replacing them with cheaper and faster file servers; but who'll suggest to the CEO that the company write off the $10 million investment in those old machines?

CONSEQUENCES OF MYTH #8

The results of industry and corporate nonstandardization go far to explain how unproductive most computer systems really are. They are identical to the results of ad hoc computing discussed in connection with Myth #6: difficult system expansion, high support costs, low flexibility, poor communications, and inefficient resource use.

THE PROBLEM

The computer industry tries to maintain a delicate balance among three goals:

- Providing a sufficient variety of products to meet the full spectrum of customer needs;

- Maintaining profit margins in the face of stiff competition; and

- Adhering to practical and sensible standards in order to reduce customer costs.

The industry has done a great job providing variety, a pretty good job (up until the early nineties, at least) maintaining profits, but a rotten job developing and adhering to standards. The reasons find their roots in historical and market forces, and the situation isn't likely to change quickly or soon.

Business customers are slow to create and adhere to their own in-house standards, partly because of the bad habits of ad hoc automation and partly because of management and organizational changes; "custom" solutions that generate extremely high life cycle costs; and a reluctance to abandon older, nonstandard systems.

Incompatibility exacts a heavy penalty in system life cycle costs. As those costs balloon, the computer system's value plummets, along with the likelihood that it will provide a net benefit to the company using it. If organizations can get past the myth that the computer industry is moving toward greater standardization, what are the steps they *can* take to minimize obsolescence and reduce the costs of incompatibility?

ACTION PLAN

Maintaining a balance between specialization on the one hand, and standardization and connectivity on the other, challenges modern computerized businesses but need not defeat them. Some computer vendors are finally taking baby steps toward improving connectivity and reducing incompatibility costs. Some of those steps are described below, with the suggestion that customers reward vendors of open systems with their business.

But customers will have to do most of the work to create their own efficient, standardized computer environment. Companies that have reached this goal follow three rules:

- ❑ Standardize where feasible.

- ❑ Connect everywhere.

- ❑ Hold fast to automation plans.

The first step is to build a case for making these changes by measuring the dollars they can save.

Warm Up the Calculator

Myth #1 stated that computer productivity is unmeasurable; at this point, it's clear that measuring is an important first step to improvement, even if it can't be done precisely. Figures accurate to plus or minus 50 percent are much better than nothing, and will suffice to justify much of what a computerizing organization will need to do. After making a run at quantifying the costs of incompatibility, automators can analyze their options intelligently based on the projected costs and benefits, and justify required actions in dollar terms.

Examples of nonstandardization costs include:

- ❑ Expensive system expansions, conversions, and upgrades.

- ❑ Redundant or unnecessary training covering similar but incompatible systems.

- ❑ Excess time spent by help desk staff troubleshooting non-standard systems.

- ❑ Inability to move computer power around where it's needed.

- ❑ Lost time due to the inability of one computer to use another's data.

- ❑ Lost time from not being able to get to desired data quickly.

- ❑ Cost of programming to overcome incompatibilities.

- ❑ Inability to use desirable off-the-shelf products because of nonstandard systems.

Reports estimating the costs of incompatibility using some of the above hints provide a powerful and persuasive document for managers wishing to improve their automated systems.

Standardize Where Feasible

Smart businesses standardize on hardware or software *if* it's feasible to do so without unduly impairing the effectiveness or capabilities of the system and *if* the standard systems meet most of the business's needs. Okay; how?

CREATE AN INTERNAL STANDARDS BODY

A happy medium *does* exist between the ineffective chaos of decentralized, unguided computer decision making and the inflexible autocracy of traditional IS departments. The organization can create a body responsible for setting guidelines and standards. This body should then consider requests to deviate from those standards when a valid business reason drives the request.

"Met Life, for example, established an eight-member standards group . . . it sets standards for how information should be stored and computers programmed. Changes to those rules occur only if they give the company a really big technological advance" (*Business Week*, June 10, 1991).

The standards group may include representatives from IS, the Help Desk, the user community, and even major vendors to ensure that the group's recommendations are not too political or accrue to the benefit of a small number. It should stay small, however, so that it may act quickly. It should also have teeth. For

Figure 5   Navigating the Chaos

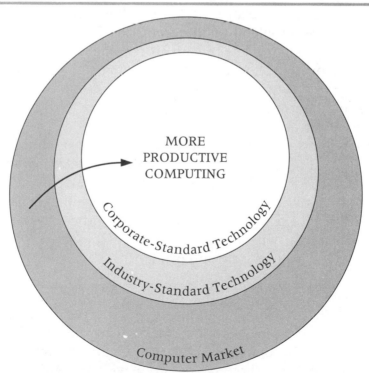

example, the organization may limit its internal computer support services, such as Help Desk, training, and documentation, to users running standard, recommended hardware and software. Departments or work groups wishing to stray from that product list have to provide for their own end-user support. Such teams also obtain permission from the standards group before *connecting* their systems to the mainframe or network.

The standards committee could allocate time to keep abreast of industry trends, either by reading relevant trade journals, periodically meeting with manufacturers, attending conferences and trade shows, or a combination of the above. In this way, the committee can make recommendations that reflect computer industry directions. Realistically, medium or small organizations may not be able to devote the necessary time to this responsibility; they might consider using expert independent consultants who track the volatile marketplace for a living.

To avoid the problems of unnecessarily customized systems, organizations can stipulate that no off-the-shelf product could do the work anticipated for the custom system before that system is okayed. One policy option is to require the group or individual requesting the custom solution to demonstrate to the standards committee the absence of commercial products by presenting a market survey. The survey process need not overburden the applicant, as some directory publishers offer computer-searchable CD/ROM disks as well as on-line databases through services such as CompuServe and Dialog. Consultants can provide this type of service as well. Considering the costs and dangers associated with custom software, the market survey requirement is appropriate and prudent.

HEAD FOR THE OPEN ROAD

While some computer customers are large and powerful enough to work with the computer industry to create appropriate standards, such as General Motors has done with the Manufacturing

Automation Protocol (MAP), most customers don't have the resources for that kind of effort. *All* customers, however, can put their money where their mouth is and buy products from vendors that seem to understand the need for open systems, connectivity, and standardization. Voting with dollars influences the industry over time. Meanwhile, those customers are increasing the standardization and flexibility of their systems.

Vendors help customers deal with nonstandard environments using different approaches. Some simply make their products compatible with *every* standard if no single standard dominates the market. This drives up development costs but may pay off handsomely over the long term, as with NEC's MultiSync monitors. These displays automatically adjust to different video signals, so they work with a wide variety of machines. Customers who appreciated the design's openness and versatility have rewarded NEC by making the MultiSync the most popular microcomputer display line in history. Other manufacturers, such as Sony Corporation, have taken the hint, building similar models that have also enjoyed strong sales.

Other vendors attempt to *define* the standard; Bill Gates, chairman of Microsoft, stated modestly in *Fortune* that "my approach to the PC market has been the same from the very beginning. The goal of Microsoft is to create the standard for the industry." Large computer companies wield such influence in the marketplace that this goal may be a realistic one if the vendor is very clever, very persistent, closely tuned in to customer needs, and a little lucky (as Microsoft was in receiving only a light wrist slap from the Justice Department in July 1994 for alleged unfair trade practices).

❏ A preeminent example of "defining the standard" is Microsoft's Windows software, which provides the developers of user programs a single set of device drivers for communicating with printers, displays, and other external devices, while also providing users with a consistent appearance and command structure.

The single set of device drivers frees the software developer from having to rewrite a program every time a new device hits the market. It also protects the customer, who can buy new hardware without having to upgrade every program that runs under Windows—just the one Windows driver. *Business Week* reports that Windows software accounted for 32 percent of the PC market in late 1992. Microsoft estimates it had sold 100 million copies of Windows 3.1 by mid-1994.

Such attempts don't always succeed, however, even for industry giants. IBM began promoting an ambitious internal standard called SAA (*Systems Application Architecture*) in the spring of 1987, claiming that the uniform software environment it specified would allow IBM's vastly different product lines to look the same to programmers and end-users alike. According to the February 22, 1993, *Business Week*, "Top IBM executives promoted the concept heavily for years in an effort to get some thirty thousand IBM programmers to focus on it and to get the software industry to adopt it." Despite that effort, SAA never really got off the ground, largely because of its extraordinary complexity—it incorporated over three hundred separate standards—and, in 1991, IBM stopped marketing the concept.

Other computer companies recognize the fast pace of change and build *upgradability* into their products. Examples:

❏ A spate of upgradable PCs hit the market in 1992 and 1993. In these machines, the electronic brain, or CPU module, is easily replaceable as opposed to older designs that soldered the CPU permanently in place.

❏ The *firmware* used in computer circuit boards consists of program code burned into silicon chips, which sit in sockets on circuit boards. Technology changes often render firmware programming obsolete, requiring technicians to obtain new chips from the vendor, dismantle computers, remove circuit boards, pull out the old chips and insert the new ones: a time-consuming, tedious operation that often simply doesn't get done. Some circuit-board builders now supply software that updates firmware without requiring chip replacement, reducing time requirements tenfold and making it easier for customers to keep their systems up-to-date as standards change and technology advances.

❑ System vendors—DEC and Apple occasionally do this—may offer to accept old computers as trade-ins on new equipment: a simple "upgrade" practice long-established in the car business but rare indeed in the high-tech world. Even the odd circuit-board manufacturer will accept trade-ins; Daystar Digital, a builder of speed-up boards for the Macintosh, does so. Bravo.

Many computer makers design their machines around industry standards, at the same time others are focusing on proprietary technology that they can rigidly guard and control. Sun Microsystems, a dominant builder of engineering and scientific computers, incorporates standards such as Motorola processors, UNIX software, and Ethernet networking into all its products. Customers who appreciated this commitment to standardization have helped Sun grow from $116 million in 1987 to $4.31 *billion* in 1993, eclipsing such established competitors as DEC and HP and garnering nearly 40 percent of the workstation market, according to *The Wall Street Journal* and *Newsbytes*.

If the security, compatibility, low price, and upgradability of a standardized computer outweigh the unique performance advantages of a proprietary computer, customers will select the standardized machine every time. Companies such as Sun enjoy success by delivering systems that perform well *and* follow existing standards better than most, recouping in volume more than they give up in profit margin.

The software industry, too, is beginning to recognize the importance of standards. Database programs manage structured sets of related information, such as inventory and personnel records. Most computers don't understand English yet, so database vendors provide a special, limited language for posing *queries* such as "How many employees in advertising make over $40,000 per year?" The traditionally wide variety of query languages has presented the same kinds of problems as the variety of macro languages.

Most database vendors now support a standard language called Structured Query Language, or SQL (pronounced "sequel"). SQL works with *relational* databases, a popular type because of their easily understood and flexible structure. SQL has become popular on PCs, minicomputers, and mainframes alike, and "offers a strong measure of transportability across platforms and products" (*Data Based Advisor*, 1993). The American National Standards Institute (ANSI) standard for SQL, SQL-92, lays out the standard in sufficient detail so that users should be able to move between database programs and between computers with minimal relearning, even though complete program portability between SQL platforms does not yet exist. The benefits in reduced training costs alone will be enormous.

In the area of operating system software, UNIX, as mentioned earlier, is an example of how a standard can be "improved" by so many companies that it fragments into a nonstandard. A standard called POSIX (Portable Operating System Interface) attempts to provide a compromise between standards adherence and product differentiation. A coordinated effort on the part of three major industry standards organizations and several large computer firms, begun in earnest in 1985, has now produced a standard defining how any particular UNIX variant should appear to users and programmers.

POSIX, an "interface standard," recognizes that different operating systems will remain different on the inside but need not look different on the outside. The goal is for users and programmers to be able to work on different UNIX machines without having to learn all their idiosyncrasies. DEC, IBM, and Unisys demonstrated their operating systems' compliance with POSIX at the 1992 UniForum conference.

Since then, POSIX products "have found a measure of acceptance in the marketplace," according to *Software Magazine* (March 1994), but it's by no means an unqualified success. The project has grown so large (forty-three committees at the IEEE) that critics call it unmanageable, and POSIX must now compete with other standards from vendor consortia. Nevertheless, it's shown more staying power than consortium-based standards such as UNIX International and Open Software Foundation. There's even a chance it may open up some traditionally closed computer environments, such as minicomputer systems from DEC and HP, if customers support it strongly enough.

Another software problem discussed earlier is inconsistent macro languages. Microsoft has taken a step in the right direction by announcing that its Windows applications will all use a language called "Visual BASIC" for macros in the future. Vendors have also begun providing a simple way of using macros that doesn't vary from program to program: they include commands for START RECORDING, STOP RECORDING, and PLAYBACK. The user sends the START RECORDING command, types the keystrokes for the job to be automated, issues the STOP RECORDING command when done, names and saves the macro, and later invokes PLAYBACK to repeat the recorded sequence when desired. This technique makes it unnecessary to learn even one macro language. Customers should look for this capability when evaluating application software—and stop teaching macro languages altogether.

Organizations that move to open systems over time as they buy new computers and devices will create a more manageable, lower-cost environment even as they push the industry to create products that are flexible, upgradable, interchangeable, and standardized. The above examples illustrate that the industry will listen if customers demand open products adamantly enough and long enough.

EXTERMINATE THE DINOSAURS

Occasionally, consultants have the unpleasant duty of advising a company to abandon its sometimes considerable investment in expensive proprietary computer systems in favor of newer, more standardized systems. Though painful in the short term, because the salvage value of such older hardware and software is usually near zero, such a step may be necessary for the company's long-term ability to wring productivity gains from their systems. We'll explore this issue further in Myth #13.

Connect Everywhere

> *"Why are computers connected to networks? Why do people talk?"*
>
> —ROBERT E. KAHN, *Scientific American* (October 1987)

ENSURE NONSTANDARD SYSTEMS CAN AT LEAST COMMUNICATE

When achieving a desirable goal requires departure from a standard, the equipment and programs in the nonstandard system should connect as well as possible with existing, standard systems. The highest level is *application* connectivity, in which a program created on one system can run on another system. At a lower level, *file* connectivity ensures that valuable information created on one system can move to another system and be used there. The lowest level is *data* connectivity, which means merely that one can plug a cable into two systems and move bits and bytes between them. *Organizations should at least require file-level connectivity for nonstandard systems.* The usual way of connecting disparate systems is with a network.

Computer networks are among the most sophisticated and complex technological achievements in the high-technology business. Given the diversity of systems, it's remarkable that different machines can interact at all, much less speedily and productively; but it's important that they do. Connected workstations enhance employee communications. Electronic mail can allow people to work more flexibly, in both time and space. Shared data means everyone has access to up-to-date information, and the right hand is a little more likely to be aware of what the left hand is doing.

Computers connect for the same reasons people connect: communication is vital to a business organization's success. Networks can improve the communications grid, enhancing flexibility and quickening response time. Further, networks can help link different systems, breaking incompatibility barriers and providing a backbone for standardization efforts. It's easier to update software programs on a network, for example, than to update individual machines.

In 1989, only about 15 percent of all business microcomputers were connected in a network. In 1994, the figure is closer to 70 percent. Clearly, organizations are beginning to appreciate the benefits of connecting.

A warning, however: Networks themselves, which vendors design to overcome some of the problems of nonstandardization and incompatibility, can and often do *introduce* incompatibility. Customers implementing networks need to tread carefully and pay great attention to standards.

NETWORK STANDARDS

Multivendor coalitions have helped increase standardization in some cases. Xerox, DEC, and Intel jointly developed the popular Ethernet networking architecture. Other network protocols without multivendor support, such as the proprietary Xerox Network System, have not fared as well; Xerox made an effort to involve DEC and Intel, but they demurred, and XNS has not been successful.

The enormous influence exerted on the computer industry by the U.S. Department of Defense has brought some substantial benefits to networking, most noteworthy of which is the TCP/IP standard. (The acronym stands for Transmission Control Protocol/Internet Protocol; an *internet* is a network of networks.)

TCP/IP is actually a *group* of data communication standards. Nonproprietary, over fifty different hardware and software vendors support it; yet all TCP/IP products look about the same to the end-user. Its advantage is that it allows a wide variety of computers to connect to each other, insulating users from the details of the various conversions taking place "under the hood" as the network translates data between machines. Customers can layer TCP/IP on top of existing networks, and in many cases can use existing communications hardware.

Network management is a broad and very important field addressing such topics as fault isolation and software installation, some of the trickiest network jobs. Several different standards exist for network management software, including IBM's NetView, the International Standards Organization's CMIP and CMIS, and SNMP (Simple Network Management Protocol).

These standards are at different stages of evolution and present different advantages and disadvantages; NetView focuses on the IBM environment, CMIP is comprehensive but rather slow in coming, and SNMP is gaining popularity but remains loosely defined.

As usual, however, industry standards don't go nearly far enough. Smart businesses will not only adopt networks conforming at least partially to industry standards where possible but will also create their own internal standards for choices such as network hardware, cabling systems, and user accounts, perhaps through the standards committee structure. Those businesses will also hire administrators to manage the complex systems, trainers to teach users how to access network resources, and support staff to answer user questions and problems.

The message is "Connect—but connect carefully."

Dropping the Keel in Rough Weather

The computer plan, discussed at length earlier, should have management support at a high enough level so changes in midlevel management positions and minor reorganizations don't disrupt it. *Most companies create and implement computer project plans at too low a level,* making them too vulnerable to the organizational winds of change. One reason is top management's traditional aloofness from automation issues. IT implementers will therefore spend whatever time it takes to convince senior managers of how important industry and corporate standards are to the long-term productivity of their systems.

Mergers and acquisitions present a tougher situation as sometimes there is nothing one organization can do to prevent the sudden incompatibilities that arise. All one can do is hope to manage the transition and integrate the systems in an intelligent, stepwise manner. Organizations can create a plan for merging disparate systems. Here the standards committee can provide a valuable service in deciding which components of the different systems to keep, which to convert, and which to abandon. Additionally, using networks to link the systems can facilitate migrating programs and data from one platform to the other.

THE REALITY

Management should want its computer systems to become as flexible, adaptable, connectable, and easy to use as modular office furniture. As needs change, the organization should be able to redeploy computer power as easily and rapidly as moving partitions and cubicles. Employees should be able to move from one area to another without encountering a new learning curve at every turn, just as they can change offices without having to relearn how to use a chair. As organizations grow, it should be possible to add modules without rendering older systems functionally obsolete, just as one may add new desks and file cabinets to existing workspaces without discarding the old ones.

Can companies achieve such a difficult goal, given the fast pace of change in the computer industry, the historical diversity of products, and the market pressures that conspire against standardization? Those that at least *approach* it have a better chance to make their information systems truly productive.

Approaching this ideal will require enhancing standardization and connectivity dramatically at both the industry and corporate levels. Companies will first quantify the costs of incompatibility, then reduce them by forming an internal standards body to define and enforce corporate standards where feasible. Such a body would allow departures from the standards only when valid business reasons exist and no commercial products fill the need. It can encourage the industry to develop flexible, standard, upgradable products by buying them where they already exist and by rejecting proprietary products that have no compelling advantage compared to open, standard products. Organizations may need to phase out obsolete systems sooner than they'd like in order to rein in the hidden costs of supporting nonstandard environments.

Nonstandard systems can connect to corporate networks at least at the file level so that companies can share valuable information. Smart organizations won't rely solely on industry standards for networks but will add their own criteria to ensure high compatibility, easy data exchange, and low ongoing costs. Finally, if top management embraces (read: is *persuaded* to embrace) automation strategies at a high-enough level, it can minimize the disruptive effect reorganizations and management changes impose on automation projects.

Any organization that follows these suggestions and is able over time to create a highly standardized computer system will save the significant dollars associated with incompatibility costs.

However, a company still may be tempted to deviate from "standard," off-the-shelf software by commissioning custom programs designed especially for its particular business needs. Does custom software pay off in the long run? The answer might be surprising, as we'll see in the next chapter.

MYTH 9

Custom Software Gives Us an Edge

THE MYTH

A southwestern building materials company spends a few hundred thousand dollars on a state-of-the-art minicomputer to handle its accounting, billing, and inventory chores. It purchases a highly customized software system to ensure the best possible fit with its operation; the price is high but less than double that of an off-the-shelf system, and the vendor pledges it will fit the customer like a glove. The company buys more modules than it needs right away to get the best package price, but plans to grow into them later on. The vendor works with the customer on a customized chart of accounts and a few reports. The general ledger component works well.

In a few months, "later on" arrives, and it's time to activate the order entry system. One problem: The company sells in different states and counties, with different sales tax rates. The solution seems simple—add a program module that will look up the appropriate tax rate based on the place of sale. The customer calls up the software house and makes the request.

No problem, says the software house, we can do that for about $200 an hour; shouldn't take more than a couple weeks' work. (You never mentioned you had multiple locations, so we didn't include that capability.) The customer doesn't like that much but understands and says Okay, we need it, and sends the tapes up to the software house for modification.

Two weeks later, the phone rings. "The programmer's had a look at your tapes, and your software's outdated." (It's nine months old at this point.) "We'll have to update some of the modules before we can work on it." How much? "Five thousand for each of the eight modules." (That's what they originally cost.) Can't you just modify the software without updating it? "No, we don't have any programmers around anymore who worked on that old stuff." Let me talk with George (who worked on the general ledger customizations). "He quit six months ago."

The president of the building materials company doesn't like being held hostage for an extra $50,000 and change just to handle a sales tax problem, so he calls the reseller that put the original deal together. Phone disconnected, out of business. He next calls a consultant and asks if *his* company can modify the system. "Sure," says the consultant, "but I'll have to learn the system first. That could take a couple of months, if I've got phone access to the original programmers; three or four, if not." But you'll guarantee it'll work after that? "That's just like asking a surgeon for a guarantee the operation will succeed," says the consultant. "There's no telling what I'll run into once I get in there. Of course, I'll do my best."

Six months and many fruitless conversations later, the entire accounting system is history. The vendor blames the customer for not thinking of all relevant requirements in advance, and for not buying the support plan that would have kept the software up-to-date. The customer blames the vendor for not being able to make a seemingly simple change for a reasonable charge. The building materials company buys a new system and starts all over.

◻ A 1992 study by International Data Corporation suggests that more than half of all application software is custom software, tailor-made for a specific customer. It's a $15 billion industry in the United States, even larger in Europe.

It's no wonder, either. Much of computers' attraction is their malleability. Programmers can make a general-purpose computer do just about anything except print money. (That's possible too, just illegal.) Writing software that will make computers jump through very specific hoops is a powerful idea with a lot of appeal.

Customers often think of their needs as so highly specialized that only a custom program will do. Sometimes they're right, and in those cases, custom software can be a genuine boon to their business and even provide a competitive edge. One Texas credit-collections business successfully touts its highly customized software program to gain new accounts.

But the phrase *caveat emptor* goes triple for custom software buyers. Businesses often don't understand the risks involved with major software projects, or the hidden costs associated with them. Our myth for this chapter, then, is: *custom software gives us an edge*. It may, but it's no guarantee; and that edge can cut two ways—painfully.

DEBUNKING MYTH #9

Common Denominators

Businesses aren't as unique as they think they are. Every business shares many of the same needs:

- Managing cash flow;

- Tracking receivables and payables;

- Budgeting and forecasting;

- Helping employees interact productively;

- Developing employees;

- Communicating with customers;

- Keeping up with the competition;

- Developing new products or services;

- Improving quality;

- Improving service.

The software industry has addressed many of these needs with tools that will work equally well for a golf club manufacturer or a yacht builder. While there are nuances to every business, many of their information needs are similar enough that standard off-the-shelf software will meet them well.

Commercial Software: Embarrassment of Riches

There's a lot more commercial software available today than in years past—a *lot* more. According to a report from the Business Software Alliance, the software industry grew 269 percent in real terms between 1982 and 1992. It was a $34 billion market in 1992. As of 1994, there were over forty-six thousand different commercial software products available in the United States.

Admittedly, probably half of those products are junk (anybody with a PC and some spare time can write software), and a goodly percentage aren't applications but rather operating systems or utilities. Even so, there are thousands of good commercial software packages out there. Many address very specific vertical markets, too: everything from architecture to zookeeping. Many businesses commission custom software, only to find out later that a good commercial application existed all along.

What are the typical benefits of commercial software?

- It costs less than custom software.

- It can be implemented faster.

- It comes with better documentation and support.

- There are many sources for training instead of just one.

- It's maintained by the vendor rather than the customer's computer staff.

- Its makers can devote more resources to improving and upgrading it because of the much larger customer base over which to spread costs.

- It's more likely to become reliable over time as more customers are testing it in the field and alerting the manufacturer of bugs.

New Kinds of Applications

Applications used to be very cut-and-dried: They'd do what the feature list said they could do, maybe provide a report writer for custom printouts, and that was it. No more. Modern commercial applications have become programmable, flexible, and extensible.

PROGRAMMABILITY

Microsoft's Word for Windows comes with its own programming language of about 470 rather powerful commands. Spreadsheet products ship with their own programming languages, too. Users can write "scripts" to make applications walk through a sequence of steps automatically on command, or every time a program starts.

Screen layouts are more customizable in commercial applications now, too. "Roll-up" windows offering groupings of related commands can be created, hidden, moved around. Users can create "buttons" on a "button bar" to do things they need to do with one mouse click. Operators can change menu options, removing unneeded functions and adding new ones.

EXTENSIBILITY

Commercial software is becoming more extensible, too, through mechanisms that allow add-on modules. Sometimes, the application vendor sells such add-ons; a spreadsheet vendor might offer an add-on to perform statistical regression analysis, for example, to fit the best curve to a set of data points. In other cases, third-party vendors sell add-ons, such as the graphics firms that augment image-editing software with "filters" for producing watercolor or fisheye-lens effects on scanned photos. Database systems can be augmented by predefined forms and report formats. Even computer network operating systems are extensible: to add sophisticated security or backup features to a Novell network, for example, one can buy a "NetWare Loadable Module" that inserts itself into the core of the network system.

Linkability

Finally, commercial programs can now create *compound documents* by linking data elements. For example, one can "graft" a spreadsheet or picture into a word processing document. When someone modifies the original spreadsheet, the changes reflect in the WP document. Linking has opened up a new world of commercial applications.

Customizing, extending, and linking commercial software has its own set of caveats, of course. Modifying an application introduces an element of nonstandardization, and this requires extra documentation, support, and maintenance for the changes. The people doing the modification don't always understand good programming or design practices. Debra Haverson in *MIDRANGE Systems* magazine points out, "As the number of customized programming patches to a system rises, it becomes harder to use vendor support services such as hotlines." And when a product's upgraded, guess what—it's often necessary to make all the modifications all over again for the new version! Extensions typically apply only to one particular program or computer environment. And links between applications often just don't work, partly because it's a new way of thinking for many software builders and partly because it's just so complicated to implement.

The point, then, isn't that customizable and extensible commercial software is perfect. The point is that it's often a less agonizing route than developing custom applications from scratch.

Dangers of Custom Software

LATE AND EXPENSIVE

> *"Because software often seems so easy to use, people are lulled into thinking it is easy to create. Just the opposite is true. Software is incredibly complex, and our expectations for it are rising faster than the ability of programmers to keep up."*

> —ROBERT MECHALEY, VP, McCAW
> CELLULAR COMMUNICATIONS, INC.

Why is software always behind schedule and over budget? Robert Mechaley mentions one reason: complexity. There are many other reasons, too:

- ❑ The hardware underneath it is in constant flux.

- ❑ Developers pay more attention to product than to the design process.

- ❑ Project estimation is difficult; models are inadequate.

- ❑ Programmers don't like testing, so they often skip it. Fixing bugs late in a project costs an order of magnitude more than fixing them early.

- ❑ Projects always change along the way, creating new bugs.

- ❑ Customers always think of new things they want halfway through.

Aside from initial development costs, the day-to-day operating cost of custom software far exceeds that of off-the-shelf software. The programming firm can't spread the cost of product support over a large number of customers, because the product is unique;

yet the level of support the customer expects in phone assistance, troubleshooting, and conversion assistance is the same as the customer would expect from a software firm supporting a widely sold commercial product, if not greater. For this reason, custom programmers charge high prices for after-sale support.

UNDOCUMENTED SYSTEMS

Custom software is expensive, and the last thing a customer wants to do is add to its cost. Writing good, thorough documentation is also expensive because there aren't very many people who can do it, and those who can are beginning to understand their own value, so software shops charge a lot to provide documentation.

For reasons we've already explored, companies frequently overestimate system ease of use and scrimp on user documentation. The result is a system that's hard to learn and hard to use. Customers also tend to skip technical documentation, believing the relationship with the vendor will last forever; when it doesn't, the lack of tech manuals makes it hard (or impossible) to modify and enhance the system.

UNSUPPORTED SYSTEMS

Because of the relatively small number of experts who know and understand the inner workings of a custom program, the customer becomes exposed to great risk if the programming firm dissolves or key designers leave. What does the organization do if it needs a program modification and the original designer has moved to Hawaii to grow orchids? If employees created the software, what will happen when they're gone?

The converse situation, when the customer decides to switch programming firms, presents similar difficulties. Maintaining custom software can suddenly become much more expensive. The new programmers will charge a fair sum just to *learn* the custom program, much less perform any useful work on it. Even if the original programmers did a good job documenting their work, which most don't, the time needed for a new firm to read and understand a custom program can cost more than the original program—in which case, it might be cheaper to redo the whole project from scratch.

INCOHERENT SYSTEMS

Software-by-committee is about as successful as symphonies-by-committee. Many programs reflect the influence of so many different programmers that users struggle with inconsistencies and contradictory design practices. A good program is a highly creative blend of art and science, best done by one or two chief designers supported by a competent programming staff to fill in the details. Too many programming firms, however, parcel out pieces of a project to different teams, resulting in a hodgepodge final product.

Hidden Costs of User Programming

Why can't a business have its custom programming done in-house? Programming's getting easier and easier, isn't it?

Well, yes and no. Programming tools *are* getting better, but then customers are expecting more of programs, too. The need for reliable, reusable, and flexible programming has put some tough new demands on those who would create applications. The client/server network environment is much more difficult to program for than the central-mainframe or stand-alone-PC environment. And new awareness of "human factors" has raised the bar for user-friendliness, too.

The definition of *programming* has blurred over the years. Once, it meant writing superdetailed programs in *machine language*. Such programs can run faster than any other kind, but they're tedious and time-consuming even for experts. With the advent of *high-level languages*, such as BASIC, FORTRAN, COBOL, Pascal, and the like, programs became more English-like and certainly easier to write and read, but the rigorous design rules and principles remained. Now, with so-called *fourth-generation languages*, macros, and visual programming tools, the programming activity is being performed by persons with no formal background—sometimes with fine results, sometimes not.

Patricia Seybold's *Office Computing Report* suggests that "Visual programming can be deceptively seductive. Sophisticated environments are not for the typical end user—and sometimes not even for the power user." Many seemingly friendly programming tools work easily for simple tasks but drop off like the continental shelf once the user tackles tougher tasks.

The road to bad programs is paved with good intentions. Good programming technique comes from study, training, and practice. It may be well worth learning, and intelligent noncomputer types can certainly learn it, but it still isn't easy and the money saved up front may not be worth the headaches later on. Some of the hidden costs of user programming include:

- Systems no one other than the programmer can understand;

- Programs limited to a very specific computer platform;

- Programs that can't exchange data with other company systems;

- Applications that violate company computer standards of practice;

- Programs with no plan for documentation, support, or maintenance;

- Employees who need to be doing other things who are doing programming instead.

THE PROBLEM

Custom solutions often generate extremely high life cycle costs, yet are common in business automation because managers believe the myth that custom software is always better than commercial software.

Custom software is no panacea and it's often not necessary. Most businesses share many information processing needs in common, however unusual or unique they may be in other respects; for example, it's almost never necessary to commission a customized general ledger package or e-mail system. Commercial software has exploded in quantity and variety; it's also much more customizable than it used to be, a trend that continues apace. On the other hand, custom software is always late; always costs more than anyone thinks it will; is often poorly documented, and even more poorly supported. End-user customization (that is, programming) is a little like cooking: Everyone thinks they can do it, but only a few have the talent or the training to do it well.

ACTION PLAN

The action plan presents the key decision points in analyzing the "buy versus build" decision, and it suggests ways to avoid the most common pitfalls if a business decides custom software is the way to go.

Buy Versus Build

SCAN THE MARKET

The first step in making the "buy versus build" decision is to see if an existing product meets the business's needs. If the goal specified for the project is one that many other companies share, there's a good chance commercial software exists. Even in a unique situation, the possibility that someone, somewhere, has already invented that particular wheel suggests a thorough market survey before committing to customization.

There are no very good ways to find out about all the commercial software packages that might be relevant and useful for a given company. In a market as cluttered and immature as this one, it's difficult for even the gurus to stay on top of all the changes. If the business employs people to keep up with high tech, they'll be doing a lot of reading, attending trade shows, etc., and may have some ideas. Outside consultants may know of some vendors, too; sometimes they can do market surveys economically if it's impractical to do them in-house, and they can offer a second opinion on the wisdom of customizing.

For businesses who want to do their own research, on-line services can be a boon. Computer company directories are available via services such as CompuServe, which also has product descriptions. Customers can run financials of prospective suppliers on-line, too, to help protect against buying from "flash-in-the-pan" companies. There are a lot of start-ups and shut-downs in this business. Directories such as those from Datapro Research, Inc., can also help. Database vendors such as Oracle publish directories of Value-Added Resellers (VARs) who have developed niche applications not listed anywhere else. Investing some time up front to canvass the market can save a business from a costly custom solution.

The 100 Percent Solution

Sometimes companies feel that if commercial applications, even after tailoring, can't meet 100 percent of the desired needs, then custom software is the way to go. This is very thin ice on which to skate. *ComputerWorld* reports that if a custom program brings only a 5 or 10 percent gain in efficiency over off-the-shelf products, that usually won't make up for the higher development costs. If commercial software can meet 90 or 95 percent of the stated needs, it's almost always a better bet than custom software.

Is there some flexibility in business procedures or program goals that would permit a commercial solution? Are there ways to link commercial programs with customizable report writers or screen design utilities to make the commercial software a better fit?

INSOURCE OR OUTSOURCE?

Once a business decides that custom software's benefits outweigh the risks, it next decides whether to pursue the programming in-house or to contract it out. Some decision factors here are:

- Availability of in-house expertise (for example, in object-oriented programming);
- Opportunity cost of pulling staff away from other projects;
- Budget;
- Time-to-completion requirements;
- Outside vendor's long-term support capabilities;
- Importance of "owning" the end product;
- Importance of confidentiality.

USER PROGRAMMING GUIDELINES

Savvy computer users will always want to create their own programs, and companies must weigh the costs and benefits according to the scale of the project. Small computers promise great flexibility for knowledgeable and talented end-users willing to invest time to develop programming skills. New, so-called visual programming tools permit rapid coding and testing that shorten the development cycle.

Far be it from me to suggest that users ought never to create their own custom programs. The stern warnings of the IS staff must be taken in context with their need to protect their jobs. However, forward-thinking companies come up with *guidelines* for user programming that consider the following elements:

- Will other people than the user-programmer be using the program?

- If so, who'll teach it to them?

- Can the program be productive running on a single platform? What are the dependencies built into the proposed application, and are they overly limiting? (For example, does it require Windows 3.1 and DOS 6.2?)

- Does the program need to communicate with other systems for maximum benefit?

- If so, do corporate standards apply? Will the user-programmer adhere to them?

- Will the user-programmer document and support his or her work?

- Who will maintain and upgrade the application?

- How important is it for the user-programmer to be doing other things besides hacking away at custom programs?

- Are computer staff available who could do the job faster and better?

- What education has the user-programmer had in software development? Is that adequate to ensure a reliable product?

- Is it more important to get something done quickly by a user-programmer, even if it isn't perfect, than to wait for trained staff to get to it?

Embarking on the Project

GOING TO THE CHAPEL

> *"When customizing, you are tying yourself into lifelong product maintenance and support."*
>
> —BYRON ISAACS, *Computing Canada* (1994)

Think before saying "I do."

Because of the high costs of switching software firms, the customer should be prepared to enter into a long-term relationship with the software vendor for any major project. In many ways, the customer and developer are going into partnership, and many of the same questions arise:

- Is the vendor financially sound?

- Is the vendor large enough to withstand the loss of key people?

- Is the vendor "compatible" with the customer in terms of style?

- Does the vendor have the resources to keep up with customer growth?

THE PRENUPTIAL AGREEMENT

Once the decision's made to customize, and the vendor is chosen, the smart customer covers all bases. No one enters into a major software project anticipating that it will fail, but given that the success rate of custom software projects is probably worse than that for marriages, it's good to consider what will happen if it *does* fail—especially since this is *business* and not love. Assuming a total meltdown, answer the following questions in advance:

- ❏ Will arbitration be used to settle disputes? If so, how?
- ❏ Does the customer have the right to resell the software if desired?
- ❏ If the customer pays for development hardware, who keeps it?
- ❏ Does the customer have the right to receive copies of all work notes?

Part of the prenuptial agreement will pertain to source code rights, which deserve special mention.

A SOURCE OF TROUBLE

One question for companies hiring out software development is whether to purchase *source code* or just *object code*. These terms sound obscure, but their meaning is simple: Object code is the version the *computer* can run, and source code is the more or less English-like version that *humans* create and modify. (Typically, programmers generate object code from source code using tools called *compilers*.) The question boils down to whether the customer wants to be able to modify the software in the future, or pay the vendor to do it.

It might seem that buying source code would always make sense, as it gives the customer the greatest flexibility. Not so. For one thing, it can cost a lot more because the vendor knows he's giving up future business by providing it. Second, modifying source code is fraught with peril. Usually, all bets are off with the vendor when it comes to warranties and support for modified code. And for good reason: When someone who's not intimately familiar with a program tries to modify it, there's a large chance of introducing new errors when making the change, particularly in badly designed software with unclear dependencies and labyrinthine structure. This danger prompted Warren S. Reid, of Laventhol & Horwath, to say, "If you're tempted to modify a package, lie down until the urge goes away."

THE WELDING VOWS

When putting together a software development project, even a small one, there's wisdom in hiring a lawyer with relevant experience, including him in negotiation sessions, and listening to his advice. When software projects blow up, a leaky contract can cost a company big bucks and much time. Contracts I've seen usually address the following issues, among others:

- ❑ What's the customer actually buying? The right to *use* the software, or the software itself? Who owns the copyright? (Usually, the "author," under U.S. law.) Can the customer use software *objects* developed by the vendor in other future projects with other vendors or in-house developers?

- ❑ Would it be possible for vendor employees who work exclusively on the customer's project for extended periods to be considered employees of the customer, rather than of the contractor? This can be a gray area!

- ❑ Everyone's heard horror stories about software development projects gone wrong, in which the customer withholds payment, the vendor allows a "time bomb" to go off, and the customer can't use the program or maybe even related data. Customers who agree to make progress payments based on milestones have the right to ask vendors to agree in writing to no time bombs.

- How will the vendor protect your business's confidential data? Will the vendor sign a nondisclosure clause that protects the customer?

- Consider 10 percent holdbacks and postproject performance bonuses to ensure the vendor's continuing commitment.

- Likewise, consider penalties appropriate to cover the pain of project delays to your business. The law only requires "reasonable skill and care" of software contractors, not that their products fulfill their intended function. What can the business do contractually to protect against programs that don't work?

WHAT THE SOFTWARE WILL LOOK LIKE

> *"Buildings conceived and completed by a single architect are usually more beautiful and better planned than those remodeled by several persons."*
>
> —RENÉ DESCARTES, FRENCH
> PHILOSOPHER AND
> MATHEMATICIAN (1596–1650)

To avoid the mishmash of inconsistencies associated with software-by-committee, custom software vendors designate team leaders or "point" programmers to guide development of all modules and ensure cohesiveness. Having one individual assume primary responsibility also facilitates communication with the custom software vendor.

HOW IT WILL FIT IN

Developing custom software with object-oriented programming, or OOP, may bring considerable future benefits. Reusable software objects build up a modular library over time to help avoid customers starting every new project from scratch.

Can the custom software communicate with other company databases, information services, PCs, mainframes, networks, etc.? Can users access data in the custom program for display, graphing, and printing using standard commercial tools already in place?

Another question concerns *platform independence*. As *Fortune* reports, "The cost of rewriting software in order to switch from mainframes to smaller machines can be almost inconceivably high." The same can be true of *horizontal migration*—from Windows to UNIX, for instance. Some development tools are more amenable to platform migration than others; it's a good issue to discuss with the provider.

HOW WELL IT WILL WORK

How fast will the software run in the business's typical computer environment? How fast will it run if the business's network grows to five times its present size? Prototypes that work acceptably on stand-alone workstations might degrade quickly as the number of users grows.

Customers should also ask software vendors how they'll ensure product quality. Have the vendors heard of clean-room software engineering, or functional verification? (It doesn't matter if *you* understand those terms; see if the *vendor* does!) What methodology will developers use to avoid bugs? And how will developers test the end results to confirm reliability? Who *are* the developers, anyway, and what are their qualifications?

One can't test quality into a program; it's the outcome of a well-considered and disciplined creation methodology. If a vendor doesn't seem too concerned about the software engineering process but claims they'll test the heck out of it once they're done, run—run like the wind.

The Aftermath

TRAINING AND DOCUMENTATION

Software vendors usually supply some level of user training as part of any project. Will that training be an off-the-cuff recital by one or more programmers, or will it include printed outlines and exercises? Smart customers also buy technical training for in-house staff, who may just be faced with managing the system two years hence.

Technology winners will always specify full technical and user documentation for any custom software project. What constitutes "full" is usually spelled out in the development contract, but it ought to allow users to learn the system and technicians to extend and enhance it.

KEEPING CURRENT

◘ Case: A software company creates a graphics application built on programming tools from two vendors. Six months later, when one of the vendors upgrades its toolkits, the application developer re-creates the graphics application with the new toolkit, making the user program run 50 percent faster. The program also becomes more reliable and able to run on a broader range of machines.

Things are always getting faster and better in the world of software (though not always as quickly as one could wish). When advancements in toolkits promise faster or more reliable applications, does the support or maintenance contract allow the customer to benefit at a reasonable cost?

THE REALITY

Today's incredibly wide variety of commercial software can adapt to most business needs. Using good commercial software where possible is cheaper, faster, easier, safer, and smarter than building programs from scratch.

Can't custom software's benefits justify its costs and risks in *any* circumstances? Of course, especially for groundbreaking, creative applications or unusual business situations. Custom programming can be a key that unlocks computer power and provides a competitive advantage. Organizations just need to know about the expenses and risks, so that when they *do* embark on custom software projects, they have an idea of what they're in for and can make that decision with eyes open wide. And please don't rely just on the information in this brief chapter; experienced consultants and attorneys are your best friends when launching custom computer projects and are worth ten times what they charge you. (Well, maybe *five* times.)

So far, the chapters in this part have dealt with the planning and purchasing processes. Now, the focus shifts to managing existing systems: specifically, user education and support, where computer myths abound.

MYTH 10

Computers Are User-Friendly, So We Don't Need Training

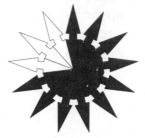

"Human history becomes more and more a race between education and catastrophe."

—H. G. WELLS, ENGLISH AUTHOR
(1866–1946)

THE MYTH

A small real estate office in Dallas buys a microcomputer to automate word processing and billing functions. The managing partner hires a computer expert to set up the machine's hardware and install the programs. The consultant does so, then recommends a series of classes for the office manager, a computer neophyte. The managing partner loses his temper, furious that he will have to send his office manager to school to use the system productively. "I just keep pouring money into this thing," he complains. "And I can't have my office manager out for two weeks. She can read the manuals and learn as she goes."

The office manager gets advice on managing the computer from a secretary in the same building; unfortunately, that secretary says nothing about the importance of making backup copies of data on the disk drive, so when the drive fails three months later, all the data is lost. Three months after that, the office manager quits in frustration and the managing partner dusts off the old typewriter.

The misconception that information systems are easy to use accounts in large part for the dismal state of computer education and the unfulfilled promise of high tech. Often, people *don't* know how to use the systems they have, and their employers don't teach them. Our topic for this chapter: are today's computers *really* so user-friendly that training isn't needed?

DEBUNKING MYTH #10

"People are still uncomfortable with the idea that a computer is a friendly, easy thing to use."

—Mal D. Ransom, VP,
Packard-Bell (1994)

Why aren't computer systems easy to use? And why don't organizations compensate by aggressive end-user education?

Ill-at-Ease of Use

A SECRET VOCABULARY

"The personal computer industry says it is moving toward making the machines as easy to use as toasters, but purchasing one still is more like buying a jet fighter than a household appliance . . . advertisements appear to be aimed at those with a degree in electrical engineering."

—*The Wall Street Journal*,
(October 1, 1987)

Unwieldy, verbose, and cryptic product names, descriptions, acronyms, and abbreviations get between users and their computer systems. Here are a few examples:

INDUSTRY TERM	REAL MEANING
Direct Access Storage Device	Disk drive
Initial Program Load	Computer start-up
EEPROM	Programmable chip
PCMCIA*	"Credit-card" device
CMOS RAM	Configuration memory
Abend (short for "abnormal end")	Failure
And my personal favorite, courtesy of IBM:	
Data Migration Facility	Cable

Even the *names* of computer products are difficult. Would you have guessed that an IBM 4579 Model 516 is a type of System/88? Or that a #9 GXE VLB Level 5 is a video card? The IBM PC/AT microcomputer was also known as a 5170 Model 339. This book was written on a Dell Dimension XPS/466V. Lately, com-

---

* My colleague Gerry Routledge informs me that PCMCIA, which I'd always thought was Personal Computer Memory Card International Association, is really short for "People Can't Memorize Computer Industry Acronyms."

panies have tried using more English-like names, but they sound so similar it's hard to remember even them: Performa, Prolinea, Proliant.

The jargon isn't even unique; it's rife with synonyms. A printed-circuit board is also called an *adapter*, a *feature adapter*, an *add-in board*, an *expansion board*, and (simply) a *card*. On a PC, *conventional* memory is the same as *low* memory, *DOS* memory, *base* memory, and *application* memory. But *upper* memory is quite different from *high* memory, which isn't the same as the *High Memory Area*. Got that?

Computer jargon is worse than medical or legal jargon, because even a smattering of Latin won't help you here. The whole problem traces back to a bygone era, when learning the lingo was the price of admission for dealing with the only game in town, IBM. All that technojargon means that user manuals are much harder to read than they should be; and woe betide the intrepid novice who picks up a trade journal in the hopes of learning something.

SECRET HANDSHAKES

Walter S. Mossberg, longtime computer columnist for *The Wall Street Journal*, calls the unintuitive, complex keyboard commands many programs use "secret handshakes." Want a list of programs running on your PC? No problem, just hold down the [CTRL] and [ESC] keys at the same time. Want to change to a different program? The secret handshake is [ALT]-[TAB]. To copy a block of text, one types [CTRL]-C; okay, C for *copy*. But to *paste* that text elsewhere, one doesn't type [CTRL]-P for *paste*, one types [CTRL]-V, for—I'm not sure what. The most popular word processing software in 1992 made the user type [SHIFT]-[F8]-3 to set a margin. Wow.

About the most user-friendly program I ever saw was Digital Equipment Corporation's WPS-Plus word processing system, popular in the late eighties. The computer keyboard had a gold-colored key in one corner. When you wanted to do something to your text, such as center it on the page, you first hit the gold key, then a single letter (*C* for center, *B* for bold, etc.). This approach went a long way toward avoiding secret handshakes. Too bad no one was paying attention.

USER-IGNORANT SYSTEMS

> *"Designers of computer systems seem particularly oblivious to the needs of users, particularly susceptible to all the pitfalls of design."*
>
> —DONALD NORMAN, DIRECTOR OF THE INSTITUTE FOR COGNITIVE SCIENCE AT THE UNIVERSITY OF CALIFORNIA, *The Design of Everyday Things* (1990)

Some writers label non-user-friendly systems as "user-hostile." I think that's a little harsh; no programmer I know sets about his or her task with the express and malicious intent of befuddling system users. "User-ignorant" is maybe a better term. System designers just don't understand how people interact with machines.

Maybe the most user-ignorant program ever written was the wildly popular database manager, dBase II from Ashton-Tate. When the user ran the program, he was faced with a completely empty screen save for a single dot at the upper left corner. This was the program's way of saying it was awaiting a command; however, for the novice, the "dot prompt" said instead, "Good luck, you're on your own."

Donald Norman makes the point that there's no reason in the world why programmers should determine the user interface of their products; he believes they don't have the skill set, and shouldn't worry about developing it. It may well be that "interface specialists" should handle the human aspect of software and hardware design; but in today's world, it's a fact that the people who work on the internal structure of computer products also often create the user interface, including the on-line "help" system.

We could easily spend an entire book on the flaws with modern computer design, but here are some typical examples:

- Most modern computers don't have a "Help" key on the keyboard. Unbelievable.

- Some systems put the power switch at the back where users can't reach it, but they put the dangerous "reset" switch right up front where it's easily bumped by accident.

- Some computers don't have a push button to eject a floppy; you have to use an unbent paper clip if the computer malfunctions and you want your disk back.

- Printers have no front-panel displays, so you can't tell what's going on by looking. Those that do are sometimes too dim to read in normal light.

- Programs let users enter inappropriate data, such as letters when the situation calls for a number, or impossible numbers, like month 13.

- Program error messages are cryptic and uninformative: "A system error has occurred." (Okay, *now* what do I do?) or: "Application ZETA01 has caused a General Protection Fault in module ZETA01 at 0025:0001." *That's* the helpful message I got *every time* I used one of the research tools for this book.

MANGLED MANUALS

> *"[Computer experts] seem incapable of putting themselves in other people's places and seeing how what they are saying and doing must appear to others."*
>
> —THOMAS SOWELL, *Forbes*,
> (September 13, 1993)

The books that accompany computer systems don't make it easy for users to learn about those systems. They're often written by programmers who don't remember what it was like to be a novice. Typical problems include:

- Manuals written for the convenience of the software vendor instead of the user. For example, the manual for Microsoft's Word version 6.0 combines Macintosh and PC manuals into a single volume, forcing users to slog through dozens of paragraphs of irrelevant material.

- Assuming knowledge users may not have. The above manual for Word is over eight hundred pages long but has *no glossary*.

- Manuals that don't distinguish between core features and frills. These books go through features one by one, sometimes (incredibly) in alphabetical order, rather than starting with the functions most users will need and breaking out advanced or little-used features in separately designated sections.

- Perfect binding rather than loose-leaf binding, which makes annotation, page replacement, and updates impossible for all intents and purposes. (This binding also makes manuals impossible to lay flat when using them—a mundane but fundamental flaw.)

Rampant Feature-itis

As software becomes more complex and as systems take on new tasks such as video conferencing and digital imaging, there's much more for users to learn. Certainly, graphical interfaces such as Microsoft Windows are easier to use than old-style command-line prompts, but that advance is more than counteracted by the hundreds of new commands users must master to use new programs to their potential.

Access Denied

Just gaining access to the computer system may be an exercise in frustration. The old corporate mainframe, the new departmental network, and the work group network probably all have their own unique *passwords*, each of which change every ninety days. Most systems today don't have a "single point of entry" that would grant access to all connected resources with a single password. As a result, users wind up putting their passwords on sticky notes that they attach to their computer screens. Too much security = no security.

Why Don't Organizations Train Users Adequately and Properly?

Naïve Management

Here are three quotations from different companies that advertised in a randomly selected issue of *Business Week* (June 18, 1990):

> *"You glide effortlessly, even seamlessly, from one application to another . . . your productivity will soar. With the greatest of ease . . . even non-programmers can create everything from applications to animation."*
>
> (Zenith Data Systems/ Groupe Bull)

"You don't need a degree in nuclear physics to operate a MultiPersonal Computer—only a little intuition. . . . A MultiPersonal Computer comes ready to roll, right out of the box."

(MOTOROLA COMPUTER GROUP)

"Using Microsoft Excel and Word together requires very little brain power."

(MICROSOFT)

Even allowing for ad copywriters' usual hyperbole, one marvels at such outright absurdity. There's *never* been a computer that is "ready to roll, right out of the box." Naïve business managers who believe these sorts of ridiculous claims are loath to spend money and time on user education. They're also more likely to cut user training budgets early in the downsizing process. A recent *Government Computer News* article begins: "What's the first thing that gets cut when Defense Department budgets shrink? Training—even crucial software development and computer training."

BUSY EXPERTS

Mark Klein of Gateway Management Consulting in New York suggests that one reason so many companies don't offer formal computer education is that the computer staff is too busy "fixing what's broken." In addition, IT experts are working hard to keep up with demand for new networks and new applications such as Electronic Document Interchange (EDI) and Executive Information Systems (EIS). Who's got time to develop and teach computer classes?

WHAT TRAINING THERE IS DOESN'T WORK

U.S. organizations spent $3.2 billion for outside computer training in 1992, according to market researcher Dataquest. Much of that money was thrown away. Why?

❏ Outside trainers may know their product well, but they may not know how a given company's employees use that product. One result: wasted time learning features that employees won't ever use.

❏ Courses from one vendor don't address issues in making that vendor's product work with other vendors' products.

❏ Courses cover a specific *version* of a product, which the vendor updates within six months, sometimes rendering much of the prior training obsolete.

❏ Employees attend vendor courses that address features and functions but never touch on limitations and problems. As a consequence, the users pick up about half of what they need.

❏ Companies send users and technical staff to public technical seminars. When employees return to work, they're inundated by the mail and memos and voice-mail messages that have stacked up during their absence. They never get a chance to practice or reinforce what they've just learned, with the result that they forget half of it within two months.

❏ In-house training often doesn't work because employees get interrupted every few minutes for phone calls, problems, meetings, etc. Computer classes are tough enough without constant distractions derailing the train of thought.

❏ Groups are too large and too mixed in technical background. In large classes that include both novices and veterans, beginners get confused, experts become bored, few students ask questions, and no one learns very much.

CONSEQUENCES OF MYTH #10

The best-designed computer system is worthless if employees only use it grudgingly and haltingly—or not at all. Uneducated users can render millions of dollars of capital equipment sterile. Keeping training costs low merely shifts costs to local "gurus" who may or may not know their stuff, or how to communicate it efficiently. The local gurus don't look at user education as a primary job responsibility, either, because it may only represent 10 percent of what they do and may not even be reflected in their job assignments. In addition, the costs shift to computer support resources, such as in-house help centers or pay-by-the-minute vendor hot lines. And one of the worst side effects of inadequate and inappropriate user education is *technophobia*.

Technophobic Users

Technophobia is the fear of anything high-tech, a feeling of discomfort with computers. A poll conducted by Dell Computer Corporation in 1993 reports that 55 percent of all Americans are technophobic to some degree, 23 percent of adults aren't comfortable using computers, and 25 percent of adults surveyed miss the days when typewriters rather than computers sat on their desks. Technophobia hinders the assimilation of technology into the workplace. It prevents companies from enjoying the full benefits of the expensive systems they've purchased. Its elements include:

- A fear of damaging the computer;
- A fear of irrevocably destroying valuable information;
- A fear of having to type at a keyboard;
- A fear of being replaced by the computer;

❏ A fear of ignorance, a correctable temporary condition, being misinterpreted by peers, subordinates, and/or superiors as stupidity.

Over time, technophobia will wane as employees who grew up with computers move up the corporate ranks. Meanwhile, however, it's a major productivity barrier.

Figure 6   The Education Gap

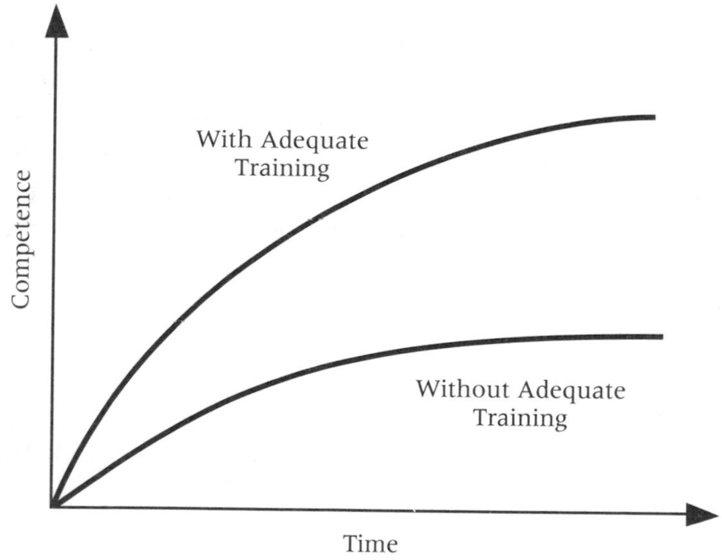

THE PROBLEM

Plato wrote, "The tools that would teach men their own use would be beyond price." Alas, information systems don't even begin to approach that ideal. Computers really haven't become easier to use over the past several years, despite the hoopla. The graphical interface has helped, but at the same time, software features have grown beyond the user's ability to keep up.

Programs still impose intimidating and inflexible user interfaces, difficult-to-remember commands, and inconsistent conventions. They fail to keep users properly informed, they handle errors poorly, and they don't discriminate between reasonable and unreasonable responses. On top of all that, software vendors redesign their products every few months. On the hardware side, computers are a long way from "plug and play."

ACTION PLAN

Computer education isn't a panacea. It won't fix systems that didn't take people into account in the first place; it won't make hard-to-use systems easy-to-use; it won't smooth over the incompatibilities of unplanned systems. But it can make just about any information system more useful and more used. It can also pay off in a big way: Motorola estimates that each dollar spent on computer training pays back $30 in improved productivity within three years.

User-Helpful Systems

Individual companies can't do much right away about the current sad state of user-ignorant systems, but they can take the following steps:

❑ Evaluate commercial products on the basis of usability as well as feature lists, speed, and cost. In-house computer support specialists can help with this function.

❑ Let hardware and software vendors know how their products fall short in the human-factors area, so they can do something about it in the future; in short, become activist customers. If they see enough money in it, computer companies will eventually make their products easier to use. For example, manufacturers are starting to focus on the home and small-office markets. To sell in those markets, they'll have to make their products more user-friendly because those customers don't have IS staffs to help them figure out the systems.

▢ Add layers of user-helpful technology onto standard commercial products. Replace vendor manuals with shorter, clearer ones from computer publishers or in-house support staff. Augment on-line help systems with annotations (Microsoft Windows, for example, has this capability, but almost no one knows about it).

The Right *Kind* of Education

Whether in-house staff or outside trainers provide IT education, the subject matter, style, and types of training are critical success factors.

TECHNOLITERACY

Just as language skills are vital to meaningful and efficient communication, technoliteracy determines how effectively employees can use the sophisticated new tools of today's workplace. Technoliteracy is no longer a luxury for the technically inclined; it's a necessity for the successful, progressive corporation, as we've already seen.

The first place to start in moving toward a technoliterate organization is a class in *general computer concepts*. Product managers and plant engineers don't all have to understand the fine details of programming, but every employee should have a chance to learn what a network does and how RAM memory differs from disk memory. As Peter Stephenson comments in *LAN Times*, "I have no objection to seminars that take a product-oriented turn. But I think there is a need for a 'core curriculum' in network technology."

Such a class—which could be as short as one or two days—would also cover essentials such as backing up data files, virus prevention techniques, where to get computer help within or outside the company, and how to tell when the computer's not working right. Users who have in-depth training on specific programs but lack these fundamentals of computer literacy are likely to make time-wasting mistakes and spend a lot more time than necessary to calling tech support.

Another example of appropriate education: classes that teach people *how to type*. Knowing all about the company's electronic mail system won't make the financial executive who types two words per minute an efficient e-mail user. Like it or not, the technology for reliably communicating with computers by voice alone is a ways off; in the meantime, the primary way of interacting with a computer, mouse or no mouse, is through the keyboard. Typing skills are no longer only associated with administrative assistants; they're helpful for high-powered managers, too. Which brings us to the next topic.

THE CASE OF THE RELUCTANT EXECUTIVE

Managers and executives have particular education needs that don't jibe well with typical end-user training. They don't want to appear ignorant in front of peers or subordinates. They need generalist rather than specialist IT education. They can't easily carve time out for two- or three-day classes. But they need a working knowledge of IT basics as much as anyone.

Creative approaches to executive education are emerging. Computer Associates and CEO Institutes offer a "boot camp" for executives with seminars targeted to their needs and interests. Organizations such as AT&T have support staff prepare "executive briefings" on Saturday afternoons, when there aren't any meetings or ringing telephones. Those briefings cover technology trends rather than details on using specific products. Classes that focus on communication technology such as electronic mail and "groupware" are well received by senior managers. The most important thing when developing an education plan is not to neglect these key participants in the company's IT future.

TARGETING TECHNOPHOBIA

It's fine to provide education on specific computer applications, but people have to feel comfortable with computers if they're to use them effectively as tools. Some types of education target technophobia specifically:

- Workshops that demonstrate you can't hurt a computer by typing the wrong thing, and how difficult it is (in a properly designed system!) to accidentally destroy computer information.

- Classes that show users how they can quickly realize productivity gains by learning some fairly simple computer applications.

- Computer dictionaries, put together by the support or training groups, that come with every workstation to help users gradually but surely overcome the jargon barrier. (These can be on-line, too, to make it less likely they'll be lost.)

SPECIAL DELIVERY

The most effective technique for training users on specific programs is personal "hands-on" instruction, where a professional instructor (not necessarily an employee "guru") familiar with how the company uses the program guides a small group of students with similar abilities through the program's use while they work through examples on a PC or terminal at their desks. Employees learn by doing (the catch phrase is *kinesthetic learning*), and the instructor can easily identify students having trouble.

Straight-lecture classes can also be effective if accompanied by projection of a "live" computer screen for demonstration and examples. These kinds of classes can address larger audiences than feasible with hands-on instruction, and they can cover more topics in a given time. However, it's difficult to know how well the people are assimilating the material. Many students feel too self-conscious to speak up when something's unclear to them; and missing one key concept can mean losing the benefit of the rest of the lecture. Without hands-on reinforcement, retention also suffers. So these kinds of classes need to be as interactive and informal as possible. Fortunately, with portable computers and LCD panels that fit onto a traditional overhead projector, the cost of this type of class has dropped quite a bit since the days when one had to build or rent an auditorium with a giant Barco or Electrohome projector built into the ceiling.

Many organizations are using more creative techniques for instruction delivery. One large insurance company filmed a fifteen-minute video on fixing common laser printer problems, and sent copies to all its office managers nationwide. As video production costs continue to drop, this is no longer a cost-prohibitive option. It may be cheaper than holding classes or adding staff to the help desk.

Computer-Based Training, or CBT, is another technique gaining in popularity because of its low cost compared with personal instruction. CBT uses an individual, self-paced, hands-on approach in which a user learns from a specially designed educational computer program. The program presents information (usually with color graphics and perhaps with sound and animation also) and periodically asks questions to test understanding. If the user answers correctly, the computer moves on to the next topic; if not, the computer might analyze the error and provide an explanation of why the answer is wrong.

A new industry is forming of companies specializing in designing CBT systems ("courseware") using multimedia development tools ("authorware"). The on-line tutorials now packaged as part of many popular application programs are examples of low-end CBT. Sophisticated CBT programs can change the lesson sequence on the fly to adapt to a particular student's needs and abilities. It's self-paced, repeatable, and interactive. And today, digital video technology is making it possible to distribute CBT on CD/ROM disks instead of the more expensive laser disks.

Whatever the type of user education—personalized hands-on, straight-lecture, or CBT—it's got to happen in an atmosphere conducive to concentration. This means a closed room away from telephones, and checking pagers and portable phones at the door. Computer concepts can be abstract and difficult to grasp. Interruptions are one reason most people become frustrated trying to learn about computers by reading manuals at their desk, where the phone rings every five minutes. They're the reason I read trade journals on airplanes instead of in the office.

Finally, companies such as Hewlett-Packard and Apple Computer are experimenting with "just-in-time" training: CD/ROM disks that users consult when they need specific information, rather than structured classes or CBT sessions. While *kanban* training doesn't replace structured education, it can certainly *supplement* it.

THE REALITY

Through vigorous programs of computer literacy courses, technophobia workshops, and specific application instruction, businesses can motivate workers to overcome user-ignorant interfaces to use the tools they have. Businesses that also emphasize usability and ergonomics more strongly when evaluating new software will reduce the need for training over time.

The *TSD* model of computer support specifies three components: training, support, and documentation. We've looked at the *T*, now it's time to look at *S* and *D* in the next chapter.

MYTH 11

Computers Are Reliable, So We Don't Need Support

" 'Tis not enough to help the feeble up, but to support him after."

WILLIAM SHAKESPEARE,
Timon of Athens (1608)

THE MYTH

A large California defense contractor adopts a "zero-defect" philosophy and charges midlevel managers with implementing it throughout the organization. Those managers sally forth to adjust processes and budgets to reflect the new attitude. One side effect is a cutback of funds to the computer support team. One member of that team tells me, "We're understaffed, but we can't get more personnel or resources because the very existence of our group flies in the face of zero-defects. If our systems are supposed to be perfect, why do we need a support team? Management has told us to expect more cutbacks; meanwhile, users are up in arms because they can never reach us."

Even with the best systems, the best end-user training, and the most laudable management philosophy, IT users will still run into problems. What happens then is a matter of support, which for the purposes of this chapter means *documentation* and *problem solving*. Support is the great productivity secret of successful automators. Many companies give it short shrift, though, introducing the next in our series of myths: *computers are reliable, so we don't need support.*

DEBUNKING MYTH #11

"Why can't we build computer systems with the same inherent reliability that we find in other designed artifacts such as bridges and buildings?"

Tom Forester and Perry
Morrison, *Computer Ethics* (1994)

Computer downtime is an ongoing problem. A 1991 study of *Fortune* 1,000 firms by FIND/SVP in New York estimated its cost at $4 billion a year. A 1993 study by Infonetics Research, Inc., estimates that firms with over a thousand employees waste an average of $3.8 million a year from network downtime. A 1993 Gallup poll indicates that although downtime hours are slowly decreasing in the nineties, more organizations report that downtime *cost* is increasing, to thousands of dollars per hour. Why, indeed, aren't computer systems reliable? And why don't customers do more about it?

The Nature of the Beast

IT computers are *digital* computers, which represent everything in terms of "on" or "off" signals (zeros and ones). This explains part of their essential vulnerability: When they're wrong, they're completely wrong. If a signal isn't a one, it's a zero; there's no middle ground. Compare this to an *analog* device, such as the aneroid barometer hanging on my living room wall. If the barometer's wrong, it's most likely just off by a little bit; it reads 30.1 for atmospheric pressure instead of 30.2, for example. It'll still work, just not as accurately. Analog devices, in this sense, are much more stable than digital devices, as anyone who's ever had a digital watch go on the fritz can attest.

A digital computer is a "discrete state machine," a fancy way of saying that the accuracy of the end result depends upon the accuracy of everything leading up to it: All those ones and zeros, millions of them, have to be right for the machine to work. It doesn't take much of a mistake, therefore, to create a major problem in a digital computer. For example, in the event of a slight power dip, a "1" in a computer's memory could change to a "0," changing a yes command to a no command. If that computer is running a nuclear power plant, it could open a valve when it's supposed to close the valve. The computer won't just open that valve partway, either; it'll open it completely because there's no gray area between yes and no.

Dozens of Achilles' Heels

Many critical failure points lurk in a typical computer:

- Power supplies can go out, disabling the entire system.
- Processors can fail (the von Neumann computer design relies heavily on a main CPU chip).

◻ Memory chips can fail, causing the machine to shut itself down.

◻ The disk storage devices that provide the computer's "consciousness" every time it's turned on can fail, again rendering the system unusable.

◻ Video circuitry can break, blanking the user's window to the machine.

◻ Network cables can loosen, breaking off contact with the rest of the company.

◻ One program can try to use an area of memory allocated to another program, bringing the computer to a screeching halt.

◻ Viruses, programs that multiply and propagate more-or-less invisibly, may damage data, corrupt programs, and necessitate a lengthy and costly "disinfection" process.

It doesn't have to be this way, of course. Reliability costs money, however, and (especially in small computers) manufacturers pass over extra features because they'd add cost and reduce sales. (And because customers don't demand them. . . .)

Multivendor Environments

Today's computer systems mix and match hardware and software from many different vendors. Design practices used by some vendors aren't used by others. Sometimes, "shortcuts" that work as long as everything is from the same vendor *don't* work when other suppliers' products connect in to the mix. As we've seen, industry standards lag product development by several years in some cases, so there's not a unified set of rules to guide product design.

A good example is SNMP, or Simple Network Management Protocol, a design "standard" supposed to make it easier to manage networks from a central point. One company's SNMP product might not work with another's, because the standards are still loosely defined. These incompatibilities often mean a more failure-prone computer system.

Power to the People

Not so many years ago, nearly all computers lived in large, glass-walled rooms protected by doors with passcard locks. Today, most computer power is on desks in unsecured offices, where neophytes have access to hardware and software and network cables. The trend toward "distributed" computing has many advantages, but its downside is a much-increased risk that novices will try to add hardware or modify software setups themselves, without full knowledge of the procedure. Other risks include plugging small computers into the same circuit as coffee machines and photocopiers; spilling soda on tape cartridges; disconnecting and reconnecting devices without turning them off first, and so forth. The physical environment is no longer a controllable variable.

Trend to Complexity

We've discussed the modern trends toward linking small computers in "client/server" networks, moving data out into the workplace in "chunks" rather than keeping it all in one central repository, and using "fatware" programs with dozens or even hundreds of features no one may need. Add to this a new dynamic of intense price competition, and you have all the elements for an explosion in the complexity-per-dollar ratio. Companies can keep their IT budgets constant and buy a lot more complexity than they had last year.

Is complexity *necessarily* a cause of lower reliability? Biological organisms, like people, are far more complex than computers but still reasonably reliable. Consider, though, how many millions of years living things have had to get it right. Digital computing is about forty-five years old. That's a lot of complexity to digest in a very short time.

Vendors Wash Their Hands

More and more, vendors are getting out of the "free" or "bundled" support business—even companies that have offered such service for over a decade. This means that computer companies have much less incentive, economically, to build reliable products. If the customer has to pay $2 a minute for support calls, that might be a nice profit center for the vendor; it's even possible that the vendor will make more money with a mildly defective product than with a defect-free one!

When support was free, there was every motivation to reduce the need for it by designing in ease of use and reliability. That motivation is waning, if it hasn't disappeared entirely. As Stratford Sherman commented in *Fortune*, "One of the remarkable aspects of the business is the way it first causes you horrific problems, and then takes your money to solve them."

WHITHER SUPPORT?

If, then, computers are largely unreliable (and not getting much better very quickly), why don't companies provide adequate resources for documentation and troubleshooting? Managers don't *know* their systems are fragile; they don't see the problems that fragility causes; and they don't perceive the benefits of providing proper support. As a result, computer user populations are growing faster than support staff. Further, managers believe vendor and dealer support to be much better than it is. They don't appreciate the rapid rise in complexity-per-dollar. And finally, businesses have used their mainframe and minicomputer experience as a basis for budgeting client/server network support, while local area network support actually costs much more than mainframe support—three times as much, in one recent study by Forrester Research, Inc.

CONSEQUENCES OF MYTH #11

The "support gap" (see figure 7) results in several problems that ultimately cost a lot more than adequate support up front would cost:

- Employees who avoid using systems entirely;
- Employees who avoid using advanced system features;
- More downtime;
- Employee frustration and mistrust;
- Problems that don't get fixed;
- Time wasted by experts hired to do other things;
- Time wasted by users trying to fix things inefficiently (the "futz" factor).

The net effect is a shift in costs from IT to the end-user community, where those costs become hidden and unbudgeted—making it even tougher to measure IT productivity. Thus does one problem beget another.

ACTION PLAN

Our "action plan" suggests, first, that companies start paying for reliability features and preventive-maintenance programs they haven't wanted to pay for in the past. Next, we address what an

Figure 7   The Support Gap

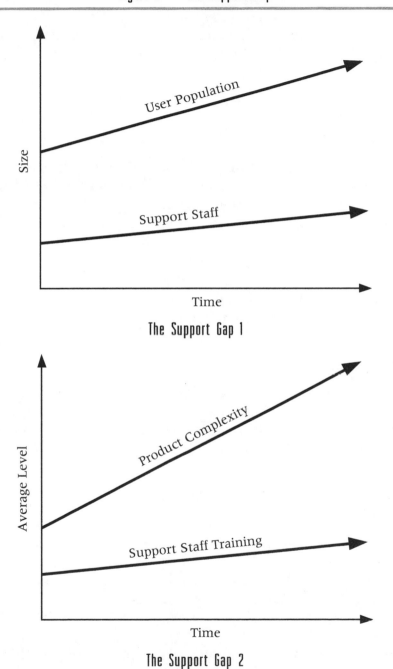

The Support Gap 1

The Support Gap 2

appropriate IT support plan might look like: Who should provide it, what functions should be provided, and how.

Pay Me Now or Pay Me Later

BUILDING IN PROTECTION

The more reliable the systems, the less need for expensive support resources to minimize even more expensive downtime. So step one in any support action plan should be to maximize reliability by intelligent deployment of some cost-effective technology.

Not much can be done about the inherent fragility of a "discrete state machine" or a von Neumann design because these are fundamental characteristics of today's digital computers. Some of the other failure points, however, can be addressed at reasonable cost:

❑ Battery backups can help prevent power interruptions. Today, these can cost as little as $200 for typical PCs and $1,000 for typical network servers. Often, all that's really needed is enough battery time to perform an orderly shutdown of the computer so files don't get lost or damaged.

❑ "Error-correcting" memory can tolerate failure. I've seen mainframes where a technician actually pries a memory chip out of a circuit board while the computer's running, and it doesn't miss a beat because it detects the problem and works around it. This technology isn't generally available for small computers, though; it's not that hard to implement—but computer customers haven't demanded it, or indicated they're willing to pay for it.

❑ "Hot fix" systems can detect disk problems on the fly and avoid them. This, too, is old technology; it's been around in minicomputers and network servers for years, but it's only recently finding its way into small-computer disk systems. Add about $200 to the cost of a PC and you've got hot-fix capability. Do many buyers specify it? Do I need to ask?

❏ Virus detection and removal utilities have become quite sophisticated, able to protect mainframes, networks, and PCs against 99 percent of the virus threats out there.

By implementing some of the above technology, organizations can move their systems from *normal commercial availability* (99 percent) to *high availability* (99.9 percent) without the costs of *fault tolerant systems* (100 percent), which ensure continuous operation under all conditions. Fault tolerant systems are great; they often have two of everything and can even call up their manufacturer when something goes wrong and order the appropriate part so it's sitting on the system administrator's desk the next morning! But they're better than necessary for many applications where high availability is good enough.

EARLY DETECTION

After a company does what it can reasonably do to improve reliability, the second step is to institute a program to catch computer failures before they become catastrophes. Most computer failures in my experience provide a little early warning time, but customers have to have the stethoscopes out periodically to detect the wheezing. That means *preventive maintenance*, something a lot of firms give lip service to but not many actually implement.

The irony is that preventive maintenance and diagnostics routines don't have to take that much time or cost a lot. For small systems, users can run diagnostic suites themselves to test memory, disk storage, the central processor, and printers—as long as support technicians set up the tests. For large systems, there aren't as many to deal with, so the procedures aren't too burdensome. If a company claims its technical people don't have time for PM and diagnostics, fine; outsource it! The world teems with computer companies that can perform routine diagnostics on a contract basis.

"Docs Okay"

What should proper support look like? We begin with documentation.

Don't Rely on the Vendors

As we saw in the last chapter, computer product vendors generally create poor-quality product documentation. Even when the writing quality is high, the *quantity* may be intimidating; too much documentation is as bad as too little. Vendor documentation has gone downhill in terms of physical format, too; the old looseleaf binder has been replaced by a dozen separate booklets and books that are difficult to keep track of.

To some extent, the commercial book publishers have stepped in to fill the gap, usually outdoing the software vendors. But no book for the general market can address in detail how a given company uses a particular product.

❏ One Chicago company helps computer users approach their nine-hundred-page user manuals by producing one- or two-page summaries of key product features in bullet format, with references to chapters in the manual.

❏ Every time a new version of a program comes out, that company's IT gurus issue a "What's New" and "What's Changed" memo to users—again in bullet format, with user manual references.

WRITERS WHO KNOW WRITING

When programmers try writing user manuals, the results can be abominable. Some programmers have an economical facility with English and can put themselves in the novice's shoes when writing, but they're few and far between. (If some of them work for you, get them frequent pay raises.) Their very familiarity with the products, alphabet soup, and technojargon works against their ability to write manuals that users can understand and use.

CREATIVE DISTRIBUTION

Massive user manuals may not be as useful as single-topic "tech notes" distributed to users on an as-needed basis. One new technology that facilitates such targeted distribution is the *fax-back*, or *fax-on-demand*, system. Support staff prepare one- or two-page notes on common problems, which they then store on a computer equipped with fax circuits. Users can dial up the fax-back computer, request the relevant document (the first one they get is the tech note *index* with each note's code number and a brief description), key in their fax machine's number, hang up, and receive the tech note within minutes. The beauty of this system is fourfold: most users have ready access to a fax machine; the tech note becomes part of the user's permanent documentation; the system's entirely automated and available round the clock; and users avoid information overload by getting help only on the topics giving them trouble.

VIRTUAL DOCUMENTATION

Why should all, or even most, computer documentation be on paper? Putting it "on-line" has many advantages:

- It's usually cheaper to produce and always cheaper to distribute;

❑ It's easier to update, especially if it's stored in one central place;

❑ It's available to everyone with a workstation;

❑ No one can "lose" it;

❑ It gets new users accustomed to the machine;

❑ It lends itself to automatic indexing and "key word" searches.

On-line documentation requires different design than paper documentation; the "page size" is about half the size of paper, for example. Putting graphical illustrations on-line can be a bit tricky, and navigating on-line documents has to be fairly simple. So it makes sense to hire people with these design skills to help assemble electronic help. But it's worth it; with the advent of multimedia hardware and software, it's now possible to create digital documents that use color graphics and even animations to get ideas across. And vendors such as Adobe are working on software to help workers on different systems read the same digital documents.

NEED-TO-KNOW BASIS

Finally, to help computer users avoid being overwhelmed—and to avoid inciting users to make system changes they're not trained to understand—companies can limit user documentation on a "need-to-know" basis. For example, after a standard installation of Microsoft's Windows products, several "read me" files reside on the user's PC, some of which cover topics that should only be addressed by experienced technicians. Restricting distribution of such documentation makes sense, at least until users have completed an appropriate training course on the system.

The IT SWAT Team

Contrary to popular belief, good documentation can't *replace* human support resources, though it's great for many situations and can reduce the need for "live" help. When a computer user has a problem, support staff can dispatch a technician if needed; suggest a way to get by in the meantime; and arrange to change the user's software setup. When a user has a question, support staff can explain concepts understandably and answer specific questions quickly. In both cases, a support tech can provide something no book or on-line system can provide: a calm, reassuring presence to help overcome the feelings of inadequacy, ignorance, frustration, and impatience that are so frequent when people meet the "dark side" of computers.

WHO SHOULD DO IT?

There are real dangers in relying on software vendors to provide 100 percent of a company's support needs. Frankly, I just don't recommend it.

For one thing, as Ed Foster, editor of *InfoWorld*, points out in the July 25, 1994, issue, in the modern multivendor environment, one can't reasonably ask individual vendors to be responsible for testing and warranteeing their product with everyone else's products. "If they were," Foster writes, "no vendor would ever ship a product again." One winds up wrestling with Finger-Pointing Syndrome, where everyone blames the others' products for causing the problems. (Thankfully, one organization is addressing this problem: The Networking Technical Support Alliance is a group of internetworking companies that agree to work together to solve customer problems when the customer's multivendor environment includes companies that belong to the NTSA. But, as of this writing, the NTSA is the only such group I'm aware of.)

For another, the costs are moving right up there with phone-sex lines (and if that analogy seems a stretch, consider that many software companies are now using "900" numbers). Can a company really afford to pay $2 a minute for end-user support once they use up their *one* free support credit (Corel, Adobe)? Can it afford to pay $25 per "incident" (read: call), or $15,000 a year to support a *single product* (WordPerfect)? Will employees hesitate to use such expensive options when it's not *their* money they're spending? Users can become defensive about such charges: "The company forced this #@$% program on me, they can darn well pay for the support calls."

Third, the level of expertise vendors provide is variable, to say the least. I've heard from hundreds of end-users who feel they've known more about the product than the vendors' support staff have. My personal experience bears that out; I frequently end up instructing vendor support techs when I run into a problem, and I've often identified the problem when they couldn't.

So, should customers train their own support staff, or contract the function out to third-party Help Desks? Much depends on how much uniqueness characterizes the customer's systems; the more unusual or customized they are, the less the chance that third-party support contracts will work. Cost is a factor, too. The database of problems and solutions that accumulates over time can be a valuable tool in making the environment more productive; in-house support ensures the availability of that database. Finally, convenience plays a role. As long as customers can call on an outsourced support team for *all* their IT questions, it can work; otherwise, you lose the benefit of "one-stop shopping."

A SUPPORT SUCCESS STORY

A good way to approach this question is to look at a success story. Stac Electronics makes disk-compression software for personal computers. In early 1993, it was facing the usual support problems: long telephone hold times, frustrated customers, and burned-out technicians. A few months later, hold times were down to three minutes from thirty, customer satisfaction ratings were higher, and technicians were both happier and more productive. What did they do?

For one thing, Stac started logging calls in a computer database. Computer support just can't be done effectively without some form of *automated tracking system*. If support staff, whether internal or contracted, don't log problems and questions, there's no documentation to form a basis for charting a course of improvement. There's also no database of history for support analysts to use as a reference; the result is a lot of wheel-reinvention.

Sometimes, technicians resist using a call logging tool because documenting calls takes time. Properly designed systems minimize that time, however, allowing technicians to enter problem and solution information into the database while the user's on the phone. In the long run, this *saves* time because technicians can find past solutions in the database using key word searches, and because the company can use the database to identify and correct the problems that generate the most calls.

Next, Stac started asking its computer users what they needed. (What a radical concept!) Fast response was number one on the list.

Third, Stac changed its priorities in accordance with customer needs. Computer users don't necessarily need immediate solutions in every case, but they always want quick response from support techs. By focusing on answering the calls quickly and faxing appropriate tech notes within a few minutes, instead of trying to solve each problem with the user on the phone, 90 percent of the users got what they needed much faster. Response time doesn't obviate the need for good resolution time, but it's more important to most users to get a quick response than an instant solution.

Quick response times also result in fewer hang-ups. In 1993, IBM's PC HelpCenter (which has hundreds of technicians) logged average hold times of about two minutes, with an 11 percent hang-up rate. By 1994, hold times had dropped to about thirty seconds, reducing hang-ups to 3 percent.

Fourth, Stac began to prioritize calls instead of treating each one equally. Users with current versions of the product got preferential treatment. In a corporate Help Desk, a similar policy might provide better service for users running corporate-standard software and hardware. This policy, in turn, reinforces the benefit to the customer of adhering to standards.

More Implementation Tips

For companies setting up internal IT support staffs, I'd just add a few key elements to the Stac formula for success:

❏ Make sure there's some sort of *feedback mechanism* so that the training, documentation, and system design people find out what sort of problems users are having out in the field.

❏ Get the support group involved in the *design and/or selection* of new computer products. These people are the experts in supportability. Too often, IT managers say to support teams, "Here's what's out there; support it." Looking at supportability from the earliest stages of product development or selection is, in the long run, a more productive approach.

❏ Have the support team focus on *user productivity* above all else. This might mean swapping components, rerouting reports to a different printer, or falling back to a previous version of a product while the tech staff researches the problem off-line. Getting the customer up and running should be job one.

❏ Try to provide *one-stop shopping*, so that computer users don't have to keep half a dozen support numbers on their Rolodexes—one for software, one for hardware, one for networks, one for upgrades, and so forth. This means consolidation of formerly autonomous support groups, and a lot of cross-training. As support expert Ralph Wilson states, "Eventually a single help desk for all technology questions will probably have to emerge if users are to be helped quickly and efficiently."

❏ Ensure adequate *education* for support staff. Most computer users would rather put up with a short wait and talk to an expert than get routed immediately to someone who doesn't know what they're doing.

❏ Train support staff in *customer service and communications skills*. These people have to interact with all levels of user expertise, and they have to be good listeners as well as good explainers. Just putting top technicians on a telephone hot line won't work. Good support communicators also make better educators who can help computer users learn to help themselves on routine issues.

❏ Be wary of interactive voice response (IVR) phone systems, the kinds that say, "Press one for this, press two for that," etc. These systems can take forever to navigate, route users where they don't want to go, and ask questions users can't answer. They're also woefully inflexible compared with humans. Systems offering prerecorded answers to common questions are enormously inconsiderate of users' time and far inferior to the fax-back systems discussed above. Until voice recognition technology and artificial intelligence are much further along than they are today, IVR systems are a good way to frustrate users, as customers of Lotus Development Corporation will attest.

❏ Improve support staff's ability to troubleshoot local area networks by investing in software to help *map* the network so technicians can know what equipment and software is where, and won't have to play twenty questions with users who may not know the details of their own workstation's setup. Intel's chief executive, Andrew Grove, commented in *The Wall Street Journal* (October 18, 1993), "Nobody has a clue where all that stuff is. . . . At Intel, there are literally tens of millions of dollars that ooze through the organization."

❑ Explore *pre-emptive troubleshooting*: ways of communicating known problems and their solutions to the user community. An IT newsletter, for example, can become a vehicle for support staff to answer common questions en masse.

THE REALITY

Companies that recognize the fallibility of information systems even as they're relying on them more each day will take steps to improve reliability and catch problems in the bud. Next, they'll provide the kind of end-user documentation and technical support that users need, without relying entirely on vendors or dealers. Most important, they'll track what kinds of problems and questions users run into, so systems and training and documentation can be improved continually. The most forward-looking companies will bring support experts into the loop when designing new IT systems and considering commercial products to ensure that supportability is built in rather than tacked on. In this way, those companies can turn computer support from a necessary evil into an opportunity for systems improvement.

So far, we've identified six principles of successful IT implementation that will make problem computer projects much rarer and increase the chances of the customer getting its money's worth. The next chapter looks at how to deal with projects that *weren't* built on those principles—and aren't working as a result.

MYTH 12

If It's *Not* Working, Throw Money At It

"If making money is a slow process, losing it is quickly done."

> —SAIKAKU IHARA (1642–1693),
> JAPANESE NOVELIST, *The*
> *Millionaires' Gospel*

"When I was young I used to think that money was the most important thing in life; now that I am old, I know it is."

> —OSCAR WILDE (1854–1900),
> IRISH PLAYWRIGHT

THE MYTH

In January 1981, Roger B. Smith takes over the reins as chairman of General Motors. Sometime that year, rumor has it, he attends a robot demonstration wherein a mechanical arm picks up an egg without even cracking the shell. It's confirmation of a long-standing belief for the chairman: the answer to GM's productivity deficit compared with Japanese manufacturers is high technology. Later in the year, Smith makes a speech in which he says, "Technology leadership is what will keep us ahead in world competition."

Over the next nine years, Smith shovels $80 billion into automation projects. GM buys Electronic Data Systems (EDS) for $2.5 billion. It buys Hughes Aircraft for $5.2 billion. *Ward's Auto World* magazine was to call this massive expenditure "the mother of all technology buying binges." And it creates a new factory of the future in Hamtramck, Michigan, near Detroit, to build the Cadillac Seville and Eldorado.

The Hamtramck plant opens in 1985, sporting over 250 robots and 50 automated guided vehicles (AGVs) to move parts around. Smith gives a speech saying that "inspired and almost miraculous inventions and innovations are ready to usher in a new and golden age of opportunity." Laser measuring devices test quality. Television cameras monitor the plant floor. Lasers, controlled by fancy computers, also weld the car bodies together. The new plant will make sixty cars per hour, declares Smith, with higher fit and finish than ever before.

One year later, Hamtramck is struggling to make half that number. Robots are taking each other apart and denting car bodies; AGVs are refusing to budge on command; paint machines miss the parts they're supposed to paint. Computer experts search for software bugs. Entire production lines shut down for hours at a time. The computers linked to the laser measuring devices spew so many figures at such a speed that operators can't read them in time to make adjustments.

Surely these are merely growing pains, and technicians will iron out the bugs in time. Any new technology has its warts. Give it time.

By 1991, six years after opening its factory of the future, GM's U.S. market share has dropped from 46 percent in 1979 to 35 percent, and its North American auto operations is losing money at the rate of about $7 billion a year. By 1992, the Cadillac plant is still running a single shift and building fewer than thirty cars per hour. *Forbes* calls it "a major moneylosing operation." *Fortune* calls it "perpetually uneconomic."

What happened? The clue comes from a senior executive at one of GM's competitors, quoted in *Fortune* as saying that "GM has been operating by the philosophy that, one, there is no problem that is so intractable that we cannot solve it by throwing money at it, and two, we've got all the money in the world, and if that isn't enough, we'll get some more." Which leads us to our twelfth myth: *if it's not working, throw money at it.*

Though this book has concentrated on office systems rather than manufacturing systems, the GM story contains lessons for all high-tech projects. After all, as a VP at ABB Robotics, Inc., commented, "A robot is just a computer with mechanical arms." The disastrous miscalculations GM made in roboticizing the Hamtramck plant parallel mistakes businesses make trying to fix *any* business problem with computers. The GM story is dramatic because of its sheer magnitude, but the issues are much the same for a small business spending a few thousand dollars on a computer system.

As the reader will appreciate by now, a hundred reasons exist why computer projects can underperform or go awry. Any business that attempts to apply technology creatively or on an unprecedented scale is vulnerable to snafus; that does not imply they should never experiment. When things *do* fall apart, however, businesses can either make a realistic assessment and recover intelligently, or throw money at the problem in the mistaken belief that enough dollars can fix anything. It's inconvenient but true: There are very few computer projects that the desperate infusion of dollars alone can save.

DEBUNKING MYTH #12

Two Heads Are Worse Than One

> *"Men and months are interchangeable commodities only when a task can be partitioned among many workers* with no communication among them. *This is true of reaping wheat or picking cotton; it is not even approximately true of systems programming."*
>
> —FREDERICK P. BROOKS, JR., IBM PROJECT LEADER, *The Mythical Man-Month* (1974)

When computer projects run long, the knee-jerk reaction is to "put more people on the job." That's usually the worst possible thing one can do.

The reason is that the team must bring any new member up to speed on the project's goals, the technology involved, the work plan, and what's already been done. All that takes time away from moving the project forward. Fred Brooks, leader of IBM's System/360 project and the OS/360 operating system, has coined "Brooks' Law": Adding personnel to a late software project makes it later.

The new member also has to establish *communications* with every existing team member in a cooperative and complex endeavor. The more organizations build interdisciplinary teams to reengineer business processes, the more communications channels there are, and the longer the time necessary to bring a new member to the point where he or she can contribute to the effort.

Finally, the more people on the team, the greater the likelihood that core design concepts and consistencies will become muddled and violated. This is especially true of software projects, where individual developers have their own ideas about style, speed, and human factors design. In the extreme case, right hand–left hand syndrome creates inconsistencies that jeopardize the reliability of the finished product.

More Power

> *"Hardware is advancing almost an order of magnitude faster than software. The capabilities of the machines that are being produced today ... are ahead of our capabilities to use them in the software sense. The industry is becoming constrained ... by software."*
>
> —NEIL COLVIN, PRESIDENT,
> PHOENIX TECHNOLOGIES, LTD.

One of the more popular shows in television's history is *Home Improvement*, whose hero, Tim Taylor, lives by the single guiding principle of *more power*. If the dishwasher isn't cleaning the dishes without a prewash by hand in the sink, install a bigger pump— one that will "blast that flowery pattern clean off." If the vacuum cleaner doesn't pull all the dust off the carpet, upgrade the motor to "turbo-suck" mode. Of course, what usually ensues is one or more explosions, injury, destruction, and havoc.

Powerful office computer hardware won't shred data into bits or explode from overloading (though I have seen circuit boards that melted chips). But pouring money into hardware isn't always the best way to fix information systems that aren't working, even though plenty of business managers have the "more power" syndrome. (There's a *reason Home Improvement* is popular;

it strikes a chord.) Why do companies throw so much more money into hardware than software?

The computer industry has always treated software as a second-class citizen. The major manufacturers have historically regarded programs as products that they must offer in order to sell more high-profit hardware. IBM's lack of both interest and success in developing application software is legendary and reflects the hardware bias. The industry's subtly deprecatory view of software is contagious and infects customers. It infects the trade press: I sampled six 1994 industry magazines at random and found about two-thirds of the editorial pages devoted to hardware issues. It infects dealers: Walk into a computer store, say you want a PC, and see what the salesperson spends 90 percent of his time talking about.

Hardware is tangible, touchable, concrete; software is abstract, amorphous, vague. Most people would rather buy a *machine*, however complex, than something as wispy as the right to use a set of commands to make a computer act a certain way. One readily understands the difference between a slow machine and one twice faster; it's harder to understand the difference between user-friendly and user-ignorant software. Some benefits of good software aren't even *visible* when it's running. A program built with reusable modules may look identical on the screen to one built with a "one-off" design.

The company that buys powerful, expensive hardware to improve an underperforming system, but leaves the system saddled with unsophisticated software is wasting its money and its time.

The Component View

> "Engineers still tend to concentrate on the constructions which they themselves build rather than considering them within a context."
>
> —ARNOLD PACEY, *The Maze of Ingenuity* (1974)

Fools Rush In

The *component view* is looking at system parts instead of at the whole system. Companies may approach computer systems that aren't working with this view, asking, "What part do we need to fix?" instead of "How is the *system* letting us down?" Or they may initiate projects by thinking in terms of components, as GM did by focusing on robots and laser-welding machines instead of on systems that included people. The component view suggests that fixing parts of the process will fix the whole process, and blinds automators to the criticality of evaluating processes *before* applying technology.

The first step in improving work flow is to assess the present system. Thomas H. Davenport in *Process Innovation* points out the four benefits of mapping out process data flows in an underperforming system before trying to fix that system:

- ❏ It helps those concerned communicate with each other.

- ❏ It helps the organization plan to move from an old system to a new one.

- ❏ Understanding the old system's shortcomings helps avoid repeating the same problems in the new system.

- ❏ It provides a baseline for predicting improvements and justifying change.

Companies that funnel funds into an underperforming computer network without first mapping data flows to fully understand the problems aren't likely to spend their money wisely. One of the things they're likely to do is fix elements that don't need fixing.

Widening the Road in the Wrong Places

At GM during the eighties, communication barriers limited plant productivity more than capital equipment did. An internal 1988 memo from a top executive admitted that "our culture discourages frank and open debate." Design engineers weren't brought up to speed on how to make cars amenable to robotic assembly. *After* installing the high-tech equipment, the bottleneck was not technical so much as educational: No one knew how to run the machines.

The component view ignores the human factor and minimizes the importance of involving users, buying people-centered systems, and teaching and supporting system users.

Even on a small scale, setting aside human factors entirely, the component view comes up short. A small financial services company decides to digitize all customer correspondence and store it on a computer network server. The massive size of the digitized files quickly fills the available disk storage. Network managers rush to buy more and bigger hard drives and tape drives costing tens of thousands of dollars. Months later, a part-time employee and computer hobbyist suggests that the scanned documents be saved in a compressed format one-tenth the size of the current files. The extra storage turned out to be unnecessary after all; but it was a reasonable response from the component standpoint.

The Technofix

A manufacturing firm in a small Texas town decides to manage its inventory system with an expensive mainframe spreadsheet program. The program is quite capable of managing all the data and manipulating it to produce the variety of reports the company wants. But its data-entry facilities aren't up to the task; it can't easily verify the accuracy or appropriateness of entered data, communicate well with the operators, or easily handle more than one clerk entering data at a time. Halfway through the project, the company's president decides to put a few thousand dollars into upgrading the spreadsheet to the latest version, which is somewhat better but still not good enough. The firm would have been better off abandoning the project and starting anew with a more appropriate tool—which it eventually does.

Businesses don't like to "start over." It seems wasteful to throw away effort, time, and money. It's also impolitic to admit a mistake; if the problem can be fixed rather than replaced, perhaps the project leader's face will have only a bit of egg on it instead of an entire omelet.

Sometimes it *is* possible to fix a renegade computer system. In the case of the Cadillac plant's laser-welding computers, for example, an engineer reprogrammed the system to produce simplified charts instead of reams of figures—a classic case of reworking data *format* to explode the "more information is better" myth discussed earlier. But sometimes hanging on to fundamentally flawed systems, such as inflexible robot assembly lines or tools ill suited to the task, is the wrong move, and the business is better off junking the systems and starting fresh, however painful and embarrassing.

THE PROBLEM

The standard response to dissatisfied users and unsuccessful systems is to "put more people on the job," which causes delayed projects to slow down rather than speed up, while endangering reliability and consistency in the bargain. The second usual reaction is to buy a bigger, faster system. While upgrading hardware can help some systems work better, it won't do a thing for systems that aren't performing because of fundamental design problems, user-ignorant and buggy software, or people who don't understand how to use the technology. A component view tends to downplay human factors and ignore optimum solutions, and a reluctance to abandon sunk costs leads businesses to throw good money after bad.

ACTION PLAN

Keep the Team, Change the Project

> *"Conceptual integrity is* the *most important considera-tion in system design. It is better to have a system omit certain anomalous features and improvements, but to reflect one set of design ideas, than to have one that contains many good but independent and uncoordi-nated ideas."*
>
> —FREDERICK P. BROOKS, JR.,
> *The Mythical Man-Month* (1974)

The first thing that happens when a business puts more people onto a computer project is the loss of conceptual integrity. A far better approach is to keep the team and change the project, either in scope or in schedule.

Changing the *scope* means looking at the project's planned goals and benefits and cutting away all but the most important ones. It demands a willingness to sacrifice 100 percent func-tionality for 60 percent to avoid 0 percent.

Changing the *schedule* (which assumes there was a schedule to start with) means looking at what the project team has accom-plished and how much time it's spent, and then extrapolating a realistic schedule the team can meet. Evaluating what's been accomplished is tricky; if a project has five parts, and each is half done, is the project half done? Probably not, for the last half of any subtask invariably reveals problems and challenges that didn't surface in the first half. Brooks points out that the schedule can either be trimmed in a careful and planned way or in a haphazard and hasty way; it'll get trimmed in any event.

Giving team members better tools and a better work environment may also help rescue a runaway project, though they usually won't eliminate the need for adjusting project scope or schedule. Especially in software development, the tools of the trade—prototypers, editors, compilers, debuggers, version control tools, test utilities, all manner of esoteric-sounding stuff—can slow or speed work significantly depending on their quality and design. The "gotcha" here is not to add new tools that *no one's ever used before*. Late in a project is no time to learn a new tool.

Regarding the work environment, the business can make sure project members aren't distracted and have a quiet, well-equipped facility, preferably with access to exercise equipment or a jogging track to help clear the cobwebs. I doubt the productivity of the romantic "skunkworks" basement where team members lock themselves up for weeks of fourteen-hour workdays without coming up for air until a project's done. Who wants to be operated on by a surgeon who's been up for seventy-two hours straight? And who'll have confidence in a project created, in the end, by bleary-eyed, caffeine-soaked system designers?

According Software Its Due

A computer depends upon software in the same way, and to the same extent, that a human being depends upon his brain: Software guides the computer's resources and channels its processing power. Any athlete knows that strength and speed is useless if not controlled and directed with intelligence. Most modern business computers exhibit impressive strength and speed but are driven by inadequate software; the programs that should bring the computer's power to the customer stand in the way instead. These systems are like giants with infants' brains.

One of the lessons that emerges from the case studies and

examples in this book is that *software is more important than hardware*. Changing business attitudes is difficult, but the following steps will facilitate it:

❑ The more business people understand software, the more clearly they'll see its value. Computer literacy education and better business-side–technical-side dialogue can help remove the veil of mystery surrounding programming and make software less abstract.

❑ Once customers realize that the computer industry even now makes more money from hardware than from software, customers can adjust for that bias in evaluating new systems and expanding existing ones.

❑ Businesses that monitor the impact of computer projects can track whether software-first projects have more success vis-à-vis hardware-first projects. It will become clear that projects putting software decisions above hardware decisions are the more profitable ones.

Holistic Computing

> *"A systems approach provides a single conceptual framework. . . . Within this framework one can study the whole, move from the whole to the parts, and move back again to the whole. . . . The real world operates as a system; to better understand it requires the use of a systems approach."*
>
> —LORNE H. RUSSWURM, *Man's Natural Environment* (1974)

BOTTLENECK HUNTING

I never really understood electricity—voltage, resistance, and current—until an EE professor used the water pipe analogy in a class I took about twenty years ago. *"Voltage,"* he said, "is electrical pressure, just like water pressure in a pipe. *Resistance* impedes flow; narrow, rough pipes resist moving water more than wide, smooth pipes do. And *current* just means how much water flows through that pipe in a certain time." Suddenly, volts, ohms, and amps weren't so abstract, now that I could visualize circuits as piping networks. (I still didn't get an A, however.)

That old water pipe analogy works pretty well in computer system performance analysis, too. Substituting data for water, and cables for pipes, helps one visualize where the bottlenecks are. It doesn't do any good to widen an upstream pipe if a downstream pipe is creating the bottleneck; the flow will still be restricted by the smallest pipe.

Here's an example in computer network design. Each computer in a Local Area Network contains a circuit board that links it to the network cable. Think of it as a pipe connection with a one-inch diameter. That network cable connects to a central "server," with shared programs that everyone accesses, with a similar circuit board (another one-inch fitting). If every workstation needs access to the server, and there are thirty workstations but only one server, the one-inch connection at the server is the factor limiting performance. So it makes sense to put a two-inch connection, or even a four-inch connection, at the server: in computerese, a 32-bit or 64-bit wide circuit card, instead of the 16-bit wide circuit cards at each workstation.

Going one step further: Wouldn't data "flow" better if there were not just one, but two pipe connections to the server, and if half the workstations were on one pipe run and half on another? Of course; and the technical gurus will confirm that one of the best ways of improving network performance is to *segment* the network by dividing workstations onto different cable segments, each with its own circuit board at the server. This technique can be much more effective than putting superfast disk drives in the server computer.

This book wasn't written to teach anyone how to make computer networks run faster, so we'll leave the discussion at that point. But the concept of *bottleneck analysis* is enormously powerful, especially when it's extended to the entire system—which includes *human beings* at both ends of the pipe.

DATA FLOW ANALYSIS

Data flow analysis, or "work flow" analysis, considers *people* and *procedures* as well as electrons. At the receiving end of any information system is a person reading a report. Consider the eyes and brain of that person as a pipe connection, too. (This is an unusual visual image, I know, but bear with me here.) If the report presents a table of figures, this final pipe connection is a narrow one. If the report presents a well-designed *graph*, however, the connection is wider; people assimilate numbers much quicker from graphs, as we've seen earlier. If that graph has some *colors* to help differentiate various quantities, we've made the final connection wider still, and the person understands the data more rapidly and completely.

At the information system's origin are people as well. In inefficient systems, people fill buckets with water and hand-carry them to a water tower a mile away. This is what happens when sales reps in the field write information on paper, which they then mail or fax to an office for entry into a computer terminal. The system becomes more efficient when the pipe network extends to the point where the data is initially created: Give the sales rep a laptop with a modem link.

Some principles of data flow analysis are:

- ❑ Put data into the computer at the earliest possible time to eliminate redundant effort and the chance for introducing errors.

- ❏ Identify points in the data flow where the system is making people wait, and direct more computer resources to those points first.

- ❏ Make sure that data is available to people who might need it, but don't waste time building an intricate network that makes all the data available to everyone all the time.

- ❏ If outside companies participate in the data flow, make sure their links to the system are efficient; use modems, public data networks, satellite links, etc. (This in a nutshell is what Electronic Data Interchange is all about.)

- ❏ Get old data out of the "fast lanes" at the earliest possible time. Keep it, put it into "holding tanks" so it's there if it's needed, but don't let it slow down the whole network.

- ❏ Make sure that when data comes out of the system, it's in a format most quickly accessible for, and actionable by, human beings.

Every component of a computer system, from the brains and hands of data entry personnel, through the workstations and cables and servers and disk drives and printers, to the eyes of those reading the reports or viewing the screens, is a channel through which information flows. The system's productivity impact relates directly to how well each of those channels does its job. Using the above principles, one can identify problems and make major improvements in computer systems with minimal investment in new equipment or programs. And since the critical bottlenecks are often at the human ends, interviewing those people and watching how they interact with the system becomes a natural and necessary part of making systems work better.

BALANCING ACT

> *"Now in building of chaises,* I tell you what,*
> *There is always somewhere a weakest spot . . .*
> *And that's the reason, beyond a doubt,*
> *That a chaise* breaks down, *but doesn't* wear out."

> —OLIVER WENDELL HOLMES,
> AMERICAN AUTHOR AND
> PHYSICIAN (1809–1894),
> *The Deacon's Masterpiece*

The object in designing a computer system for maximum "up-time" is to make sure no weak spots exist. In the case of the Deacon's Masterpiece, the Deacon fitted his horse-drawn carriage with every component so carefully matched that all failed at the same moment, turning the carriage to dust. In the case of the computer system designed for balanced reliability, economics dictate that the business will replace the system with a newer one before it ever "wears out." The goal is to ensure it doesn't break down before it's replaced.

Here again, the systems approach suggests a broad perspective. Some of the least reliable parts of an information system have nothing to do with the computers themselves: power from the electric utility, noise on modem phone lines. For large systems, another relatively unreliable component is the cooling equipment used in the computer rooms; if it fails on a hot day, the tanklike reliability of the computers won't matter.

The systems approach suggests that organizations put their money into improving the reliability of the least-reliable devices in the system. These are, in order:

---

* Chaise = horse-drawn carriage.

- People;

- Computer software;

- Power, phone lines, etc.;—and

- Computer hardware.

The radical but inevitable conclusion is that to improve up-time, *don't spend money on more reliable computers!* At least, not at first, and if the machines work reasonably well to start with. How does one improve human reliability? First, by fitting systems around people. Then, by involvement, education, motivation, documentation, and support. Software reliability is improved by using commercial products, adhering to industry and corporate standards, doing usability and supportability testing, and reusing modular code components.

Do these topics sound familiar? Systems thinking supports many of the suggestions made in earlier chapters. Once one gets far enough along in myth busting, the realities start connecting, reinforcing each other.

Replace or Repair?

Professional programmers have learned through painful experience that it's easier to rewrite custom program modules that don't work than to debug them. Why so?

- Debugging requires understanding existing code, which can take more time than writing from scratch.

- Poor code has so many dependencies and hidden assumptions that it may never be possible to fully debug it— especially if its author(s) didn't document those assumptions.

- Software written without stringent quality control procedures may never be reliable, because complete testing is
  almost never possible. If the process is flawed, the product
  will inevitably be flawed also.

It's also often better to abandon commercial software than to
try fixing it through customization, vendor troubleshooting, or
workarounds.

- The more commercial software is customized and modified,
  the less supportable it is by the vendor.

- Vendors don't typically like pouring resources into fixing
  bugs in modules they're likely to rewrite for the next release
  anyway, so they drag their feet.

- New software may be available that's a better fit for the job.

Of course, when a business abandons software, whether custom or commercial, it's lost some investment in user education as
well as dollars and time. The point is that such losses may be less
than the cost of continued reworking and troubleshooting.

Technology writer William E. Perry writes about the "rat hole
theory" that describes organizations throwing money down a rat
hole with no resultant gain. He stresses that a reluctance to
assume or assign blame keeps employees from blowing the whis-
tle on "rat hole" projects, citing three U.S. Health and Human
Services Department systems that soaked up $32 million before
managers pulled the plug. Perry suggests that by blaming *processes*
rather than groups or individuals, whistle-blowers can avoid
censure and finger pointing. (He also suggests blaming recently
departed employees, which I *don't* agree with.) I'd also suggest
that employees with a stake in the company, be it profit sharing
or employee ownership, might be more likely to raise alarms
even if it means some personal discomfit.

Pursuing the abandon-and-move-forward reality one step further, Fred Brooks suggests that in any innovative computer project the first attempt won't work, so management should first build a pilot project that it *intends* to abandon. This removes the problem of assigning blame entirely because the organization never expects the pilot project to work perfectly. If that sounds expensive, think about $32 million at HHS (or $80 billion at GM). Unexpected, unplanned delays are more expensive than anticipated ones every time.

THE REALITY

Faced with a failing (or failed) computer project, the last thing a business should do is sink more money into it. What *should* it do, then?

- ❑ Keep the project team intact, resist the temptation to add to it but rather reassess and adjust project goals and schedules.

- ❑ Forget hardware for a bit and take a serious look at software: Can new programs make the system work as intended?

- ❑ Use a holistic approach to map information flows and identify bottlenecks, including those at the users' brains.

- ❑ Improve hardware to create systems with balanced performance and reliability, targeting the weakest links in the chain for enhancement.

- ❑ If none of the above works, throw the whole thing out and start over, chalking the failure up as a pilot project that just wouldn't pretend to be the real thing. Learn from the failure and try again, reconsidering the entire project process from estimating to implementing, and ask the core question that GM didn't ask: Is the project addressing the right problems? Or is it doomed to fail even if it succeeds?

If a company avoids all the pitfalls identified so far (and that's quite a few), and implements a successful information system that's well planned, appropriate for the job, conforms to reasonable standards, is well supported and properly balanced, that company is *not* out of the woods. It now faces the most difficult computer myth of all: Don't mess with success, or, if it works, leave it alone. The subject of constant improvement brings us to the next chapter, which will close part IV's discussion of implementing computer systems.

MYTH 13

If It *Is* Working, Leave It Alone

"The despotism of custom is everywhere the standing hindrance to human advancement."

—JOHN STUART MILL, ENGLISH
PHILOSOPHER AND ECONOMIST,
(1806–1873)

"When I try to summarize what I've learned since 1981, one of the big lessons is that change has no constituency. People like the status quo. . . . When you start changing things, the good old days look better and better. You've got to be prepared for massive resistance."

—JACK WELCH, CEO, GENERAL
ELECTRIC COMPANY, *Fortune*,
(January 25, 1993)

THE MYTH

As you've read this book, you've no doubt thought of a number of things your business seems to be doing right as well as perhaps a few things it seems to be doing wrong (or, in today's bland politically correct parlance, *nonoptimally*). Perhaps you are even fortunate enough to work in an organization that is not fooled by very many of the various Computer Myths at all, and has managed to install smooth and successful computer systems that have reduced costs and moved the business to new levels of performance. Perhaps you feel pretty good about that, even a little bit smug.

Watch out; for tomorrow, the world changes. *Leaving well enough alone is a risky business.*

DEBUNKING MYTH #13

Forces operating outside and inside the business inhibit change. Let's look at some common ones.

External Change Inhibitors

PROBLEMATIC PRICING

> *"In the DEC marketplace, the most popular licensing scheme is pricing by potential capacity, which is something like weighing restaurant patrons at the door and charging them according to how much they might eat. . . . A better scheme—at least for application software—would be to charge for the actual use of the software . . . this strategy would encourage people to purchase software that they might use only occasionally."*
>
> —RICHARD LaFAUCI, *Digital Review*
> (November 9, 1987)

Until late 1992, DEC charged customers thousands of dollars to move the same software from a smaller to a bigger machine. Computer Associates, a preeminent mainframe software vendor, likewise based pricing on the size of the computer running the programs. Those pricing policies make a powerful argument against buying bigger systems, even if the organization needs them. Though DEC and others have moved away from such pricing schemes, some haven't.

Even less biased licensing schemes don't really allow charges for actual use. In *metered* applications, where the system imposes a limit on the number of simultaneous users specified in the license, programs loaded into a computer's memory count as active users even though they might be in the "background"—that is, not being used! These problems jack up the cost of licenses and help inhibit companies from buying the software they need. Eventually markets will fix this sort of problem, but it may take years.

ONE-WAY SOFTWARE

To change from old to new, one must usually remove the old first. Removing a program from a computer seems like it should be a fairly simple chore. In reality, it's often difficult, tedious, time-consuming, and impossible to verify. In the small-computer industry, companies have sprung up to supply programs whose *sole purpose* is to help administrators remove programs they no longer want. Software vendors take the attitude that "our product is great, why would you ever want to remove it?" The harder it is to deinstall software, the harder change becomes.

THE IMPERFECT MARKET

We've already seen that the industry is sometimes motivated to hold new technology back instead of getting it to market as quickly as possible (Intel delaying the Pentium's release, for instance). The role of the industry in inhibiting change is even clearer in the shift from large, centralized mainframes to networks of smaller PCs and workstations. The industry doesn't want to do anything to endanger high profit margins until its customers drag it kicking and screaming into the present day.

Internal Change Inhibitors

We can't examine all the factors inhibiting organizational change in one chapter, but here are a few relevant ones.

LIVING WITH WARTS

In 1992, a computer technician makes an annual junket to visit remote branch offices and see how things are going. This visit is a good policy in that remote business locations often feel they're low on the totem pole when it comes to getting their computer problems corrected. The technician is working away on one of the terminals when suddenly it locks up. She finds the local office manager and asks what happened. The office manager scurries away for a moment, returns, and the terminal's back up. "What did you do?" asks the support tech. "Oh, I just reset the terminal controller," replies the office manager. "How many people are connected to that controller?" "Thirty." (So thirty workers' terminals just went down and came back up when the office manager reset the controller.) "Wow, how often does this sort of thing happen?" "Oh," says the office manager, "only once or twice a day."

Talk about job stress: Imagine knowing that every day your terminal is bound to freeze up once or twice, causing you to lose a few minutes' worth of work. But the workers in the branch office didn't think it unusual; they just assumed it was one of the warts of the system with which they'd have to live. People have an amazing capacity to work around what they *perceive* as computer limitations, to the point that they won't even complain about them anymore. (Of course, they might also feel that no one would care enough or be competent enough to fix the warts, also.) These workarounds, or *substitute processes*, are very expensive.

GIVING UP PRIVACY

The move from "stand-alone" workstations to networks meets some resistance because users no longer feel that their systems are truly personal, in the sense of being private. If a technician has to explore someone's personal file structure to rebuild a corrupted disk, or update workstation software for greater reliability, users accustomed to sole authority over their machine may balk. They don't call them "personal" computers for nothing.

GIVING UP CONTROL

Traditional computer systems followed the functional department organizational model rather than the process model. They also were developed when mass production was the rule, instead of flexible, "agile" production. Newer systems feature an unprecedented level of information sharing and availability, threatening established layers of control. Knowledge is power, and new systems that spread knowledge around mean those at the top may have to relinquish some of that power.

The control concern applies to technologists, too. Old-guard MIS/DP professionals became comfortable with a rigid, highly controlled, well-modeled computer architecture. They became used to dealing with one company for everything (IBM). Today's flexible, decentralized, even chaotic LAN/WAN architectures and multivendor systems are anathema to such managers.

Much of the entrenched IT establishment just doesn't trust distributed computing; it isn't safe in the sense that they've come to know safety. Those professionals have a valid viewpoint, but the world is changing, and the new systems need some of the discipline and order that they're afraid will vanish with the corporate mainframe.

At the more basic level of survival, many old-line IT professionals worry that more efficient systems might remove the need for their jobs. Their worries may be justified: Many companies lay off IT staff, for example, when moving from mainframe systems to "client/server" networks. At Turner Corporation, a large construction firm headquartered in New York, over 60 percent of the mainframe staff was let go in 1991 after the company decommissioned its mainframe in favor of a network.

Ironically, the earlier companies jumped onto the computer bandwagon, the more difficult it is for them to change today. Mike Sheehan, director of corporate planning for the Washington, D.C., Blue Cross and Blue Shield, says, "We were one of the first industries to adopt computer technology in the 1950s and we swiftly became entrenched in mainframe culture. As a result, we're slow to adopt personal computers and PC links between departments, slow to use technology to facilitate coordination-intensive structures such as cross-functional teams."

NOT KEEPING UP

Organizations can't use technology they don't know about. Companies that don't designate some individual or group to track what's going on in the computer industry will miss out on innovative new products. Granted, brand-new technology might be a risky proposition due to bugs and glitches. But this industry moves products from version 1.0 to version 1.1 in a matter of months or even weeks. Forward-looking companies may even *want* to get their hands on version 1.0, not to deploy it "live," but rather to get an idea of what it's like.

Who's tracking the computer industry for your organization?

It'll Be Obsolete Tomorrow

Companies sometimes don't buy new systems because they're afraid those systems will be obsolete tomorrow with the next of the high-tech breakthroughs that seem to occur every few weeks. The trouble is, the opportunity cost of *not* computerizing in the meantime is usually greater than the savings from waiting.

But the Old System Isn't Worn Out Yet

It used to be thrifty to run capital equipment until it broke beyond reasonable repair. John Frank, former chief engineer for a division of manufacturer John Deere, states that the company "takes great pride in making money with well-maintained, 'obsolete' machine tools." Some managers feel that well-maintained, obsolete computers that still operate must have a place within the organization, so they hang on to them. After all, they're already written off, and the company probably couldn't *give* them away.

I meet people every month trying to run 1994 software on vintage 1986 computers. The machinations they go through to make those old systems hobble through their tasks represent a tremendous drain of time and effort, not to mention ingenuity.

No One to Roll the Dice

Most companies discourage risk taking, which has the negative side effect of also discouraging experimentation and innovation. Consider Xerox's failure with its Star computer, which inspired the Macintosh and Microsoft Windows products but which almost no one outside the industry has ever heard of. The company didn't want to take the risk of marketing such a radical design.

Risk means trying something different and moving away from old ways, but, as management consultant Karl Albrecht writes, "abandoning [old ways] is often difficult because they are woven into the psyche of the culture and they have become so fossilized that no one thinks of them as options any more." In today's organizations, everything should be an option. Nothing can stand immune from examination. Existing business processes, policies, and structures that served well in the past may not serve well in the future. Nobel-winning economist Robert Solow suggests that organizations clinging to old ways of business may find the results similar to the man striking a match over and over because it worked fine the first time.

If there are no incentives to employees to take risks by changing those old processes and policies and structures—indeed, if there are *disincentives* to do so—how can change take place? Who's going to propel it?

No Way to Try It Out

> *"Knowledge must come through action; you can have no test which is not fanciful, save by trial."*
>
> —SOPHOCLES (495–406 B.C.),
> *Trachiniae*

Many technology projects don't make it past the proposal stage because there's no easy way of trying them out on a small scale. Few companies have "computer labs" where innovators can test new programs and devices without putting any on-line data at risk. It's a bit of a hard sell to get the controller to spring for a local area network that the company will use only for "playing around on."

High-tech advocates can be their own worst enemy, too. They become so enthusiastic about a product or system that they want the whole company to start using it right now. By pitching their project as a company-wide mandate, they almost ensure it won't happen.

THE PROBLEM

The rate of change in the computer field has made investing in computer tools an evolving art. Opportunity cost, fast depreciation, and human adaptability converge in a cauldron of activity that we all find confusing; and that confusion can immobilize. "If it ain't broke, don't fix it" is one of the more damaging computer myths in the long run. Systems that appear to work well (or, at least, to work at all) may have the hidden potential for great improvement. Those systems rarely do get improved because businesses don't evaluate them periodically; don't want to abandon significant investments; learn to live with their shortcomings; and generally resist change.

Many factors prevent companies and work groups from taking advantage of appropriate new technology when it becomes available. Some such factors are lack of knowledge about product advancements; fear of rapid obsolescence; desire to "wear out" existing systems before migrating to new ones; and no champions willing to risk prestige if a new system fails.

ACTION PLAN

Goading the Industry

Though few individual computer customers are large enough to make the industry stand up and take notice, the collective voice can be heard. Customers should goad the industry into doing the following to help facilitate beneficial change:

- ❑ Price software sensibly. Don't tie license fees to the size of the system on which the software runs. With licenses that specify a maximum number of users, make that *simultaneous* users, and *active* users at that—not just users who have the program loaded in memory but not doing anything.

- Help customers remove products when they're no longer wanted by providing precise information on what files get modified or added when new programs are installed; and by providing uninstall utilities to automate the removal process.

- Don't hold back on new technology unless you want your customers to consider switching vendors. As soon as the latest and greatest is ready for prime time, bring it to market. Replace your winners.

Encouraging Internal Change

There *are* a number of things companies can do internally to encourage beneficial change, however.

Not Tolerating Second Best

Earlier we discussed the importance of imagining or envisioning an "ideal" computer-assisted business environment. That skill comes into play with underperforming systems, too. Business managers and computer users who can visualize how a system *ought* to work aren't likely to tolerate deficiencies in how they *do* work. Encouraging constructive criticism of information systems is the only way to identify and eventually overcome system problems. Companies that frown on any kind of complaint ensure that users will sweep computer glitches under the rug, and live with the warts.

Privacy Policy

It's important that whatever the organization's policy on privacy may be, everyone understands it up front to minimize the chance of resentment later. I've found that if a company needs to ask computer users to relinquish some privacy, it can lessen the negative reaction by simultaneously showing some new benefit to the users as a result of the change. "Yes, we're going to network the department and the system administrators will have access to all your files. But, because of the network, those administrators will be able to back up all your files every night without you worrying about it anymore."

DEMISE OF THE DICTATORS

Global competition has made the days of organizational dictators obsolete. Businesses simply can't afford to waste the brains and ideas and imaginations of their employees anymore. Authoritarian, top-down control is fading as a viable management concept and being replaced by the "manager as coach" organization. If companies wish to benefit from new information-sharing technologies, they'll have to release their stranglehold on business data—and teach employees what to do with it. Business men and women who don't add much value to the organization will find their positions threatened or eliminated as data and information flow more freely.

On a more local scale, IT management's cultural shift is also a difficult one, because just when computer experts are starting to understand mainframes and get them really running efficiently, companies are walking away from them. The new system architectures are unknown quantities. Excellent tools exist for modeling mainframes but none that really work for modeling complex networks. Mainframe security is well understood; network security is almost an oxymoron. Mainframe standards are clear and precise; networks are heterogeneous, multivendor, and messy. In the old world, the technical staff did their job without much interference; now, they're expected to be business experts as well as computer experts.

In addition, they're expected to build more efficient systems that may threaten their livelihoods. Overcoming this barrier to change may be possible only if organizations begin managing their computer departments on an *incentive* basis—tying compensation to business performance metrics instead of meaningless criteria such as lines of programming per person per day.

Forward-thinking organizations emphasize to managers and technologists of the "old school" that new ways of doing business will require their expertise more than ever. Top managers will have to educate newly empowered information workers on techniques for decision making and evaluating alternatives. Top technologists will have to bring their discipline to bear on the chaotic mess of computer networks. The old ways may be changing, but the old *skills* remain vital for success.

Tracking the Trends

Because software is often easier to change than hardware, and often has a greater productivity impact, industry watchers should concentrate on new application programs to a somewhat greater degree than on new devices. Note, too, that organizations running standardized, general-purpose computing equipment will be better able to try new software than those with unique and specialized equipment.

Those who track technology trends can periodically inform senior management about new products that could help the business. Quarterly "technology briefings" build understanding and lay the groundwork for appropriate new investments.

Getting Comfortable with Obsolescence

In computers, technical obsolescence per se really doesn't matter.

First of all, it's all but guaranteed from both the power and price standpoints. My wife's computer was the most powerful Macintosh available when we bought it five months ago; now it's fifth on the list and sinking. The $500 disk drive I bought for an office PC a month ago costs $400 today.

But you don't worry about it because it doesn't matter. The "obsolete" Macintosh is, of course, still able to do what we bought it for, and will be for a couple of years. It didn't suddenly get slower when the new models came out. The disk drive was worth $500 to me when I bought it, and if I'd waited a month, I would have had to put up with inconveniences costing well over the $100 difference.

Certainly, organizations can minimize obsolescence by tracking the industry and timing discretionary purchases accordingly. And by sticking with industry standards (as well as creating their own), the long-term usability of hardware and software can be reasonably assured. The question hesitant organizations should ask is not "Will it be obsolete in a few months?" but rather "Is this technology worth what it costs *right now*?," "Is it appropriate for meeting a business need?," and "What will it cost the business to wait and do nothing?"

OLD COMPUTERS NEVER DIE, THEY JUST GET EXPENSIVE

Computers wear out their welcome long before they wear out. The costs that grow over time include:

- User time spent working around hardware limitations;

- Support and maintenance costs;

- Add-on products to inject a few more months of life into old systems;

- Lost productivity due to slow system response times;

- Downtime from poor parts availability;

- The cost of not being able to run new and improved software.

When one compares the above against new equipment costs, it usually becomes clear that any small system over four years old is costing more to keep than it would to trash and replace. Large systems have a longer useful life span, but they, too, become uneconomical long before they physically break. Companies that spend some time developing spreadsheet models for evaluating when to replace old technology will find it's sooner than they think.

REWARDING RISK

> *"Success is never final."*
>
> —J. W. "BILL" MARRIOTT

The consensus structure of some modern matrix organizations can sometimes thwart the innovators and risk takers. One high-tech company in New Mexico provides a special vehicle for frustrated "intrapreneurs": Individuals can prepare an informal project proposal and submit it to a committee that meets monthly. If the committee sees some promise in the idea, it grants the individual time to develop it and even try it out, allocating appropriate personnel to the project in consultation with the innovator. The criteria for granting proposals aren't easy, but the mere act of going before the committee carries respect and prestige. Successful projects get written up in share-holder newsletters and even the annual report.

Companies such as Safeway are beginning to support rewards for risk takers by evaluating employees based on improving margins and increasing market share. Any project champion who meets those goals is rewarded handsomely. The flip side is for companies not to come down too hard on those who experiment and fail. Those individuals are the company's driving force.

REDUCING RISK

> *"There's a substantial element of psychology in success-ful technology introduction. The secret is making workers feel part of what would otherwise seem a wrenching and foreign set of changes."*
>
> —DAVID KIRKPATRICK, *Fortune*
> (Autumn 1993)

Having stated that progress requires a business culture that re-wards risk takers, it remains true that reducing risk is a good plan when implementing new technology. What are some of the ways organizations can encourage experimentation but limit the downside?

❏ For one, getting new technology into a company is easier if the innovators conduct a *pilot project* before trying to convert the whole organization. Starting small is a way to demonstrate a project's potential benefit without asking everyone to commit to the technology. It wins employees over and establishes cred-ibility. For example, Robert M. Rubin, VP/IS at Elf Atochem North America in Philadelphia, created a computer application designed to reimburse employee expenses immediately, while checking the math and receipts later. Everybody liked *that* idea, and it helped break down some of the doubts in employees' minds about whether computers could really help them.

❏ Another risk-reduction technique for IT projects is to phase out the old and phase in the new in modules rather than all at once. For example, bring groupware on-line by department: engineering, manufacturing, etc. Overnight transitions are very dangerous and not suited for mission-critical systems.

❏ When moving from manual to automated systems, the busi-ness can run old and new systems *in parallel*. This is expensive in that employees must enter data twice during the parallel test, but it's a way of building confidence in the new system—and finding flaws before the return bridge has been burned.

THINKING ABOUT BIG CHANGE

Computer projects can bring incremental change or "big change." Ambitious, "big change" projects are the toughest to start up because the implications for failure are great, and so much inertia must be overcome. Steven Rayner, in *Recreating the Workplace*, presents prerequisites for fundamental change that apply as well to computer projects as any other:

- A strongly and widely felt need;
- Change that ascends to the top;
- Clear leadership commitment;
- Perception of immediate payback;
- A single, grand theme;
- Vigorous publicizing of results;
- Motivating description of potential benefits;
- Integration to the business's cultural fabric.

"Big change" entails the biggest risks . . . but promises the biggest benefits.

THE REALITY

Innovative companies, departments, and teams maximize returns from their technology investment by using new devices and software to improve operations and help reengineer business processes. They encourage experimentation, respect innovative thinking, and reward risk takers, while simultaneously reducing risks by means of pilot projects, phased implementation, and parallel operation. They also find ways to build a consensus for change by involving users rather than imposing change authoritatively.

That's the last of our thirteen computer myths. The final section, part V, discusses a new framework for making computer decisions: one based on reality, not mythology. It concludes with an "editorial" about the future of business computer systems . . . and *people*.

Part V

A New Framework for Decisions

"An attitude of orientation, is what the pragmatic method means. The attitude of looking away from first things, principles, 'categories,' supposed necessities; and of looking toward last things, fruits, consequences, facts."

—WILLIAM JAMES,
AMERICAN PHILOSOPHER
AND PSYCHOLOGIST,
Pragmatism, LECTURE 2
(1907)

MOVING TOWARD A REALISTIC APPROACH

This book has identified thirteen computer myths organizations can abandon, and thirteen computer realities they can accept, in order to deal with information technology realistically and profitably. The discussions have ignored "supposed necessities" and concentrated on "fruits, consequences, facts." The goal has been, very simply, to get more benefits out of information systems while reducing their costs.

Some suggestions may not work for a given company. But most of what is here works for most companies I've seen.

Some changes may require years or even decades. But you can't get there from here, unless you know where you'd like "there" to be.

All the suggestions involve an element of risk, though, I believe, less risk than maintaining the status quo. But nothing worth doing has zero risk.

One book can only scratch the surface of the complex topics involved. But one book can sound a few alarms, stimulate debate, and suggest a point of view.

Ultimately, reading about ideas—however challenging it may

be when the subject is unfamiliar and complex—is the easy part. Taking ideas and *applying* them to specific organizations is the hard part. The first step in that effort is to build a new framework for computer-related decisions, a framework based on how things *are* as opposed to how things ought to be.

We've created two views of this new framework: a long-term, "big picture" view, and a nuts-and-bolts near-term view. The long-term view rests on five key tenets:

1. An organization dedicated to measuring and monitoring true, life cycle computer costs and benefits, if only approximately, will learn over time which IT applications pay and which don't—and will be able to make more informed decisions about the types of projects to pursue in the future.

2. An organization where business managers and IT managers communicate, cross boundaries, pursue projects in teams, and share expertise is the only kind of organization that can realize the potential benefits of automation. Isolated IS departments no longer work, if they ever did; and managers who get more involved in technology projects help ensure success.

3. Organizations that think of creative ways to apply IT, not just to traditional "back-office" functions like accounting but also to functions such as improving customer service, designing better products, and responding faster to the market will enjoy great productivity gains.

4. Successful computer projects always put people rather than technology first in defining project design and implementation, to ensure system relevance, acceptance, ergonomics, trainability, and supportability.

5. Organizations that successfully convert raw data to useful information recognize that one relevant fact is worth a

thousand trivial ones and design systems to focus on facts and numbers most important to the business.

The nuts-and-bolts, or "implementation," view of the new framework has eight linchpins:

1. Ongoing planning is necessary for long-term successful projects, and it involves management, the user community, and the technical community if it's going to work. Uncoordinated departmental purchasing is the wave of the past.

2. The latest, greatest technology isn't always appropriate or necessary and may hurt more than it helps. Smart organizations focus on expandability and matching tools to tasks, investing dollars where they do the most good.

3. Organizations that adhere to industry standards where possible, create their own internal standards in addition, and emphasize links to nonstandard systems will enjoy lower costs, greater flexibility, and less obsolescence.

4. Commercial software is always much less expensive, both initially and over the life of the application, than custom software. Where custom software promises an overwhelming benefit, insistence on professional design practices increases up-front costs but pays back many times in reduced life cycle costs and customer vulnerability.

5. Computer systems aren't easy to use; nor are they getting easier to use because user interface improvements are counteracted by growing product complexity. Therefore, aggressive user education, far above the norm, is a prerequisite for productive technology applications.

6. Vendor support is getting more expensive and poorer in quality every year. Companies will benefit from responsive, competent in-house technical support, not just to keep

users up and running but also to determine how to improve systems, documentation, and training based on problem histories.

7. Fixing, enhancing, and expanding computer systems requires a "holistic" or systems approach to make best use of capital. Software projects in particular are resistant to improvement by infusing dollars and bodies. Money is no substitute for balanced hardware design and an intelligent software development process model.

8. Organizations must find ways to overcome the numerous institutional, cultural, economic, and political barriers to change when change seems to hold promise. Technology labs, rewards for successful innovation, risk reduction techniques, and IT education can all help drive appropriate change.

One person alone can't build such a structure, even in a small firm. But if enough people in an organization begin to think pragmatically about automation, there's a chance of creating it. So part of the job of applying the insights from this baker's dozen of computer issues is to become a persuasive advocate of the pragmatic point of view: someone who will raise the arguments in memos, meetings, and private conversations; who will do so diplomatically, sympathetically, firmly, clearly, and enthusiastically.

Although this book has done a fair amount of myth busting, lambasting computer companies and customers alike, and advocating a healthy skepticism toward the claims of the technological cheerleaders, I wouldn't have bothered to write it and you wouldn't have bothered to read it unless we felt that computer technology can be a great enabler of human productivity. We're starting to see more and more evidence of this notion; the success stories are coming a little more often these days. Improved productivity will eventually mean job creation, rising real incomes, more money for research and development, more money for education.

The quicker companies recognize the computer myths for what they are, the sooner they adopt a decision framework based on practicality and understanding instead of idealism and ignorance, the faster they can join the technology winners and start cashing in on IT's long-heralded benefits. One of those benefits—the transformation of work—suggests a fitting topic to conclude this exploration of technology in business.

THE LIBERATING TOOL: A PERSONAL VIEW

"Hardware has not been thought of as a means of releasing human potential, but simply in terms of self-contained technical problems. So one objective of technology in the future will be to devise machines and technical procedures which will enable everybody to do work which is personally satisfying, and which will also enable them to make their essential contribution to the material needs and social welfare of the community."

—Arnold Pacey, *The Maze of Ingenuity* (1974)

"The entire focus of the information age is on people rather than machines. . . . What is now of greatest value is man's unique faculty to apply insight, discrimination, and judgment to complex situations—and then make effective choices."

—Paul A. Strassman, VP, Xerox Corporation (1985)

"If you're not thinking all the time about making every person more valuable, you don't have a chance. What's the alternative? Wasted minds? Uninvolved people? That doesn't make sense!"

—JACK WELCH, CEO,
GENERAL ELECTRIC, *Fortune*
(January 25, 1993)

The implicit assumption throughout this book has been that improving productivity will improve *profitability*, usually treated as an end in itself. But while profitability is a valid and even central goal, it might not be the *only* goal of applying IT more intelligently; it might not even be the *best* goal to keep at the front of one's consciousness. Before you shout "Heresy!," read on.

There was a tribe in Africa called the Ik. It was ravaged by drought and horrible starvation, and anthropologists chronicled the cruelty and selfishness of Ik members as they turned against friend and family and scrapped to survive. Twenty years ago, a professor of mine used this story as evidence that beneath the veneer of civilization, humans are still basically animals and revert to their true, selfish character when placed under extreme stress.

Consider an opposing interpretation to the story, inspired by the psychologist Abraham H. Maslow: that people can *only* attain true humanity if their fundamental needs are met, and material prosperity—rather than being a mask for our crude impulses— allows people to unlock their potential, develop their minds and spirits and talents, and become more truly human, if they so choose, whether they interpret that as devoting more time to family, learning to appreciate Beethoven, cleaning up a local stream, running for mayor, or taking classes in Zen Buddhism. In the case of the Ik, starvation perverts humanity rather than revealing it.

What does all that have to do with computers? These two

opposite views of human nature fundamentally affect how organizations apply technology.

Some organizations are concerned with productivity and efficiency not because of a materialism that sees wealth as an end in itself but from a desire to free employees from the drudgery and detail of mechanical jobs and physical poverty and allow them to concentrate on developing higher levels of achievement more appropriate to their capabilities, as well as to become more complete human beings. These organizations believe that people really are *human resources*, and that developing human resources is the most important thing they can do. This isn't altruism; such companies believe it's in their best long-term interest as a business to develop their people as fully as possible.

I believe organizations that embrace Maslow's philosophy will find that prosperity is a surprising side effect, just as the car racer who concentrates on driving smoothly rather than quickly automatically goes faster. Organizations that believe my old professor's view will regard employees as animals, who will probably

Figure 8   The Fork in the Road

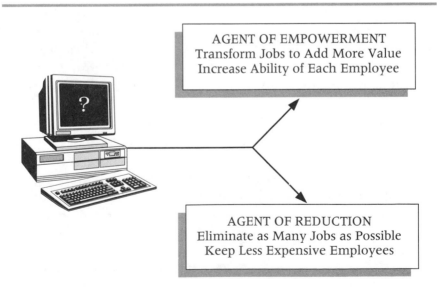

AGENT OF EMPOWERMENT
Transform Jobs to Add More Value
Increase Ability of Each Employee

AGENT OF REDUCTION
Eliminate as Many Jobs as Possible
Keep Less Expensive Employees

perform in line with that expectation. These organizations will impose inappropriate technology on the workforce in an uninvolved, autocratic, ignorant, and ultimately unproductive way.

The computer is innocent as only a machine can be: the forms it takes ultimately reflect its users' values and priorities. Technology can enslave or empower with equal effectiveness. Renaissance man Georgius Agricola commented in his 1556 book on mining, "For what good things can we not use alike for evil or for good ends?" He was writing about metals—such as the copper in computer circuit traces.

The alert reader may have noticed that every single chapter in this book suggests that a *people-centric* approach works better than a *techno-centric* approach.

This discussion is not to downplay the importance of financial return. The organization that improves its bottom line and rewards its owners merits respect and reward. The individual whose career benefits from understanding high tech a little better should take pride in his or her advancement. But perhaps the most profitable philosophy of all sees improving computer productivity as a way to enable individuals to learn and assume new and more important responsibilities, if they want to step up to the challenge. People can do remarkable things if organizations expect remarkable things of them—and provide a few good tools and some room to work. General Electric Company's vice president for business development, Gary Reiner, states, "All of the good ideas—all of them—come from the hourly workers" (*Business Week*, June 14, 1993).

Using IT to empower employees carries its own set of challenges for business managers—difficult, critical challenges. Larry Hirschhorn at the Wharton Center for Applied Research suggests that "the emergence of a new technology places new demands on management's social and cultural skills. The new worker must be matched by a new manager." That manager will not be one who imposes strict control over employees doing stressful and repetitive jobs with technocentric systems, but one who can elicit a high level of interest, commitment, cooperation, and creativity from employees doing challenging and complex jobs with ever more sophisticated technologies.

Challenges emerge for nonmanagers, too. The days of being able to throw one's mind into neutral and perform work that computers can do better and less expensively are nearly over—no thanks to Adam Smith, who convinced millions that human beings work best when doing small, simple tasks. Workers will have to learn more complex skills to stay employed. Ultimately, work will become more interesting and rewarding, but for many Americans, the shift will be an uphill climb. Why?

The country's educational system is not preparing people for such positions. Displaced workers won't be able to look to the federal government for "job retraining," despite the grandiose plans of would-be social architects in Washington. Bureaucrats don't understand what skills today's companies need and have rarely demonstrated any ability to manage anything (much less a massive education initiative) efficiently or successfully. To quote Jack Welch of GE again, "Governments set out to create Silicon Valley and wind up building the Motor Vehicle Department." In the near term at least, it will be left to individuals and their employers to develop tomorrow's skills.

Ironically, information technology can help advance that education at the same time it's making it more and more necessary. MIT researcher Peter M. Senge advocates the "learning organization." Computer systems can help companies become learning organizations by humanizing work, enhancing internal and external communications, conveying ideas in new ways and converting data into information accurately, quickly, and provocatively. Patricia Seybold comments, "A learning organization encourages learning and experimentation among its employees and is masterful at transforming itself to create and meet new market conditions."

It could be, then, that when thinking about computer systems, profitability, and productivity are secondary, freeing people to develop their uniquely human abilities should be the primary goal, from which profitability and productivity follow as a natural consequence. Maybe organizations should look at computer systems not first and foremost as a way to pare overhead but as a liberating tool to tap the reserves of human creativity and talent that currently lie dormant in the workforce. Maybe unlocking the hidden dynamo of unused and ill-used *computer* power is putting the cart before the horse, and using computers to unlock *people* power provides the real payoff.

If that's true, then thinking of computers primarily as a mechanism to improve profits by reducing "head count" is the biggest and most dangerous Computer Myth of all. This myth is perpetuated by periodic articles on technology payoff in respected business magazines that focus almost exclusively on the "cost savings" (read: layoffs) that automation enables.

Competition and global economic shifts do cause companies to eliminate jobs that add little value. It's also true that process improvement and IT deployment help identify those jobs more clearly. However, companies that use automation solely to cut employees are throwing away their greatest potential resource in exchange for a resource with remarkable, but ultimately much less, promise. If a company can't develop its human resources, it won't succeed in the long run, no matter how smoothly and efficiently its information systems move electrons around.

Once organizations outgrow their obsession with computers as agents of staff reduction, a door will open to a level of productivity barely hinted at today; a quantum leap forward—courtesy of a new generation of as-yet-unwritten computer applications, far more human-centered than anything we've seen so far in the brief history of computing.

Tomorrow's workplace will not be a place where computers do everything people used to do. It *will* be a place where computers help rather than frustrate, suggest rather than dictate, cooperate rather than obstruct, stimulate rather than anesthetize, and clarify rather than confuse. It will be a place where technology enables people to achieve extraordinary new levels of performance.

That's the image to keep in mind. Keep it in mind, and we might just get there.

References

Part III, Myth 1

Jean d'Alembert, *Preliminary Discourse to the Encyclopedia of Diderot*, 1751. One of the best books about knowledge and thinking ever written.

Dave Barry, "The Internet Zone," appeared February 6, 1994, in the *Denver Post*. Frittering away time on the information superhighway.

Janet Butler, "New Technology Bares Performance Pitfalls," *Software Magazine*, February, 1993.

Thomas D. Clark, "Corporate Systems Management: An Overview and Research Perspective," *Communications of the ACM*, February 1992. Florida State University professor raises disturbing questions.

Peter F. Drucker, "We Need to Measure, Not Count," *The Wall Street Journal*, April 13, 1993. Drucker's comments on cost accounting.

Howard Gleckman, "The Technology Payoff," *Business Week*, June 14, 1993. Much of the benefit from automation is from rethinking procedures.

Cheryl D. Krivda, "Get a Grip: Managing System Ownership Costs in Modern Midrange Shops," *MIDRANGE Systems*, March 11, 1994.

Leonard Lee, *The Day the Phones Stopped*, Primus, 1992.

Larry Light, "Software Even a CFO Could Love," *Business Week*, November 2, 1992. Applying technology in new ways to "front office" activities.

Amal Kumar Naj, "Shifting Gears: Some Manufacturers Drop Efforts to Adopt Japanese Techniques," *The Wall Street Journal*, May 7, 1993.

Adam Osborne, quoted in the text, was the first to build and market a transportable, or "luggable," microcomputer.

Jared Sandberg, "Playing 9-to-5: Video Games in the Office Can Enhance Productivity. Maybe," *The Wall Street Journal*, June 27, 1994.

David L. Schnitt, "Reengineering the Organization Using Information Technology," *Journal of Systems Management*, January 1993.

Stratford Sherman, "How to Bolster the Bottom Line," *Fortune*, Autumn 1993. The entire special issue deals with IT and productivity.

Paul A. Strassman, *Information Payoff: The Transformation of Work in the Electronic Age*, Free Press, 1985.

Part III, Myth 2

"ACM Code of Ethics and Professional Conduct," *Communications of the ACM*, February 1993. (ACM is the Association for Computing Machinery.)

Deborah Asbrand, "User Satisfaction Is Essential to Successful Projects," *InfoWorld*, February 15, 1993.

Richard Brandt, "Intel: What a Tease—And What a Strategy," *Business Week*, February 22, 1993. Story of the intentional Pentium delay.

Frederick P. Brooks, Jr., *The Mythical Man-Month: Essays on Software Engineering*, Addison-Wesley, 1982.

Dwight B. Davis, "Hard Demand for Soft Skills," *Datamation*, January 15, 1993.

Richard T. Delamarter, *Big Blue: IBM's Use and Abuse of Power*, Dodd, 1986.

Alan Farnham, "Want a Network? Read This," *Fortune*, June 14, 1993.

Tracy Kidder, *The Soul of a New Machine*, Avon Books, 1981.

Bernie Knill, "Material Handling Grounds Denver Airport," *Material Handling Engineering*, May 1994.

Naomi S. Leventhal, "Behavioral Skills for Systems Professionals," *Data Training*, October 1987.

Mark Lewyn, "The New Face of Business: Washington Bogs Down in Booting Up," *Business Week*, May 1, 1994. Various disastrous projects.

Jessica Lipnack and Jeffrey Stamps, *The TeamNet Factor*, Oliver Wight Publications, 1993. Boundary-crossing teams.

Patrick O'Driscoll, "Poll: DIA Would Lose Vote," *Denver Post*, July 19, 1994.

Kathy Rebello, "Is Microsoft Too Powerful? How the Industry's Leader Is Wielding Its Clout," *Business Week*, March 1, 1993.

Robert L. Scheier, "Software Snafu Grounds Denver's High-Tech Airport," *PC Week*, May 16, 1994.

Geoffrey Smith, "The Computer System That Nearly Hospitalized an Insurer," *Business Week*, June 15, 1992.

Jon Udell, "ComponentWare," *Byte*, May 1994.

Garrison Wells, "Baggage Problems May Delay Airport," *Denver Business Journal*, September 3, 1993.

Lauren Ruth Wiener, *Digital Woes: Why We Should Not Depend on Software*, Addison-Wesley, 1993.

Part III, Myth 3

Stan Augarten, *Bit by Bit: An Illustrated History of Computers*, Ticknor & Fields, 1984. See the chapter, "The Engines of Charles Babbage."

William M. Bulkeley, "Computers Start to Lift U.S. Productivity," *The Wall Street Journal*, March 1, 1993.

————, "Computers Keep Taking Pages away from FAXes," *The Wall Street Journal*, November 24, 1993.

Peter Coy, "The New Realism in Office Systems," *Business Week*, June 15, 1992. Hyatt's new reservations system.

Howard Gleckman, "The Technology Payoff: A Sweeping Reorganization of Work Itself Is Boosting Productivity," *Business Week*, June 14, 1993.

Michael Hammer and James Champy, *Reengineering the Corporation*, HarperBusiness, 1993. Especially chapter 5.

Richard Heygate, "Technophobes, Don't Run Away Just Yet," *The Wall Street Journal*, August 15, 1994. The ADP on-the-spot insurance claim system.

Larry Light, "The New Rocket Science: Welcome to the Future of Finance," *Business Week*, November 2, 1992. Lockheed's supply ordering system.

Bob Lindgren and Martin Luray, "Artificial Intelligence Gets Real," *Enterprise*, October 1993. GTE's "phone-clone" detection computer.

Timothy L. O'Brien, "Entrepreneurs Raise Funds through On-Line Computer Services," *The Wall Street Journal*, June 2, 1994.

Kyle Pope, "To Whom It May Concern," *The Wall Street Journal*, November 15, 1993.

Ira Sager, "The Great Equalizer: Information Power Is Getting Cheaper," *Business Week*, May 1, 1994. Andersen, Dell, and others apply IT.

Evan I. Schwartz, "Finally, Software That Slays Giants," *Business Week*, March 15, 1993. The Motorola mainframe-to-network move.

Stratford Sherman, "How to Bolster the Bottom Line," *Fortune*, Autumn 1993 Special Report. Chris-Craft's CAD/CAM system pays off.

John W. Verity, "The Gold Mine of Data in Customer Service," *Business Week*, March 21, 1994. Whirlpool and Attachmate.

John W. Verity and Evan I. Schwartz, "Software Made Simple: Will Object-Oriented Programming Transform the Computer Industry?," *Business Week*, September 30, 1991.

Ron Winslow, "Four Hospital Suppliers Will Launch Common Electronic Ordering System," *The Wall Street Journal*, April 12, 1994.

Part III, Myth 4

Stewart Alsop, "Just Give Me ISDN, A Cable Modem, and I'll Stay Home," *InfoWorld*, June 27, 1994.

Larry Armstrong and Julie Tilsner, "The Office Is a Terrible Place to Work," *Business Week*, December 27, 1993.

Pam Black, "A Home Office That's Easier on the Eyes—and the Back," *Business Week*, August 17, 1992.

William M. Bulkeley, "Software Writers Try to Speak a Language Users Understand," *The Wall Street Journal*, June 30, 1992. Usability labs.

Michael L. Dertouzos, Richard K. Lester, and Robert M. Solow, *Made in America: Regaining the Productive Edge*, MIT Press, 1989.

Susan Fitzgerald, "Global Warming: ISDN Heats Up," *LAN Magazine*, June 1994.

Tom Forester and Perry Morrison, *Computer Ethics: Cautionary Tales and Ethical Dilemmas in Computing*, MIT Press, 1994. Chapter 6 deals with monitoring and privacy; chapter 7 with expert systems.

Barbara Garson, *The Electronic Sweatshop*, Simon & Schuster, 1988.

Monta Kerr, "Ergonomics: Experts Debate Productivity Issue," *Computing Canada*, August 16, 1993.

David Kirkpatrick, "Making It All Worker-Friendly," *Fortune*, Autumn 1993. Mr. Shpilberg's quotation.

Brian McWilliams, "Information Insecurity," *Enterprise*, July 1993. A good treatment of the sea change in computer security philosophy.

Gary Marx and Sanford Sherizen, "Monitoring on the Job," *Technology Review*, November/December 1986. Suggestions for appropriate monitoring.

"Performance Support: Worker Information Systems," *Release 1.0*, August 24, 1993.

Charles Rubin, "Workstation Comfort Boosts the Bottom Line," *MacWeek*, January 3, 1994.

Ira Sager, "The Great Equalizer: Information Power Is Getting Cheaper," *Business Week*, May 1, 1994.

Michael Schrage, "Robert's Electronic Rules of Order," *The Wall Street Journal*, November 29, 1993. E-mail pitfalls.

Noel M. Tichy and Stratford Sherman, "GE: Control Your Destiny or Someone Else Will," *Fortune*, January 25, 1993.

Part III, Myth 5

William M. Bulkeley, "Databases Are Plagued by Reign of Error," *The Wall Street Journal*, May 26, 1992. A sobering MIT study.

Patrick H. Corrigan, *LAN Disaster Prevention and Recovery*. PTR Prentice-Hall, 1994.

G. Christian Hill, "New Software Helps Networks Get Smarter," *The Wall Street Journal*, January 6, 1994. General Magic's Telescript filter.

Philip Inman, "Getting Back in Touch with Business," *Computer Weekly*, October 22, 1992. Developing Executive Information Systems.

David Kirkpatrick, "Groupware Goes Boom," *Fortune*, December 27, 1993. Detailed discussion of how companies are using Lotus's *Notes* product.

Bill Kuipers, "Action-Oriented Reporting," *Direct Marketing*, June 1992.

Steven Levy, "A Spreadsheet Way of Knowledge," *Harper's Magazine*, November 1984.

Christopher Locke, "Making Knowledge Pay," *Byte*, June 1992. A stimulating treatment of distributed data and "browsing" technology.

Walter S. Mossberg, "All the News You Want, When and How You Want It," *The Wall Street Journal*, May 26, 1994.

Arno Penzias, *Ideas and Information: Managing in a High-Tech World*, W. W. Norton, 1989.

Judy Schuster, "The Soul of a Social Machine," *Electronic Learning*, February 1994. Interview with Paul Saffo, director, Institute for the Future.

Harley Shaiken, "The Automated Factory: The View from the Shop Floor," *Technology Review*, January 1985. Stress from CAD/CAM.

Benjamin Svetkey, "Whirled History," *Entertainment Weekly*, April 1, 1994.

James Burke's quotation. Burke's book is *Connections*, Little, Brown & Co., 1978.

Rick Tetzeli, "Surviving Information Overload," *Fortune*, July 11, 1994.

Part IV, Myth 6

Russell D. Archibald, *Managing High-Technology: Programs and Projects*, Wiley, 1992. Contains considerable wisdom on project planning and management issues.

Janet Butler, "How to Stay in Business When a Disaster Strikes," *Software Magazine*, August 1992. More details for managers preparing disaster plans.

Thomas D. Clark, "Corporate Systems Management: An Overview and Research Perspective," *Communications of the ACM*, February 1992.

Shannon Gaw, "Platform Politics," *LAN Magazine*, November 1992.

Jeffrey Rothfeder, "It's Late, Costly, Incompetent—But Try Firing a Computer System," *Business Week*, November 7, 1988. Good, concise summary of computer project management pitfalls.

John W. Verity, "Deconstructing the Computer Industry," *Business Week*, November 23, 1992. Summary of major industry changes in the early 1990s.

Part IV, Myth 7

Janet J. Barron, "Putting Fuzzy Logic into Focus," *Byte*, April 1993. A bit technical; explains how "fuzzy" programs differ from traditional programs.

William Bowen, "The Puny Payoff from Office Computers," *Fortune*, May 26, 1986. The Northern Telecom story and several others.

Gene Bylinsky, "Computers That Learn by Doing," *Fortune*, September 6, 1993. Focus on business applications of neurocomputers.

Paul M. Eng, "Office Machines That Do Everything But Make Coffee," *Business Week*, October 5, 1992.

David P. Hamilton, "Fujitsu Readies New Products as Mainframes Wane," *The Wall Street Journal*, May 29, 1993. Large computer vendors continue pushing high-margin products long after customers need them.

Michael Hammer and James Champy, *Reengineering the Corporation: A Manifesto for Business Revolution*, HarperBusiness, 1993.

Ernest W. Kent, *The Brains of Men and Machines*, McGraw-Hill, 1981. Difficult but fascinating early look at human and computer brains by a University of Illinois psychology professor.

Carol Levin, "Quick Thinking Neural Networks," *PC Magazine*, October 12, 1993. Details on the Intel NI-1000 neurocomputer chip.

Ian McGugan, "The Machines from MENSA," *Canadian Business*, March 1994. Nontechnical summary of the current state of the technology.

Ed Perratore, Tom Thompson, Jon Udell, and Rich Malloy, "Fighting Fatware," *Byte*, April 1993. Reasons for software bloat, with suggestions for curbing the disease.

Otis Port, "Computers That Come Awfully Close to Thinking," *Business Week*, June 2, 1986. A good intro to neurocomputing.

Jeffrey Rothfeder, "It's Late, Costly, Incompetent—But Try Firing a Computer System," *Business Week*, November 7, 1988. Good, concise summary of computer project management pitfalls.

Linda Shaw, "The Wait Is Over," *Systems/3X World*, November 1987. More discussion of user performance as a function of computer response speed.

Arvind Thadhani, "Interactive User Productivity," *IBM Systems Journal*, vol. 20, no. 4, 1981. Users work faster if their computers don't hold them back.

Part IV, Myth 8

Claude J. Bauer, "POSIX in Government," *Government Computer News*, September 27, 1993.

Barbara Buell and Deidre A. Depke, "Computer Confusion," *Business Week*, June 10, 1991.

Jerry Cashin, "Bloom Fading from POSIX Rose as Open Focus Shifts," *Software Magazine*, March 1994.

Marilyn Chase, "Sun Microsystems Juggles New Strategies," *The Wall Street Journal*, May 11, 1993. Discussion of Sun's strategy and future.

"DEC, IBM, Unisys Display Proprietary Openness," *Software Magazine*, April 1993. Major vendors commit to the POSIX standard UNIX interface.

Melissa Dunn, "Learn SQL Now," *Data Based Advisor*, February 1993.

Mary Jo Foley, "Unisys One Year Later: A Mean, Lean VAR Machine," *Mini-Micro Systems*, November 1987.

John Gantz, "Are Open Networks a Myth?," *Networking Management*, May 1992.

Bill Gates, "Beyond Macro Processing," *Byte*, Summer 1987. Discussion of macros, presaging "Visual BASIC for Applications" in 1993.

Paul Korzeniowski, "SNMP: From Underdog to De Facto Standard," *Software Magazine*, August 1992.

Jonathan B. Levine, "The Knives Come Out in Europe's Software Market," *Business Week*, February 8, 1993.

Charles McCoy, "Quarterly Net Doubles at Sun Microsystems," *The Wall Street Journal*, July 29, 1993.

John Markoff, "Ending PC Chaos in the Workplace," *The New York Times*, September 9, 1988. The role of networks in the office.

Russell Mitchell, "In Supercomputing, Superconfusion," *Business Week*, March 22, 1993.

Linda Rohrbough, "Sun Gains Market Share at Expense of Profits," *Newsbytes*, August 6, 1992.

Brenton R. Schlender, "Who's Ahead in the Computer Wars," *Fortune*, February 12, 1990.

———, "The Future of the PC," *Fortune*, August 26, 1991. Bill Gates quotation.

Mark Stevens, "Businesses Need Detailed Plan When Installing Computers," *Dallas Morning News*, June 28, 1987. Warren Reid and myths.

S. Yoder, "New World Order," *The Wall Street Journal*, December 21, 1992. Reports that MS-DOS had 89 percent of the 1991 PC operating systems market, Apple 8 percent, UNIX 2 percent, and IBM's OS/2 had 1 percent.

Bart Ziegler, "IBM's New Effort to Connect with the Outside World," *Business Week*, February 22, 1993. The ill-fated SAA standard.

For hardware and software directories, see DataPro Research at 1805 Underwood Boulevard, Delran, New Jersey 08075, phone (800) DATAPRO.

Part IV, Myth 9

Paul M. Eng, "Information Processing," *Business Week*, March 22, 1993. Exploding size of the commercial software market.

Joel B. Gilman, "How to Protect Your Rights to Custom Software," *Systems Integration*, November 1990.

Debra Haverson, "Streamlining for a Custom Fit," *MIDRANGE Systems*, July 13, 1993.

Grant E. Head, "Six-Sigma Software Using Cleanroom Software Engineering Techniques," *Hewlett-Packard Journal*, June 1994.

Byron Isaacs, "How to Make the Buy-versus-Build Decision," *Computing Canada*, April 27, 1994.

Zoe Ollerenshaw, "Tailored to Fit," *Computer Weekly*, April 8, 1993.

Laure B. Rowan, "Visual Programming: Application Design for End Users and Professional Developers," Patricia Seybold's *Office Computing Report*, November 1992.

Alan J. Ryan, "Why Remodeling Often Beats Building," *ComputerWorld*, April 8, 1991.

Stratford Sherman, "The New Computer Revolution," *Fortune*, June 14, 1993.

Bill Tolson, "Graft Windows Programs to Your Custom Software and Reduce Your Workload," *EDN*, April 15, 1993.

G. Pascal Zachary, "We're Still Waiting," *The Wall Street Journal*, June 27, 1994. Reasons why software is always late—commercial or custom.

Part IV, Myth 10

Doug Barney, "Service-Oriented Video Houses Are Making It Easier to Create Training CDs," *InfoWorld*, July 11, 1994.

Mary E. Boone, *Leadership and the Computer: Top Executives Reveal How They Personally Use Computers to Communicate, Coach, Convince, and Compete*, Prima Publishing, 1993.

William M. Bulkeley, "Basic Training: At a Boot Camp for CEOs, Computerphobes Can Show Their Ignorance—Without Too Much Embarrassment," *The Wall Street Journal*, June 27, 1994.

Joyce Endoso, "As DOD Downsizes, Brass Say IT Training Must Improve," *Government Computer News*, May 30, 1994.

Kathy N. Kendall, "A Primer: Computer-Based Training," *Data Based Advisor*, February 1994. Intro to the subject plus typical steps to a CBT project.

David Kirkpatrick, "Making It All Worker-Friendly," *Fortune*, Autumn 1993 special issue, "Making High Tech Work for You."

Walter S. Mossberg, "The Passing of a Year Leaves PCs Improved but Still Imperfect," *The Wall Street Journal*, October 21, 1993.

Donald A. Norman, *The Design of Everyday Things*, Doubleday, 1990.

Lewis J. Perelman, "Kanban to Kanbrain," *Forbes*, June 6, 1994. The concept of "just-in-time" user education.

Kyle Pope, "Packard Bell Is Planning a Makeover of Its Home PCs to 'Humanize' Them," *The Wall Street Journal*, January 6, 1994.

Peter Stephenson, "Training for Excellence," *LAN Times*, May 9, 1994.

"Technophobia Still Infects Some Americans, Poll Says," *The Wall Street Journal*, July 26, 1993. The Dell study, staff report.

Bart Ziegler, "On Their Own: Employees Need Computer Training. So, Why Don't They Get It?," *The Wall Street Journal*, June 27, 1994.

Part IV, Myth 11

Deborah Asbrand, "Lean Budgets Put the Squeeze on IS Departments," *InfoWorld*, February 7, 1994.

David C. Churbuck, "Help Is at Hand," *Forbes*, August 1, 1994. The importance of logging support incidents with automatic tracking systems.

"Downtime Cost the US $5.2 Billion Last Year," *Australian*, staff report, August 4, 1992.

T. C. Doyle, "New Era in Technical Support Dawns," *Computer Reseller News*, February 14, 1994.

"End-User Survey Digs Up Buried Costs," *I.T. Magazine*, staff report, May 1993.

Tom Forester and Perry Morrison, *Computer Ethics*, MIT Press, 1994. See especially chapter 5, "Unreliable Computers."

Barbara Gengler, "NTSA Incorporates," *LAN Computing*, February 1994.

Claudia Graziano, "Soft Costs of Net Management," *LAN Times*, April 25, 1994. PC networks can cost three times as much as mainframe networks.

Simi Grossman, "Everybody's Talking Fault-Resilience," *Computing Canada*, September 1, 1993.

Eric Hausman, "Network Downtime Is Down," *Computer Reseller News*, December 13, 1993. Down in hours, but up in dollars.

Julia King, "Hello, Help Desk? HELP!," *ComputerWorld*, November 11, 1991. Interviews with Glenn Weadock and other consultants.

Willem Knibbe, "Adobe to Charge for Technical Support," *InfoWorld*, January 10, 1994.

———, "Corel Will Begin Charging for Technical Support June 1," *InfoWorld*, May 23, 1994.

Walter S. Mossberg, "Talk Is Cheap? Not If You're Calling for Software Support," *The Wall Street Journal*, October 14, 1993.

Paula Musich, "LAN Costs Surprisingly High," *PC Week*, December 20, 1993. Results of the Infonetics study on LAN downtime costs.

Brantz Myers, "The Importance of 'Availability,'" *Computing Canada*, May 25, 1994.

"Process Reengineering: Stac's New Support Model," *Soft-Letter*, staff report, October 22, 1993.

Kelly Sewell, "No Rest for Help Desks," *ComputerWorld*, January 4, 1993.

Stratford Sherman, "The Computer Revolution," *Fortune*, June 14, 1993.

Carrie Thomas, "On the Front Line in Customer Support," *PC World*, July 1994. Insightful look at Lotus Development Corporation's support system.

Lauren Ruth Wiener, *Digital Woes: Why We Should Not Depend on Software*, Addison-Wesley, 1993.

Ralph Wilson, *Help! The Art of Computer Technical Support*, Peachpit Press, 1991. A good general book on the topic from a support tech's viewpoint.

Bart Ziegler, "Help! The PC Support-Center Worker Is Part Psychologist, Part Technician," *The Wall Street Journal*, June 27, 1994.

Part IV, Myth 12

Frederick P. Brooks, Jr., *The Mythical Man-Month: Essays on Software Engineering*, Addison-Wesley, 1974.

"A Curriculum for Change," *Economist*, June 16, 1990.

Thomas H. Davenport, *Process Innovation: Reengineering Work through Information Technology*, Harvard Business School Press, 1993. Mr. Davenport's book illustrates what insights a "techno-suit" can offer.

Jerry Flint, "Darkness Before Dawn," *Forbes*, November 23, 1992.

William E. Perry, "How to Keep Money from Going Down the Systems Rat Hole," *Government Computer News*, April 26, 1993.

Alex Taylor III, "Can GM Remodel Itself?" *Fortune*, January 13, 1992.

"When GM's Robots Ran Amok," *Economist*, August 10, 1991.

Drew Winter, "The Machines That Didn't Change the World," *Ward's Auto World*, November 1991.

Part IV, Myth 13

Karl Albrecht, "The Power of Bifocal Vision," *Management Review*, April 1994.

Peter Coy, "The New Realism in Office Systems," *Business Week*, June 15, 1992. The Elf/Atochem story.

"A Curriculum for Change," *Economist*, staff report, June 16, 1990.

Michael L. Dertouzos, Richard K. Lester, and Robert M. Solow, *Made in America: Regaining the Productive Edge*, MIT Press, 1989.

Jerald M. Jellison, *Overcoming Resistance*, Simon & Schuster, 1993.

David Kirkpatrick, "Making It All Worker-Friendly," *Fortune*, Autumn 1993 special issue.

Richard LaFauci, ed., "Pay As You Program," *Digital Review*, November 9, 1987.

Bob Lindgren, "Going Horizontal," *Enterprise*, April 1994. Methods of changing while keeping risks low.

Steven R. Rayner, *Recreating the Workplace*, Oliver Wight Publications, 1993.

Evan I. Schwartz, "Mainframe Software That Isn't as Hard on the Wallet," *Business Week*, November 23, 1992. Mainframe software pricing policies.

Noel M. Tichy and Stratford Sherman, "GE: Control Your Destiny or Someone Else Will," *Fortune*, January 25, 1993. Jack Welch, one of America's more successful CEOs, shares elements of his business philosophy.

Part V

Howard Gleckman *et al.*, "The Technology Payoff: A Sweeping Reorganization of Work Itself Is Boosting Productivity," *Business Week*, June 14, 1993.

Larry Hirschhorn, "Robots Can't Run Factories," in *Computers in the Human Context: Information Technology, Productivity, and People*, Tom Forester, ed., MIT Press, 1989.

Michael J. Mandel and Christopher Farrell, "Jobs, Jobs, Jobs— Eventually," *Business Week*, June 14, 1993.

Arnold Pacey, *The Maze of Ingenuity*, MIT Press, 1974.

Patricia Seybold, "The Learning Organization," *Byte*, April 1993.

Paul A. Strassman, *Information Payoff: The Transformation of Work in the Electronic Age*, Free Press, 1985.

Noel M. Tichy and Stratford Sherman: "GE: Control Your Destiny or Someone Else Will," *Fortune*, January 25, 1993.

For Further Reading

Stan Augarten, *Bit by Bit: An Illustrated History of Computers*, Ticknor & Fields, 1984. Excellent technical overview up to the eighties.

Frederick P. Brooks, Jr., *The Mythical Man-Month: Essays on Software Engineering*, Addison-Wesley, 1982. Essential reading for anyone involved in software projects. Brooks was project manager for IBM's System/360 mainframe and its operating system software.

Patrick H. Corrigan, *LAN Disaster Prevention and Recovery*, PTR Prentice-Hall, 1994. Required reading for networked businesses.

Katharine Davis Fishman, *The Computer Establishment*, Harper & Row, 1981. Entertaining, anecdotal treatment of the computer business in the sixties and seventies.

Tom Forester, ed., *Computers in the Human Context: Information Technology, Productivity, and People*, MIT Press, 1989. Fascinating collection of essays.

Tom Forester and Perry Morrison, *Computer Ethics: Cautionary Tales and Ethical Dilemmas in Computing*, MIT Press, 1994. Broader in scope than the title sugggests; more thought-provoking essays.

Michael Hammer and James Champy, *Reengineering the Corporation*, HarperBusiness, 1993. Many examples of process improvement, both with and without Information Technology.

Tracy Kidder, *The Soul of a New Machine*, Avon Books, 1981. Entertaining story of Data General "skunkworks" creating a new computer.

Leonard Lee, *The Day the Phones Stopped*, Primus, 1992. This dramatic book's true horror stories will shake the reader's faith in technology.

Robert W. Lucky, *Silicon Dreams: Information, Man, and Machine*, St. Martin's Press, 1989. Interdisciplinary look at text, speech, and image technology; parts of this book will interest everyone.

Regis McKenna, *Who's Afraid of Big Blue? How Companies Are Challenging IBM—and Winning*, Addison-Wesley, 1989. Concise analysis of how the computer industry changed during the eighties.

Donald A. Norman, *The Design of Everyday Things*, Doubleday, 1990. Lucidly points out how hardware and software designers often do things wrong, and how they could be doing things right.

Arnold Pacey, *The Maze of Ingenuity*, MIT Press, 1974. One of the best books about ideas and technology, ranging from the cathedral builders of the twelfth century through the Industrial Revolution.

Arno Penzias, *Ideas and Information: Managing in a High-Tech World*, W. W. Norton, 1989. Wide-ranging, engaging, and accessible meditations by former AT&T Bell Labs research director.

Glenn Rifkin and George Harrar, *The Ultimate Entrepreneur: The Story of Ken Olsen and Digital Equipment Corporation*, Contemporary Books, 1988. Chronicles of the industry's minicomputer pioneer.

John Sculley with John A. Byrne, *Odyssey: Pepsi to Apple*, Perennial Library, 1987. Readable account by a key player in the industry's microcomputer phase.

John Shore, *The Sachertorte Algorithm, And Other Antidotes to Computer Anxiety*, Viking, 1985. Entertaining and objective survey of computer technology; highly recommended and only slightly outdated.

Paul A. Strassman, *Information Payoff: The Transformation of Work in the Electronic Age*, Free Press, 1985. An insightful and exhaustively documented treatment; an update is *The Business Value of Computers* (1990, Information Economics Press), by the same author.

Ron White, *How Computers Work*, Ziff-Davis Press, 1993. PC-oriented book with many good illustrations.

Lauren Ruth Wiener, *Digital Woes: Why We Should Not Depend on Software*, Addison-Wesley, 1993. Read the foreword especially.

Index

About the Author

Glenn E. Weadock is president and cofounder of Independent Software, Inc. (ISI), a computer consulting firm in the foothills of Evergreen, Colorado, near Denver. ISI offers a range of services, including help desk planning, information system strategy studies, project management, computer system performance analysis and enhancement, software design, and training program development. ISI clients, which include several *Fortune* 1,000 companies as well as small private companies, do business in industries as diverse as telecommunications, semiconductors, real estate, high energy physics, bioengineering, and electronics retailing. Mr. Weadock, an office automation specialist, works with PCs, Macs, networks, and minicomputers.

In addition to consulting work, Mr. Weadock develops and leads seminars in the United States, Canada, and the United Kingdom with Data-Tech Institute. These seminars include technical courses on PC network design as well as managerial courses on end-user support. He has conducted over 120 public and on-site seminars since 1988. Mr. Weadock has also made three computer videos for Technology Interchange Group: *Windows on NetWare*, *The Help Desk Analyst's Workshop*, and *Accessing the Internet*.

As one of the country's top consultants on computer support issues, Glenn Weadock has been interviewed by such trade journals as *Computerworld*, *InfoWorld*, *MacWeek*, and *LAN Maga-*

zine. His technical and business articles have appeared in various international magazines as well as regional business newspapers. He received his engineering degree with distinction from Stanford University in 1980, where he was elected to both Phi Beta Kappa and the Tau Beta Pi Engineering honor society. He is a member of the American Society for Training and Development (ASTD), the Independent Computer Consultants Association (ICCA), the Association for Computing Machinery (ACM), and the Microsoft Developer Network.

Glenn lives with his wife, Emily, a computer artist, on the side of a mountain that is shared with two dogs, a herd of elk, and the occasional rabbit, fox, and chipmunk. When not teaching or consulting or writing, he enjoys skiing, hiking, and tennis.